The
Hidden
Meaning
of
Illness

The
Hidden
Meaning
of
Illness

Disease
as a
Symbol
and
Metaphor

by Bob Trowbridge, M.Div.

ASSOCIATION FOR
RESEARCH AND
ENLIGHTENMENT

A.R.E. Press • Virginia Beach • Virginia

3rd Printing, January 1999

Printed in the U.S.A.

A.R.E. Press
215 67th Street
Virginia Beach, VA 23451-2061

Library of Congress Cataloging-in-Publication Data
Trowbridge, Bob, 1939-
    The hidden meaning of illness : disease as a symbol and
metaphor / by Bob Trowbridge.
      p.   cm.
    Includes bibliographical references.
    ISBN 0-87604-358-9
    1. Medicine, psychosomatic. I. Title.
RC49.T76 1996
616'.0019—dc20   95-46753

Cover design by Veronica Reed

Contents

Dedication

I wish to dedicate this book, with love, to my family: my father, Archy Trowbridge; my mother, Evelyn Trowbridge; my sister, Darlene Smith; and my brothers, Ronny and Alan Trowbridge.

Introduction

When the body is ill, life is experienced almost exclusively through the lens of that illness. When you hurt your toe, the whole world becomes a sore toe. The pain or illness becomes the focus of your life. The body now harbors an enemy, a source of pain or discomfort, and in some cases a threat to life. When we feel our bodies have failed us, even in small ways, we feel betrayed, victimized. Whether we seek help from traditional medicine and/or alternative therapies, we often feel that our body, and its health, is out of our control. Helplessness and frustration can accompany even minor illnesses.

In holistic medicine, an individual is seen as a mind-body system rather than a mechanism to be repaired like a car. Elements such as diet, exercise, recreation, relationships, and emotional state are taken into account in the treatment of illnesses, as well as things like environment and lifestyle.

Illness is seen as a problem involving the whole person, not just isolated body systems. Prevention of illness also relates to all aspects of the individual's life. You may follow a healthy diet and exercise regularly, but if you're involved in toxic relationships, under stress at work, or worried about money, your health may still be at risk.

In this book I take a holistic approach to creating health and eliminating illness that embraces the spiritual dimension. From my point of view, every part of our life concerns spirituality and our spiritual growth or lack of it. I believe that all illnesses represent, at some level, a "dis-ease" of the soul, an imbalance of body and spirit. How do body and spirit interact?

I will show that the mind is the intermediary between the spirit and the body. The body is subject to the mind's beliefs and attitudes. This book is not simply about using the mind to heal the body, however. If the mind is capable of healing the body, it is also capable of making the body sick. If the mind makes the body sick, it does so for a reason. The illness is neither haphazard nor accidental. It is not thrust upon us by God or the devil, by our enemies, or by attacking germs and viruses. It does not attack us merely because of poor diet or riotous living. Neither is illness a punishment for our sins, real or imagined.

Our illnesses, from colds and allergies to life-threatening diseases, are meaningful, and they occur within the context of a life that is meaningful. That is the premise of this book. Illnesses have meaning in the same way our dreams have meaning. Like the symbols in our dreams, our illnesses are messages from the psyche, the inner self, which can be interpreted and understood. But our illnesses are not the problem. They are only symptoms or symbols of the real problem. The real problem is spiritual, an imbalance or distortion in our thinking, attitudes, and feelings.

An illness in the body has actually been created to give us information about a deeper dis-ease. It is the result of the incredible creative power of our own thoughts and emotions. A serious illness is like a nightmare, but even our nightmares have a healing intent. They point out problems, fears, or blocks in our lives and give us an opportunity to make changes. Our illnesses also have a healing intent because they, too, point out inner dis-eases, fears, and imbalances. They give us an opportunity to make healing changes in our lives.

In the following pages, you will learn how to understand the meaning of your illness and how to take positive steps toward eradicating its root cause. You may be surprised at the number of positive things that can occur as a result of a serious illness. You will learn to read early warning signs that can help prevent illnesses and how to recognize when certain actions or life changes are required to prevent the eruption or continuation of disease. You will become more aware of the messages your mind and emotions are sending to your body on a daily basis and the messages your body, your dreams, and your waking life experiences are sending to your mind.

I have come to the conclusion that courage is the answer to every problem, and courage is the answer to healing every illness. As you seek answers to your health questions throughout the book, you will find an underlying assumption that the correct answers are not enough. It is necessary to continually seek the courage to act on our understanding, to apply our insights, and to make the difficult healing choices and changes in our life that may be required.

Courage is the daughter of love. Whatever problems or obstacles we find in our lives, whether they manifest as an illness or in some other way, love and courage can overcome or transform them. And what are those obstacles? I will write of some of the different physical forms our obstacles or blocks can take and the many unique meanings illnesses can carry. Within this variety there is a common characteristic in these blocks to our growth, whether they manifest in our physical body or in other areas of life. The common factor in all such blocks is fear. Fear is the polarity to courage and love. Love and courage are the antidotes to fear.

This book goes beyond helping you understand the meaning of your illness and possibly helping you heal that illness. It also concerns your spiritual growth, finding and staying on your personal spiritual path, confronting and overcoming the obstacles you find, and eliminating the different forms that fear takes. The ideas and exercises in this book can help you find out who you are and what you're really capable of. You can learn to break down self-imposed barriers and stretch yourself, in spirit, mind, and body. Your illness can actually be your teacher in this process.

In the First Letter to the Corinthians Paul says, "No temptation has overtaken you that is not common to man. God is faithful, and he will not let you be tempted beyond your strength, but with the temptation will also provide the way of escape, that you may be able to endure it." (I Corinthians 10:13)[1] I believe this is a spiritual law which relates to all of life, not just to temptations.

We do not create challenges which are meant to defeat us. Challenges may feel like walls, but they always have doors. Our challenges, including serious illnesses, often provide us with what I call "course correction." Many think of illnesses as life disrupting or even life shattering. They *do* stop life as usual and seem to knock us off our path. They *do* disrupt or even shatter our lives, but illnesses also give us the opportunity to get back on a more positive, life-affirming, and spiritual path.

In working on dreams with individual clients and in groups, I have found that every dream, even a nightmare, has a resolution, and every resolution contains a gift. We receive the gift of energy, energy that had been going into the problem represented by the dream, and we receive the gift of insight and understanding. In the same way, if we have a physical challenge, there is a solution to that challenge and there are gifts in facing and resolving it.

Nonetheless, in terms of understanding the meaning of illnesses and their potential for aiding in our spiritual growth, physical healing isn't the only answer. When I discuss birth choices in chapter 4 you will see that some illnesses, especially congenital diseases or handicaps, may have the hidden purpose of helping an individual channel life energy in a direction other than the physical. For example, a developmentally disabled individual may forego intellectual development in order to focus more on the emotional side of being. A physically disabled individual may be creating a path in which the intellect or the imagination is given primacy, a path made more likely by the physical limitation.

A physical illness is sometimes created as a way to leave this life. Death by illness is often seen as a failure in our culture. Death by illness is no more a failure than is death in an automobile accident or death by any other means. It is just another way to leave this life. Living for many years is not the only measure of a healthy or fulfilling life. From a larger perspective, some individuals may actually complete their life work by age three or age seven or age twenty-seven.

The success of a life is not determined by how many years an individual lives, but by the quality of the life lived and perhaps by how much love that life contained. What is important is not the number of years in a life but the quality of life in the years. Many individuals with life-threatening illnesses find that their illnesses have shattered their lives. It is impossible to continue with family, relationships, and business as usual. The apparent shattering, however, provides an opportunity to create a new and even better life. Serious illnesses have helped many individuals reexamine their life values and priorities and make new and better choices based on that examination: "I truly believe that AIDS has made me a better person . . . I'm not so selfish, and I'm able to give love. I believe I am alive because God has some mission for me. I think it's about helping."[2]

I will give other examples, throughout the book, of individuals who actually say they are glad they became ill. The illness helped them improve the quality of their life so much that they wouldn't trade their months or years of quality living for many more years of living the old life. This doesn't mean they wanted to die nor that their family and friends wanted them to die. It means that our illnesses can help us transform our lives in a very positive way, regardless of the final outcome of the illness.

I will write of illnesses as being meaningful throughout the book, and I will use the word *responsibility*. It is important to understand I am not talking about people *blaming* themselves for their illnesses. Responsibility, although it is often incorrectly used as a synonym for blame, has to do with accountability. It's empowering because it has the sense of being able to act on your own authority. Being responsible, of course, means being trustworthy and dependable.

Physical life involves creating, experiencing, and learning. Health is one of the arenas in which we can learn about ourselves and about the world. Other arenas include relationships, work, and money. More general life arenas exist: the mental, psychological, and emotional. We tend to focus on one or two of these arenas in our lives, although we may have issues or problems in several of them.

This will become evident as you look at yourself, your family, friends, and acquaintances. Certain of your friends or family members, for example, don't seem to have much trouble with their health, but they may have a terrible time with relationships. Someone else will always be having problems with money or with settling on a satisfying career. Still another may find his or her spiritual life to be the greatest challenge.

This book is mainly directed at those who have chosen the physical body as their major life arena, the place where they most frequently play out their challenges. The principles, however, will apply regardless of your areas of life challenge. If we *do* make certain choices before we're born, as I discuss in chapter 4, the arenas in which we will face our greatest challenges would undoubtedly be selected then.

The choice to work out life issues through the body is just one choice, no worse and no better than any other. A serious physical illness is no more of a challenge for one individual than poverty is for another or difficult and painful relationships for someone else. It's important to recognize the areas in your life where you tend to be challenged and the areas where you seem to handle things well. In the section on healing techniques, I suggest that you try to apply some of the positive attitudes and abilities from areas of your life where you have feelings of competence and confidence to change or heal areas where you're having problems.

Some of you may have a serious illness, possibly life threatening. I will try to impart some light and some joy to make your reading pleasant as well as practical. Though illnesses can be serious, we don't have to be serious about them. Much has been written about the power of laughter and humor in healing, and rightfully so. As you read this book, I want you to embark on an adventure with me. Think of understanding and healing your illness as a detective story, a holy quest, or possibly a deep initiation into the mysteries. Be open to finding a healing metaphor that feels right to you. There's no reason why the healing process itself can't be fun, aside from the sometimes necessary pain and discomfort of the illness itself or the healing modality you are using.

From my own experiences with illness, I know I can compound my physical problems by my anger at being sick, my self-condemnation for creating the illness, or my inability to quickly heal myself. I confess to falling into those traps, even as I warn you about them. Such emotions are definitely countertherapeutic, as are self-defeating habits like self-pity.

I would like you to look at your physical problems as puzzles to be solved, mysteries to be uncovered, dreams to be interpreted. As you work with your own physical problems, as you peer inside your own psyche to unravel the mystery of your illness, always keep in mind the possibility of the greater healing that every illness contains and be alert for the gifts that await you.

In Part One I will look at how illnesses are built through our thoughts and feelings, using "mind is the builder" as the metaphor. I will show that illnesses are just one part of a larger feedback system that includes other waking experiences as well as our dreams. We will explore current scientific information on the mind-body dance, seeing how thoughts, feelings, attitudes, and expectations actually influence body chemistry, especially the immune system. A chapter on extraordinary physical functioning suggests the outer possibilities of the mind-body and can inspire us in our self-healing efforts. We will look at the role reincarnation might play and the possibility that some of our major choices were made before birth.

Part Two will cover the ways in which we use illness, exploring how illnesses can be used both negatively and positively in our lives. How can we consciously utilize our illnesses in a positive way to change disaster into healing? What are the opportunities for growth to be found in your illness? How does your illness serve you, positively or negatively? Is it protecting you from something you perceive to be worse than the illness? What are some of the positive things that illnesses can do for us? What are the gifts?

Part Three covers the actual work of understanding the meaning of your illness. I will show how illnesses and symptoms are like dream symbols, and how dream interpretation and noninterpretation techniques can be used to discover their meaning. Just as dreams sometimes present us with spiritual teachers, illness can be used as a spiritual teacher, and I believe that is its greatest benefit in our lives.

We will look at illness as a means of spiritual initiation, course correction, and transformation.

In Part Four you will confront the important question, "Do you want to be healed?" Because our illnesses often serve us in some way —perhaps protecting us from failure or success or just an unknown future —this question must be asked and answered at the deepest level. I will also share some of my healing techniques for you to experiment with. Some are what I call internal techniques, and some are external. There are a number of writing exercises that can be both fun and effective. You can experience the wizardry of shapechanging or take a journey to a cell in your body. You will learn the difference between *yang* and *yin* healing, and discover parallel processing. Other exercises will help you open up a healing and spiritual path.

Part Five looks at the qualities of living the healing life, qualities of Attunement, Action, and Being-Becoming. Living the healing life involves practicing attunement: attunement with nature; with your body, mind, emotions, and spirit; and with Spirit, the Divine. Action deals with the daily healing actions and choices which contribute to the healing life. Being has to do with an attitude of living in the present. Because spiritual growth is an ongoing process with no final destination, it's important to love and appreciate ourselves in the present. A serious illness can teach us to live each day more fully. Becoming is a recognition of the journey. We cannot enjoy our lives, or live the healing life, if we aren't able to enjoy the daily journey. Accepting ourselves as beings who are becoming can help us to be kinder to ourselves and not punish ourselves for not being instantly healed or enlightened.

This book is itself a journey into the self. I hope that it will be a healing journey. Bring your sense of adventure, your willingness to explore and question, and your strong determination to discover and live the healing life.

PART 1

THE BIRTH OF AN ILLNESS

1

Mind Is the Builder

Being sick is seldom fun, and sometimes it is life threat-ening. The symptoms of an illness—and the treat-ment—can range from annoying and uncomfortable to ex-tremely painful. For many, feelings of being powerless and victimized are nearly as bad as the illness itself.

What if you weren't the victim of your illness? What if ill-nesses were the result of natural or spiritual principles, prin-ciples that could be learned and applied in order to heal and prevent illness? What if you could live your life illness free and could experience a quality and fullness of life far beyond what you now know? The concepts and tools for doing just that can be found in the following pages.

When I speak of natural or spiritual principles, I mean something like the Golden Rule: "And as you wish that men would do to you, do so to them." (Luke 6:31) Another ex-ample, from a different tradition, is "As above, so below." The physical or material reality is a reflection of the Divine.

The primary spiritual principle we will be working with in this book can be found throughout history in various cultures and religions over a period of thousands of years. The Maitri Upanishad, a Hindu text nearly three thousand years old, tells us: "One's own thought is one's world. What a person thinks is what he becomes." In the Dhammapada (circa 500 B.C.), the Buddha says: "We are shaped by our thoughts; we become what we think." An inspirational little book by James Allen from the 1920s puts it this way: "The aphorism, 'As a man thinketh in his heart so is he,' not only embraces the whole of a man's being, but is so comprehensive as to reach out to every condition and circumstance of his life. A man is literally what he thinks, his character being the complete sum of all his thoughts."[1]

Edgar Cayce is a relatively modern source of this spiritual principle. He left one of the largest and most thoroughly studied bodies of information on health and spirituality in this century. Cayce will be my primary source for this and related spiritual principles.

The Edgar Cayce Legacy

Over a period of four decades Edgar Cayce gave more than fourteen thousand psychic readings, over nine thousand of which were physical readings: diagnoses and prescriptions.[2]

Although he exhibited unusual psychic abilities as a child, his psychic career didn't begin until he was a young adult suffering from aphonia, a paralysis of the throat muscles that left him barely able to speak. Doctors were unable to relieve his symptoms.

Then hypnotist Al Layne came along. He put Cayce in a trance and asked him to make his own diagnosis. At Layne's suggestion, Cayce was able to speak clearly in trance. (I'll speak of the power of hypnosis in chapter 3. It's interesting to note here that a physical problem medical science was unable to cure was instantly—if temporarily—cured through hypnosis). The entranced Cayce correctly diagnosed the problem, and then Layne asked Cayce what to do about it. Cayce said the circulation needed to be increased to his throat area. Layne gave the suggestion, and he and Cayce's parents watched as Cayce's throat and upper chest area turned bright red with an infusion of blood. After a few minutes Cayce told Layne to suggest that the circulation return to normal. When he was brought out of trance, his throat was healed and he could speak again.

Layne wondered if the hypnotized Cayce might be able to diagnose and prescribe for others as well. Cayce was dubious, but Layne, who had some physical problems himself, prevailed upon Cayce to give it a try. The next day Layne made the suggestion to the hypnotized Cayce that he would go over Layne's body, diagnose his ailments, and prescribe a cure.

Layne could hardly keep up with Cayce's words, which filled several handwritten pages. When it was all over Layne had exactly what he wanted. Cayce, looking at what had come out of his mouth, was amazed. He couldn't even pronounce some of the medical terms he had used. The prescription proved beneficial to Layne.[3]

Edgar Cayce's clairvoyant career was born. Through his psychic gifts, Cayce was able to demonstrate the efficacy of his philosophy with many remarkable healings and other beneficial life changes. Thousands of people were healed following Cayce's directions, many of whom had exhausted all medical options. Many others had the quality of their lives changed for the better.

The Basic Spiritual Principle

In his readings, Cayce frequently expressed the principle of "Spirit is the life. Mind is the builder. Physical is the result." The following quote amplifies this principle and provides some images and metaphors to work with: "For mind is the builder and that which we think upon may become crimes or miracles. For thoughts are things and as their currents run through the environs of an entity's experience these become barriers or stepping-stones . . . " (906-3)[4]

"Thoughts are things." Our thoughts literally become "crimes or miracles," "barriers or stepping-stones." How does that work? This principle can be seen as a process or formula which moves from spirit through mind to the physical result. This process or formula is what creates illness in our lives as well as everything else that happens to us. It is why illnesses are meaningful. Understanding it and seeing how it works in your own life can be the beginning of healing and the beginning of freedom.

"Spirit" here can be seen in two ways. It refers to our personal spirit, the fact that we are spiritual beings. It also refers to Spirit, the source of *our* spirit, the Creator or Original Mind, which can be called God, All-That-Is, the Creative Forces—as Cayce often called God—or any other name which is meaningful to you and identifies that Source. When I capitalize *Spirit,* I am referring to that Source. When I use a small "s," I am referring to the spirit within each of us.

Spirit can be seen as divine energy or divine "matter." Just as energy and matter are interchangeable in quantum physics, so does divine energy pass through the mind where our thoughts turn it into matter. Thoughts become things. The "things" our thoughts become—the physical result—are our bodies and our entire physical experience.

If we use Cayce's metaphor of building, as in "mind is the builder," we see that both the energy and the material we use to build our physical experience come from Spirit. So we start out with the best materials possible. That which eventually becomes our physical reality, including our bodies, comes directly from the Creator. We and all of physical reality are made out of God "stuff." Spirit is the building

block for matter. (Some quantum physicists have con-
cluded that there is no smallest indivisible piece of matter.
Perhaps the building blocks of the universe are consciousness, not matter. In this framework, God consciousness
would be the building blocks of the universe.)

Imagine your mind as a pipe. Divine energy is poured
into one end of the pipe. Inside the pipe our mind modifies
that energy. We shape it with our thoughts and feelings. We
shape it with our fears and desires, our attitudes and beliefs. Pouring out of the other end of the pipe is the physical
result, our life experience, including our body and its state
of health or illness. If we *are* made out of God material—if
God is Love, we are made out of Love; if God is Light, we are
made out of Light—the universe has a positive intent or
bias. Because of this intent, because the very material we
are made of yearns toward the image of the Creator, it takes
a great deal of energy to make ourselves poor, unhappy, or
sick. Still, we are free to take divine energy, the very stuff of
God, and build pain, poverty, sickness, and lack of love.

Our ability to make ourselves unhappy or sick demonstrates how powerful we are. This shouldn't discourage us,
however. It is possible for us to cooperate with the positive
intent of the universe, to come into alignment or attunement with it, so the Spirit can come through our minds with
very little distortion. When this happens, we can become a
channel of blessings to ourselves and others. We can learn
to create miracles and stepping-stones even more easily
than we now create crimes and barriers, or serious illnesses.

But what happens inside that pipe called the mind that
can so strongly affect the spiritual building blocks passing
through?

The Process of Creation

I use the word *mind* in a broad sense here. The mind is
the waking consciousness as well as the unconscious and

the superconscious. The difference between the conscious and unconscious, for my purposes, is quite simple. What is conscious is what we are aware of at any given time or can easily be brought to awareness from our memory banks. Obviously the line between what is conscious and what is unconscious is not fixed. There is a large gray area and differences of opinion. When you can't recall someone's name we could say the name is in our unconscious but only temporarily so. It isn't deeply hidden away. The unconscious, on the other hand, contains things that are not easily available to consciousness. Many of these things are childhood experiences (or past-life experiences) that have been forgotten or even repressed. The unconscious also contains many ideas, attitudes, beliefs, expectations, fears, and desires which affect our lives every day.

Superconscious is a word coined, I believe, by Italian psychiatrist Roberto Assagioli, the father of psychosynthesis. I use the word to refer to the realm of consciousness in which our spiritual nature resides. This is the realm of the higher self, the Christ self, Buddha self, or God self. Some of our highest possibilities and ideals reside here and much of it is as unconscious as the negative things we repress. We repress our powerful, positive, beautiful, divine selves and they reside in the superconscious. Just as the unconscious can be explored through dreams, meditation, and other avenues, so can the superconscious be explored and many gifts can be raised to consciousness.

A surprising number of our physical experiences, including illnesses, are created by thoughts and feelings that are quite conscious. We don't think of many of them as thoughts or ideas, however. We think of them as facts or truths. We create a circular feedback in which a thought—a "fact"—becomes manifested in our experience: We believe that life is difficult, and our lives *become* difficult. We will have experiences and *focus* on experiences which confirm our thought-belief. The thought then becomes even stronger, more real, and more difficult to change.

Some experiences are created by thoughts and beliefs that are beneath our normal waking consciousness, like hidden fears. These will also be confirmed by our experiences. We will attract and experience the things we fear, and our fear will grow stronger. Other experiences are created by a wiser part of ourselves. This wiser part comes from the superconscious and may be called the inner self, higher self, the Holy Spirit, or any designation which is meaningful to you. Our wiser parts create peak or religious experiences, experiences of peace, beauty, or grace. We can use these experiences to create positive feedback loops, thus creating more similar experiences, or we can consider them flukes and continue to deny them as aspects of our true selves.

In psychosynthesis, Roberto Assagioli sought to get at the individual's fundamental core, which he called the true or higher self, through guided visualization and other active imagination techniques. He saw the individual as being made up of subpersonalities, some of whom represented our blocks and fears and some of whom represented aspects of the true self.

Psychotherapist Carl G. Jung theorized something similar to Assagioli's subpersonalities, ancient and universal characters he believed dwelt in an area of consciousness we all share, which he called the collective unconscious. He called his characters archetypes. The archetypes included characters like the wise old woman, the trickster, the eternal child, and the shadow.

The shadow represents the undesirable parts of ourselves that we reject, deny, and bury in the corners of our unconscious. These shadows show up in our dreams and nightmares as dark or threatening characters. We also project our shadow qualities onto other people, groups, and even nations and then do battle against these projections.

I believe there are also what I call "golden shadows." These are parts of ourselves that we also hide from, reject, and deny. These shadows, however, represent our power, beauty, and divinity—positive aspects we are unable to accept because of feelings of unworthiness or fear. These aspects show up in our dreams as divine beings, wise old women or men, powerful animals, or magical objects. We project these positive qualities onto others while not recognizing or accepting them in ourselves. People whom we admire, respect, and look up to—people we love—represent parts of ourselves we may be denying. These positive characters may be living or dead, people we know personally, or people we know only from the news or from history. If you can see it in someone else, you have it within yourself.

All of these thoughts, whether conscious or unconscious, whether fears or desires, modify Spirit as it passes through the mind. As we look at the process of the mind molding divine energy into our life experiences, we should keep in mind the existence of these unconscious and super-conscious shadows. They will show up in your dreams, in your waking experiences, and in your bodies. As we will see later, both the dark and golden shadows come bearing gifts of healing and transformation. We also need to pay attention to our conscious thoughts and the words we speak. These will help explain the physical experiences we are creating.

Hypnosis and the Creation of an Illness

We create our world and our daily experiences with our thoughts. One way to understand this process is to consider hypnosis. Hypnosis is a technique which involves making suggestions to someone while he or she is in a relaxed and receptive state of consciousness. If a hypnotized subject is told he or she is beautiful, the person will believe the hypnotist and act accordingly. If a hypnotist tells a subject that he or she is a great singer or dancer, the person will believe it. Furthermore, the individual will be able to sing or dance far better than usual.

I have had two experiences of this, one with a show hypnotist who told a hypnotized woman that she was Barbara Streisand. The woman sang beautifully! The other experience was a film showing a Russian experiment involving piano students. The idea was to hypnotize the students and suggest to them that they were various famous piano virtuosos. It was hoped that the hypnotic suggestions would improve their playing and that the improvement would spill over into their conscious state. The hypnosis *did* help the students improve their playing. An interesting side effect, however, was that the students not only played better, but they played in the style of the virtuoso they believed themselves to be.

In a sense, we hypnotize ourselves every day with the words we say and the thoughts we think. If we believe and say limiting things about ourselves we are creating limits in our lives. When we say, "I can't . . . " or "I'm no good at . . . " we are building barriers, false limitations. Unfortunately, our subsequent experience will always support our limiting belief. Whatever suggestions we give ourselves, repeatedly, become self-fulfilling prophecies. If you say, "I can't sing," often enough, you will see it as a truth, not just a belief. You'll be able to prove it every time you try to sing, and your friends will support your belief.

The energy that comes from Spirit does not have "can't" attached to it. The "can't" comes from our minds. The divine energy does not come with limits, does not come with "I'm not good enough" or "I'm unworthy." The Divine knows Itself in you and me no matter how much we have distorted It, and It continuously yearns to experience fulfillment through our lives.

Jenny, one of my clients, repeatedly spoke of things as being hard. It was so habitual that she really didn't notice it. When she found a lump in her breast, it became evident that the hardness she found in life had manifested as the hardness of a tumor. She was fortunate because the lump wasn't malignant. She immediately began to stop saying things were hard and turned her bad mind habit into a positive one by affirming that things were easy.

Stacy, a woman in one of my groups, habitually prefaced her statements with "I don't know," especially when she shared personal matters or visualization experiences. Another group member pointed this out to her and suggested that "not knowing" wasn't something she should affirm about herself. As we go in search of unconscious thoughts we want to change and superconscious qualities we want to embrace, it would be helpful to affirm the hypnotic suggestion, "I know!" These habitual negative hypnotic suggestions are difficult to catch because they *are* so habitual. Your friends can sometimes tell you about verbal habits you have, and you can reflect on them to see if they're possibly limiting or damaging to you.

Illnesses are frequently created through this self-hypnotic process. Ruth, a nurse in one of my healing classes, had cancer of the throat. She recalled that she would frequently say, "This job is killing me." Ruth cut back on her work hours and stopped the hypnotic suggestion and her cancer went into remission. I believe Ruth's cancer had less to do with the work she was doing, which didn't involve much speaking, and more to do with a calling to go into a more spiritual work which would involve speaking in public. These things are never simple, however. In a later section we'll see that the throat cancer also had to do with Ruth needing to say "no" to her two adult children and change that relationship.

We give ourselves such hypnotic suggestions all the time. Sometimes they're less severe, such as "He's a pain in the neck" or "She makes me sick." Spoken or thought frequently enough and with enough energy, these hypnotic statements will make us sick and can, in some cases, kill us.

Pay attention to your words, thoughts, and feelings. Whenever you catch yourself saying or thinking anything of a negative or limiting nature, stop. Immediately begin to de-energize negative and limiting thoughts or ideas by saying to yourself, "That's just a belief or idea. It's not the truth."

If you deny your negative and limiting thoughts their status as truths or facts, they will begin to lose their power over you. Even those things which seem as real as money problems, relationship problems, or serious illnesses *are nothing more than materialized ideas.*

Our illnesses and other life obstacles feel very real to us and can have a powerful emotional impact. Life-threatening illnesses *are* real and their consequences are real indeed. Healing does not come through denying the reality of your experiences, but through affirming your power as the creator of those experiences, and that includes the power to change your thoughts, and therefore your experiences, from negative and life denying to positive and life affirming.

Your Healing Journal

This book can be used as part of a healing journey—a journey for healing not just your illness, but your life. It may be helpful for you to keep a "log" or "journal" on this journey. Get yourself a notebook to serve as your healing journal. On the top of the first page write a title: "Healing Journal," "Healing Journey," or whatever is appropriate for you. Below that, on the same page, write in big letters:

My physical experience is the materialization
of my thoughts and ideas.

In this journal you will write down the limiting ideas you discover as you begin to pay attention to your self-hypnotic thoughts and what you say about yourself and others. These will be ideas about yourself, ideas about others, and ideas about the world. As you do this, remember that because they are just *ideas*, they can be changed! You will also pay attention to and write down the positive and expansive ideas and experiences you can think of, ideas that are working for you, whether they have to do with your body or some other part of your life. You might want to write negative and limiting ideas in one color ink and positive and expansive ideas in another.

Positive and Negative Ideas—Affirmations

If you have an idea that you're susceptible to a certain form of cancer because of statistics or family history (or you're just afraid it might happen to you), you can write down an opposite idea: "I am in good health and will remain in good health." It's best not to include the problem in your positive idea. If you say, "I will not get cancer," you are still giving energy to the idea of cancer. Set up two columns and put your current negative belief in the left column and its opposite or affirmative belief in the right column. (See Figure 1.)

As you write down positive and negative ideas and beliefs, you may begin to see patterns emerge. Pay attention to these patterns as they may suggest larger, more inclusive, beliefs. You may find yourself saying, "My job is hard." At another time you'll tell someone, "It's hard to make close friends." If you discover a number of ideas about things being hard, you might consider the possibility that you have the more fundamental belief that my client had: "Life is hard."

If you can uncover and work with these fundamental beliefs, it's possible to heal a number of different areas of your life at once. Remember, you're not just looking for ideas and beliefs that relate to your body and its health. Any negative or limiting ideas can affect your health.

At first the affirmative idea or belief will simply seem to be false and the limiting belief true. Later we will discuss

HEALING JOURNAL

Negative Beliefs and Ideas	Affirmation or Antidote
I can't sing.	I sing very well.
I feel uncomfortable with strangers.	I am comfortable with strangers.
People don't seem to care for me.	People seem to care for me.
I'm too fat.*	I am my ideal weight.
I don't have any energy.	I have unlimited energy.
I don't like being criticized.	I accept criticism graciously.
There are a lot of dangerous people in the world.	The world is a safe place, and people are basically good.
No one is willing to make a commitment in a relationship.	There are a lot of people willing to make a commitment in a relationship.
I have serious physical problems.	I'm in excellent health.
Things never seem to get any better.	My life gets better every day.

*You may find it difficult to see being overweight as an idea or belief. Such a condition can be measured and verified by your doctor and others. But in the metaphorical world, the world of meaning, such things are not truths. Being "too fat" is the materialization of an idea or belief. Unfortunately, your bathroom scale and your mirrors continually confirm your belief. In order to begin changing such beliefs it is necessary to use antidotes and affirmations that fly in the face of the physical "evidence." When you're successful in changing your beliefs, the physical manifestation will change. You'll lose weight. As one who has been overweight for half of my life, I do not suggest any of this is easy to do.

Figure 1

ways of changing these limiting beliefs. For now, you can allow yourself to consider the possibility that your limiting belief is just a belief, just an idea about reality, not a truth. If it's just an idea, then it's possible to come up with a different idea, give time and emotional energy to the new idea, and change your physical experience.

Begin consciously inputting new and more positive ideas by stating the opposite belief as an affirmation: "Life is easy." Follow that up with some action. Do something that's easy for you. As you affirm that life is easy, begin to pay more attention to the things in your life that *are* easy.

A simple but powerful psychological principle that can change your life immediately has to do with consciously directing your attention and perception to more positive aspects of your life: Our beliefs and attitudes, our ideas about ourselves, others, and the world act as focusing agents that direct our attention and perception. We do not see things as they are. We see things as *we* are.

For example, when you buy a new car, you immediately begin to notice other cars of the same kind everywhere you look. It isn't that there is suddenly more of that kind of car. Your new car has simply opened a window of attention and perception that wasn't open before.

If you're walking down the street and you're in a bad mood, you tend to experience other people who are also in a bad mood. Conversely, when you're in a good mood you will notice other people smiling, and people will tend to say "hello" to you. The windows of your attention and perception are opened by your thoughts, feelings, and expectations. It has been said that frowning takes more muscular energy than smiling. New research suggests that smiling helps build the immune system, *even when you fake the smile!*

By creating positive affirmations to offset your negative beliefs and attitudes, you can deliberately open more positive windows of attention and perception. The affirmation becomes what I call a focusing agent, something that directs or attracts your attention and energy. You may discover that there are more positive things in your life right now than you realized because your attention and perception have been focused on the negatives, on your problems and fears.

As you continue to uncover ideas and beliefs that are limiting or negative, ideas that create "crimes and barriers," pay attention to those areas of your life that are working for you. You may be in good shape financially, or your relationships might be going smoothly. Someone else might be in excellent health but be struggling with money problems.

In your journal, write down the areas in your life that are working well. Write down the feelings and attitudes you have about those areas and about yourself in relation to them. You may assume your ideas and feelings are positive because of your success in those areas. It may take some time before you are able to turn cause and effect around and see your positive ideas and feelings as the *cause* of your successes.

Once you see the positive thoughts and feelings that led to the successes in your life, it can help you bring more positive thoughts and feelings into the areas that are not working as well. A person who is successful in business can bring some of the thoughts and feelings from that part of his or her life and apply them to an illness. In dealing with a serious illness, our feelings can be our greatest foe or our greatest ally. Wherever we can find good feelings in our life, feelings of success and competence, we can try to bring those feelings into our healing process.

Self-Image

Personality or self-image is something we tend to take for granted. We don't see it as something that can be easily changed. We may find ourselves saying things like, "That's just the way I am," or "I just don't like my body."

Your self-image is creative. What you think about your-self has a powerful effect on how you act in the world, how you treat others, and how you expect to be treated. Many limitations in your life are the result of how you view your-self. Many of the things you create in your life or are unable to create in your life are the result of your self-image.

Some of the roles we play represent powerful modelers of self-image. One of the most powerful of these is called "mother." There will be more on this in chapter 6. Ruth, the nurse with throat cancer, had a grown daughter living at home and a son away at college, a good hour-and-a-half drive. She still cooked, cleaned, and did laundry for her daughter. When her son had an emergency at school, she always drove over to help him out. Her cancer made it im-possible for her to fulfill her motherly duties, at least for a time. Something remarkable happened. When she stopped trying to fulfill the self-image of mother, her adult children suddenly became more responsible. Our roles and self-im-age also affect those around us.

Your self-image is not fixed. Your personality is not fixed. Your gifts and abilities are not fixed. Your limitations are also not fixed. Your self-image is a constellation of ideas you have about yourself. In your healing journal, list any personal qualities that are not helpful to you, that you would like to change. Then write down as many of your positive qualities as you can think of. As you go about your day, others may come to mind. Write them all down.

Remember the principle you wrote down in your healing journal at the beginning: "My physical experience is the materialization of my thoughts and ideas." This is true for your self-image or personality as well: "My self-image is a manifestation of my thoughts and ideas about myself."

In writing down negative qualities, write "I believe ... " or "I think . . . " rather than "I am . . . " If you say, "I am shy," you're stating it as a fact or truth about yourself. If you say, "I believe I'm shy" or "I think of myself as shy," you're putting it in the realm of thought and belief, where it belongs. Once we perceive something as an idea about ourselves and not a truth, it becomes more malleable and subject to change.

The Universal Feedback System

What if you're unable to catch all of your negative self-talk, your self-hypnotic suggestions? What if some of your thoughts are unconscious, your fears unknown to you? I believe that most of our ideas are quite conscious. They may *seem* unconscious. Because we take them so much for granted, they are invisible to us. We look through narrow windows of attention and perception and think we're seeing the whole landscape.

Affirm in your journal that your thoughts and ideas are conscious and available to you: *"I am open to discovering the thoughts and ideas that are causing limitations in my life, thoughts that are causing or might cause illness. They come to me clearly and easily."*

There is another avenue for discovering invisible or unconscious thoughts. Illnesses themselves represent one part of that avenue. I call it the Universal Feedback System, and it's remarkably simple in theory. Since my mind—my thoughts—creates my physical experience, all I have to do is look at what I've created in my life and follow that creation back to the thoughts that created it!

This isn't necessarily easy to do, in practice, because it requires a lot of honesty and courage. It requires taking full responsibility for what is happening in our lives. With that responsibility comes freedom and the power to consciously direct our lives.

If you have a serious illness you can ask yourself, "What thoughts, ideas, or beliefs might have created this situation?" There may not be a single idea or belief but a constellation of ideas. As you uncover thoughts and beliefs that seem related to the dis-ease (lack of ease) in your life, you may begin to see themes or patterns. Try to put your beliefs together like a puzzle. Look for constellating or fundamental beliefs, master themes such as I mentioned above ("life is difficult"). Write them in your journal.

There is no part of your life that is not part of the feedback system. You may already record and work with your dreams. Your dreams are an excellent source of feedback about what is going on in your mind. I will write more about dreams later, but for now I want to present the idea of looking at your waking experience as if it were a dream. Our waking experiences are as meaningful as our dreams. Because your thoughts create your experiences, your experiences are like dreams that tell you what is going on in your mind.

All life experiences, therefore, like our dreams, are part of this Universal Feedback System. Illnesses are like dream symbols and can be worked with and interpreted like any other symbol.

As you try to catch your negative, self-hypnotic statements and work with your illness as a dream, it is important to understand the unity of life. In other words, you can't separate your illness from other parts of your life. Julie, another nurse in one of my metaphorical healing classes, had breast cancer which led to a mastectomy. As a result of her cancer, she left her job and her husband.

The feedback in her life—the cancer—was telling her that both her marriage and her work were toxic to her. This was something she was aware of, but for whatever reason she couldn't quite find the energy or courage to do anything about it. In her case and in many other cases the imbalances or dis-eases are known, but we often follow the path of least resistance; inertia carries us forward in familiar, if unhappy, ruts.

This emphasizes a basic principle of this book: Illnesses are not the problem but are themselves simply part of the feedback system, pointing to the real problem. You may not think it's that important to change your relationships, reconcile with family members, improve your work situation, or make other healing changes in your life, but in some cases those changes can save your life. At the very least they will definitely improve the quality of your life.

It's possible that Julie could have taken some healing action earlier, perhaps divorcing her husband or getting into counseling and healing the relationship. She could have quit her job or possibly done something to make it more satisfying. Taking such actions earlier, when the feedback was less severe, might have prevented Julie from contracting cancer.

This is not to criticize Julie or any of us who let situations go too far before we take corrective action. It's just that we have a built-in mechanism that is designed to give us feedback about what our thoughts and ideas are creating. If we do not respond to the feedback in its earlier stages, the situation is bound to escalate into an illness or other life crisis. Your beliefs create a situation in your life. The situation confirms the validity of the belief, and the belief becomes stronger, creating additional similar situations or making the original situation worse.

In your journal, write down the areas in your life that aren't working for you. I realize that many people see these situations as having an external basis. It's your mate, children, or parents; your job, your boss, the economy, or your genes. I would like you to try to think differently about these situations. If things aren't working for you now, you have nothing to lose by trying a different approach, a different way of perceiving your experiences.

Think of the people and other outside influences in your life as dream characters, situations, and symbols. If these seemingly external people and influences were solely the result of your own thoughts and feelings, what would those thoughts and feelings be? For example, if you have trouble with your boss at work, and this is a pattern in almost every job you've had, your experiences may *not* be telling you something about the nature of bosses or authorities. They may be telling you something about your *own* issue with authority. You may need to change your attitude toward authority figures, but the deeper issue may be about your own sense of authority, a potentially positive aspect of yourself that you may be denying.

As you begin to see your experiences and relationships as part of a feedback system, a guidance system for helping you to improve your life, you will be able to see yourself more and more as the author of your experiences and less as the victim. Ironically, you can begin to see all of the negative experiences and individuals in your life as teachers and helpers rather than as obstacles and enemies. Illnesses are not the problem. They are, in fact, part of the solution. Our illnesses have within them a healing intent.

The negative feedback we get from our world is not a reflection of what is true about us *or* about the world. It is a reflection of our beliefs. A serious illness may be the result of many months or years of feedback that we either did not perceive or we overlooked or ignored. When you deny the power of your own thoughts and place your issues outside yourself, when you blame other people or situations for what's happening in your life, you give your power away and confirm yourself as helpless.

Any part of your life that is not working may be telling you something about an imbalance or dis-ease in your thinking. In a sense, it's a thought problem. Your problems and illnesses should therefore be seen as blessings because they can serve to heal your life, to get you back on a path of health and wholeness.

The TV program "Entertainment Tonight" had an interview with TV journalist and former NBC correspondent Linda Ellerbee. Ellerbee had undergone a bilateral mastectomy for cancer. In the interview she said, "Despite cancer, [pause] or maybe because of it, I'm having the best year of my life." It seemed she was realizing for the first time that her life-threatening illness contained a gift.

It's interesting to read and hear stories of people with cancer, AIDS, and other life-threatening illnesses. Time after time, they say their illness has changed their lives in positive ways, healing relationships and changing life values and priorities. Some actually say they are grateful for the illness because of the quality of life they have experienced as a result. Wouldn't it be wonderful if we could have such a transformation, enjoy a similar quality of life, filled with meaning and life-affirming relationships, *without* contracting a life-threatening illness?

We *can* do that if we're able to hear and respond to the feedback we are constantly receiving from our waking and dreaming experiences. We are continually being given life-giving, life-affirming, life-changing information. What we need to do is pay attention, learn how to read the feedback, and then act on that information.

Redundancy

Redundancy is one important aspect of the Universal Feedback System. Considering the various sources we have for feedback—dreams, waking life, past lives, childhood memories—it would be easy to go into information overload. That's where redundancy comes in. If people do not explore and heal negative childhood experiences, are they doomed to suffer the consequences of those experiences for the rest of their lives? If someone does not believe in past lives or is not interested in exploring them, is he or she similarly doomed? Because of redundancy, this is not the case.

A fellow dream consultant was sharing one of her client's dreams with me. The dreamer was planning on leaving her husband and was concerned about the timing. She sought advice from her dreams and brought a dream to my colleague to work on.

Together they were able to extract the dream's message. The dream seemed to indicate the woman should not leave her husband at that time. There was one symbol, however, that left both of them puzzled—won-ton soup. They didn't realize that this one strange symbol contained within it the same meaning they had worked together to find in the rest of the dream. I turned the words *won ton* around and came up with *not now!*

Dreams commonly use puns and word games to get their message across. I enjoy word games *and* puns and have found that interest to be valuable in understanding dreams. I already knew that dreams give us the same message over and over again until we "get it." Now I see that dreams sometimes give us the same message more than once in the same dream!

I have since found the principle of redundancy operating in a number of dreams. Grace, one of my clients, dreamed about her teenage girlfriends, especially one named Karen. Our work revealed that the dream was telling Grace she didn't believe her friends cared about her when she was a teenager. Later I realized that "Karen" also contained the meaning of the dream (Karen/caring).

It's not just our dreams that are redundant. The entire feedback system is based on redundancies. We are given the same messages over and over again until we receive them *and* act on them.

Some people feel overwhelmed by their problems. It has been my experience, however, that most of us are dealing with just a few fundamental core life issues. The feedback system primarily deals with core issues, not the satellite issues. Your satellite issues will always lead to more central or core issues. When core issues are healed, the symptoms and satellite issues will follow.

Since we are primarily dealing with a few core issues or challenges at any given time, the feedback system of dreams, waking life experiences, and past experiences (childhood and past lives) *is giving us the same messages/ information over and over again.*

Redundancy encompasses Carl Jung's concept of synchronicity. A synchronicity is a meaningful coincidence. Such coincidences are to be expected in a metaphorical or meaningful world, a world built by the mind. Synchronicity is further evidence of the positive bias of the universe.

Redundancy gives us more choices in terms of healing our illness and our life. One person might believe dreamwork is the only route to healing and transformation. Another believes it's impossible to heal the adult without healing one's childhood or inner child. Still another swears by past-life work. If you are overwhelmed by the many different systems for healing and making life changes, you needn't be. The psyche or inner self can cooperate with any system of healing you choose. Redundancy assures that your issues will come up in any area you choose to look at and can be worked on with just about any system or technique you choose to follow.

Divinity is not limited, and neither are we. The mind issues we are dealing with, the attitudes and emotions that are creating our current life experiences, including our body experiences, can be worked with using many different modalities. We have a multitude of sources for the same information. Each source of information becomes an arena for working with the feedback we receive to help us discover and change our current beliefs.

Whispers and Shouts

How do thoughts form our experience, and how can we follow our experience back to the creating thought or belief? The second important element of the Universal Feedback System can be called Whispers and Shouts.

Lazaris, a nonphysical entity channeled by Jach Pursel, speaks of whispers and shouts. I have borrowed his terminology for my own purposes. When we first begin exercising a certain thought or idea, early in our self-hypnosis program, the feedback we get from our waking and sleeping experiences is mild, relatively quiet, a whisper. If we don't hear or respond to the whispers—the early warning system—the feedback gets louder. After a long period of ignoring the feedback or not acting on it we will experience shouts. Shouts take the form of nightmares, serious illnesses, or other life crises.

For example, we can assume that Julie was happy with her husband and her job in the beginning. Using her job as our example, we would expect she had some ideas or beliefs about work in general or perhaps about her career, specifically, that gradually led to her unhappiness.

Any new venture may begin with high hopes and expectations, but if we have fears and negative beliefs they can begin rather insidiously gnawing away at those hopes. Our beliefs act as filters which color our perception of people and events. Our thought-filters work in two ways to bring about a physical result.

First, we tend to perceive our experiences through our thought-filters. This means we will notice and give emotional energy to experiences that fit our beliefs, and we will not notice or give energy to experiences that do not fit. Remember the windows of attention and perception? Let's assume that Julie had a belief that people don't appreciate her work. (Some beliefs are area-specific. That is, Julie may believe she's appreciated in other areas of her life, but not at work. Or it may be a larger belief or core belief that colors all areas of her life, including her marriage.)

Julie will notice experiences of not being appreciated at work, however small, will get upset, and will give emotional energy to the experiences. These small experiences are whispering to Julie about her belief regarding appreciation. Experiences are like balloons. We determine how big and important they are by how much energy we give to them, how much we blow them up. She will tend *not* to notice examples of being appreciated or will give them less emotional energy. They will become practically invisible because of her thought-filter.

The second way our thought-filters work is by getting others to cooperate with our beliefs. Julie's negative belief not only causes her to selectively perceive her work experiences, but her attitude affects or, we might say, *in*fects her co-workers and superiors, and they will begin to cooperate with that belief. Soon she will actually *have* fewer instances of appreciation and will have more criticism or lack of appreciation. And so the negative feedback loop is set up.

Our thoughts create a perception of reality, but they also ultimately create the reality itself. Julie will be able to document more and more instances of lack of appreciation. The job will become more of a burden and she will want to get out any way she can, including contracting a serious illness. The whisper gradually becomes a shout.

This is a process that takes time. Some marriages last for many years before there is sufficient unhappiness to bring about a divorce. Some people stay in a job for years before they're dissatisfied enough to leave. Some, like my father, never leave their job even when—as my father said to me— he hated every day he had to go to work.

The key to illness prevention is hearing and acting on the whispers before they become shouts. To do this requires the courage to accept the feedback from our experiences as beliefs, not truths. Early on, Julie could have asked herself, "Why do I feel unappreciated at work?" She could examine her beliefs to see if she expects to be unappreciated. She could look at her past and see if there's a pattern of lack of appreciation related to work. She also might consciously try to recall experiences at work where she *was* appreciated so she could see her selective perception in operation.

It's far easier to change our thoughts when we catch the feedback at the whisper stage. Unfortunately, it's difficult to recognize it at that stage. Aside from learning what to do when life is shouting at you, you will learn to be more aware of the whispers. You will still need to make changes, still need to find the courage to heed the whispers and act on them, but it requires far less courage and less life disruption at the whisper stage.

One simple approach that can help you catch the whispers is to think and speak of your experiences in terms of thoughts, ideas, or beliefs. You will begin to see yourself more as the creator and less as the victim. Instead of saying, "I'm unappreciated at work," Julie could say, "I think or have the idea I'm unappreciated at work." If you have a series of bad experiences during the day and find yourself saying, "People are really rude," you can change that statement into a whisper of feedback: "I believe people are really rude."

This may be the most difficult thing to understand in this philosophical framework. You may find yourself insisting that people *are* rude, and that's why you have the belief. But in the metaphorical world, *belief always precedes experience.* You can see how a belief like this can eventually lead to illness if you change it to "People make me sick!"

Even being sick is not a truth about you, even though you can show evidence in the form of symptoms. Being sick is nothing but the materialization of a belief or complex of beliefs. Being healthy is the truth about all of us. Being happy is the truth. Experiencing nurturing and fulfilling relationships is the truth. Experiencing abundance is the truth. Spiritual growth and fulfillment are truths.

Spirit is the life. Spirit, flowing through our minds, is pure Love, pure Light, pure God. The mind modifies that good energy. Our thoughts and beliefs can impede that energy: suppress, bend, and distort it. Our problems could be called Spirit-suppression devices or love-suppression devices. It is a measure of the power of our free will that we are able to take the energy of Spirit and, in Cayce's words, turn it into crimes and barriers.

In the chapters on dreams I will talk about using your dreams to detect whispers before they become shouts. There is a two-part method for detecting whispers that you can work with in your journal right now.

The first part is simply to pay attention to the persons and situations which elicit a strong emotional response in you. Positive reactions give you clues as to the kind of people and situations you want to cultivate in your life. Negative reactions may be whispers about some aspect of yourself you're suppressing and projecting onto others.

If you have a strong positive or negative reaction to a person or situation in your life, even if it's something or someone on TV or in a book, write the experience down in your journal. Notice if there are certain subjects, situations, persons, or types of persons that consistently get an emotional reaction out of you. They *may* be whispers.

For example: I was working as the warehouse manager for a software distributor. I had a man work for me as a temporary employee for one day. He was very involved in a peace organization and encouraged me and others to come to one of their meetings.

There is no doubt in my mind the man was sincere in his desire for world peace. Before the day was over, however, he nearly came to blows with another employee. Although this man's passion for peace was laudable, it also helped him mask his personal problem with peace. He projected his lack of inner peace onto the world and essentially tried to heal himself by creating world peace. His emotional intensity about peace was a whisper about an imbalance in his life.

This does not mean that every negative emotional experience you have indicates an imbalance or dis-ease. I'm not saying that all personal passions or emotional issues are whispers about imbalances. Everyone working for world peace does not necessarily have a personal issue with peace. But strong emotions can be clues to personal issues.

The healing life requires that we at least examine such issues and see if there isn't a whisper about a belief or feeling that's suppressing Spirit.

The second part is to be used in conjunction with the first. As you pay attention to emotionally charged persons, experiences, and issues, also pay attention to repetition, the redundancy mentioned earlier. Do certain issues keep coming up in your life? Do you keep encountering the same type of people and wonder why they're in your life? Do you have the same kinds of experiences over and over again?

Some men and women repeatedly end up in the same kind of unhealthy relationships. The experiences confirm their attitudes about what women are like or what men are like. It doesn't occur to them to consider the possibility that their belief about what women or men are like determines their experiences. Another "benefit" of not accepting the message in these whispers is the ability to avoid a committed relationship while blaming it on the opposite sex.

You might end up with the same kind of boss job after job. The redundancy does not show you the accuracy of your belief about bosses. It shows you the power of your belief to repeatedly create such a boss. As in the example above, it also gives you an excuse for not advancing in your work.

These redundancies can take the form of synchronicity, coincidences that are meaningful but have no obvious causal relationship. I dreamed about a duck wearing a life preserver, an unusual image to say the least. That morning in the Sunday funnies there were two different comic strips that featured ducks in life preservers. The image is quite humorous and it might seem that nothing of value, certainly nothing serious, could come out of such an image. But the inner self may not be afraid to use humor to make a serious point. The redundancy or synchronicity simply told me that the image was an important one for me. A duck in a life preserver is an image of someone being unnecessarily careful. The whisper was telling me I needed to take more chances in my life and also that it would be safe to do so.

Write these redundancies and emotionally charged situations down in your journal. You can use the dream interpretation and non-interpretation methods from chapters 7 and 8 to try to understand them. Meanwhile, you will find that simply writing them in your journal will put in motion inner mechanisms of the psyche—the whispering mechanism of the self—to give you further information and additional clarifying whispers.

The Process of Change

The most important thing about the process of change is that you have the ability to do it. It doesn't matter where your beliefs come from—your suppressing thoughts and feelings. What is important is the beliefs themselves and that *those beliefs exist in your mind in the present.* They need to be changed in the present, and it will be helpful to understand how your present beliefs, including those which are harmful and limiting, are serving you.

Your illness *is* serving you in some way. It is either bringing you something you feel you need in your life, or protecting you from something you are afraid of, or both.

There are two questions—two sides of the same question—you can ask about your illness or any other problem in your life. If you can answer honestly, it may become clear to you why you have the problem or illness and what you are risking in becoming healed and making changes in your life. The answers to these questions should be put in your journal.

"How is this problem/illness serving me?" As strange as it may seem, your illness is serving you in some way. It may be protecting a negative self-image. It may even be—in a negative way—giving meaning to your life. As you'll see in later chapters, your illness can serve you in both negative and positive ways. The ideal is to use your illness to serve the healing of your life

"What is this problem/illness protecting me from?" It may be protecting you from something you perceive to be even worse than the illness itself. Many of us use perceived limitations, including illnesses, to protect us from very positive things we say we want in our lives. When we don't believe we can really have the love we seek or the success in our work, our illness can be used to protect us either from failing at those endeavors or from succeeding. Our man or woman who can't find the ideal mate is protected from the risk of an intimate relationship. Our individual with the bad bosses is protected from career success or perhaps a larger failure.

You may be surprised at the many ways in which an illness can serve you and/or protect you, and I will write more about that later. You will also see that you may have to give up some perceived protection in order to heal. You may have to take some risks. Our waking experience is the result of the flow of Spirit through our minds. Our problems are Spirit-suppression devices. Miracles in our life are the result of the free flow of Spirit. One of the things we can practice on a daily basis is experiencing Spirit flowing through us unsuppressed, as in the following exercise.

I have done visualization exercises with individuals and groups for over twenty years. I have found that long inductions are not necessary. In fact, I want to impress upon you the idea that these exercises are easy to do and don't require a lot of preparatory relaxation or any prior experience. Those of you who are meditators or experienced visualizers should use whatever relaxation techniques you are familiar with. Those of you who are new at this will find that a few deep breaths, taken in slowly, held a second or two, and then released slowly, and a few minutes of getting the body comfortable and relaxed will be sufficient.

Exercise: Spirit-Suppression Devices

This is primarily a feeling exercise, although you may want to visualize the process. When you are finished, write your feelings and images down in your healing journal.

Give yourself ten to fifteen minutes of uninterrupted time. You may want to have music playing quietly in the background. You can sit or lie down. Be as comfortable as possible but not so comfortable you'll fall asleep. Close your eyes and take a few deep breaths. Spend a few minutes relaxing your body.

When you are ready, imagine your body, representing your mind, as a pipe with Spirit flowing through it. Think of it as pure Spirit energy, love, white light, a golden liquid, or any other meaningful image. Imagine your fears and negative thoughts and feelings as obstacles in your mind-body which suppress, impede, and distort that energy as it passes through.

Experience that for a few moments and see how it feels. Some people may experience their Spirit-suppression devices in specific parts of their bodies. In some cases they will correspond to physical problems, and in some cases they will be more symbolic. Note those places. Now imagine removing your Spirit-suppression devices, all of your limiting thoughts and beliefs. You can visualize some kind of container to hold them until the exercise is over. When you pick them up at the end of the exercise, perhaps some will be weaker, lighter, or even gone! You may choose to leave some of them in the container.

Spend the rest of the time experiencing the free flow of Spirit through your mind-body. Emotions or images may rise up. Note them with your mind, and let them flow away. You may feel resistance in your body. Don't judge it or try to make it go away. Notice it and let it go. If you feel yourself continually drifting away from your focus, it may be time to stop, or you may be able to bring yourself back to the exercise with a word or phrase. One woman used this affirmation: "I release all Spirit-suppression devices." She found it effective in keeping herself focused.

Gently bring yourself back when you feel finished.

Do this exercise frequently. Imagine the Spirit flowing through you while you're engaged in any activity, alone or while interacting with others. See if it doesn't enhance whatever you're doing, especially when you're engaged in any healing work. If you're involved with a doctor or other health practitioner, imagine Spirit flowing unsuppressed through your body, through your healer, and through the treatment itself.

As you pay attention to your thoughts and feelings, you can consciously become aware of which ones are Spirit-suppression devices and imagine releasing them from your mind.

Mind as Bucket

I have likened the mind to a pipe which acts on the spiritual energy coming through it and turns that energy into your physical life. In terms of making changes in your life, there's another image that might be helpful—mind as bucket. We all use a certain amount of spiritual energy in any given day, and we use that energy for good or ill. The mind is like a bucket that contains a certain amount of thought. We fill it with thoughts each day.

As you go through your day and begin paying attention to your thoughts and feelings, try to note how many of your thoughts are negative. How many are worry thoughts, fear thoughts, anger thoughts, judging thoughts, guilty thoughts? How many are positive, loving, uplifting, joyful, peaceful? Every day your mind bucket is going to be filled with thoughts. What will be your positive/negative ratio?

You can begin consciously and deliberately putting more positive thoughts into the bucket. This process can take the form of affirmations or prayers and creating positive goals and ideals. If your goal is self-healing, you can deliberately put more thought time and thought energy into your goal of health, energizing the desired outcome, and less thought time into worry and fear about the illness.

Melinda, a woman in one of my healing workshops, had two strokes ten years apart. When I saw her she had some difficulty walking and speaking but had recovered to a large degree. One of the questions I asked her was, "What do you imagine doing with your life once you are healed?" To her surprise, she realized she never thought about what her life would be like after she was healed. There was absolutely no energy going into life-after-stroke.

If we're going to use the mind to build health, we need to concentrate on healing. But working on healing can still focus our attention and energy on the illness, on the problem. We also need to consciously focus our mind energy, our thoughts, on the outcome, the healed self. The mind as builder needs a plan, a blueprint that represents the finished product, the goal or ideal.

Take time to write down your goal or ideal in terms of healing, but do more than say you want to be healed. What will you do as a healed person? You might finish this sentence in as many ways as possible: "I want to be healed so I can . . . " or "I want to be healed in order to accomplish the following goals . . . " Be specific and add to the list as new goals come to you.

Thoughts are things and mind is the builder. We are here to learn to be more conscious builders, to learn the wonderful art of building stepping-stones and miracles.

2

The Mind-Body Dance

Does the body dance to the mind's tune? Science is beginning to catch up with the wisdom of the ancients, and the answer increasingly is a resounding "Yes!" Body systems, once thought to be less related to one another than our feet are to our heads, are now seen as intimately connected in an ongoing electrochemical dance. Understanding this dance can help us see how something as seemingly insubstantial as a thought or feeling can affect the body and, over time, make us sick. Beyond that, however, I am suggesting that illnesses are specific metaphors that can lead back to the thoughts and feelings which gave them birth.

We now know that our nervous, endocrine, and immune systems are in continuous communication with one another, sending and receiving chemical messages by way of amino acid compounds called peptides and neuropeptides. "The neuropeptides link the nervous system, endo-

34

crine system, and immune system. They transmit, receive, and monitor the flow of information, and adapt accordingly."[1] The formerly separate disciplines of neurology, immunology, and endocrinology have given way to a new science named *psychoneuroimmunology* (PNI) by Robert Ader of the University of Rochester in 1975.

It was Ader who serendipitously broke the *psyche-soma* or mind-body barrier. He was studying "conditioned aversion" using classical conditioning. In classical conditioning, a stimulus is presented to a subject (such as food to a dog) which causes a physiological response (salivation). The first stimulus is paired with a second unrelated stimulus (the ring of a bell). After sufficient repetitions of presenting the bell and food together, the dog will salivate at the sound of the bell with no food present. In conditioned aversion, one of the stimuli is neutral and one is negative.

Ader was pairing saccharin-flavored water with a noxious drug, cyclophosphamide, which causes nausea. His subjects (rats) were given the flavored water to drink and were then immediately injected with the drug. Learning usually occurred with one trial. After associating the saccharin-flavored water with the noxious drug, the rats would become nauseated from drinking the flavored water alone.

There was a complicating side effect, however. Ader's rats were dying even though they were no longer receiving the drug. It turned out that one effect of cyclophosphamide is temporary suppression of the immune system. "The rats had not only become conditioned to the nausea, but they also seemed to learn to repeat the effect of cyclophosphamide on the immune system. The rats had learned to suppress their immune systems in response to tasting the sweetened water."[2]

This was followed by similar conditioning experiments which confirmed Ader's findings. Some of these experiments demonstrated immune system enhancement through conditioning.

The mind-body connection can be demonstrated by wiggling your finger. The decision to wiggle your finger triggers nerve cells in the brain that trace a path down to your finger. A nerve cell produces an electrical charge. The charge activates a chemical reaction at the end of the cell. The chemical, a neurotransmitter, jumps the tiny gap between one nerve cell and another and causes the next cell to fire (electrically discharge), and so it goes all the way to your finger.

When we say, "Thoughts are things," we now know what some of those things are. Every thought and feeling causes the secretion of messenger substances such as peptides, as well as neurotransmitters and hormones. These substances are secreted by the central nervous system, the endocrine system, and the immune system.

While our thoughts and feelings cause inner chemical emissions, they are also affected by these chemicals. Peptides, for example, are associated with pleasure, pain, learning, appetite, sexuality, and anxiety. These "mood regulators" may help to integrate behavior, and they definitely alter consciousness.

As Aron Belkin, director of the National Center for Psychoneuroendocrinology in Moscow, put it, "To say mind and body are one is almost a platitude . . . The ancient Greeks knew as much. The key is the interaction. We are investigating how an immaterial thought creates such dramatic repercussions in the body."[3]

Nearly one hundred years ago a young Edgar Cayce healed his throat with a suggestion that directed his body's circulatory system to a specific site—something that doctors of Cayce's time believed should not have been possible. Today that experience, while still not fully understood, is well within the realm of scientific respectability.

Mind over Immunity

One of the most common ways in which the mind interacts with the body, for health or illness, is through the immune system. Our thoughts and feelings can strengthen or weaken the immune system, our most powerful ally in preventing and healing illness. Ader's conditioned rats and many subsequent studies have shown that the immune system is subject to alteration through mind and mood.

As Robert Ornstein and David Sobel state in *The Healing Brain*, "There are numerous connections between the nervous system and the immune system, making it possible to understand how the mind can influence resistance or susceptibility to disease."[4]

The full extent of the relationship between the immune system and diseases isn't known, but it's certainly a factor in many illnesses from colds to cancer. Cold germs are routinely destroyed by the immune system unless it is in a suppressed state. Potentially cancerous cells, circulating in the bodies of healthy individuals, are eliminated by a healthy immune system.

A strong immune system is important in the prevention and healing of illness. In later chapters I will speak more about ways to improve immune functioning, including lifestyle choices. For now, the listing in Figure 2 draws from a number of studies which reveal ways in which the immune system is suppressed and ways in which it can be enhanced.

As a participant in the mind-body dance, it is important that you decide whether you are going to lead or follow. In your healing journal you may want to rate yourself on the listed items and see where you might make helpful changes. Choose two or three items from the immune system enhancement list that you can easily incorporate into your life. It can be as simple as spending five or ten minutes listening to music that you love (or playing it if you play an instru-

---

FACTORS THAT TEND TO ENHANCE OR DEPRESS THE IMMUNE SYSTEM

Immune System Depressors	Immune System Enhancers
Loneliness	Sufficient sleep
Stress	Modest exercise
Pessimism	Relaxation (meditation)
Feeling out of control	Optimism
Depression	Hypnotism (could also be
Grief	used to depress the immune
Loss of spouse	system)
Feeling powerless	Hugs (touch)
	Music
	Laughter
	Confession (speaking of
	painful experiences, if only in
	your journal)
	Love

Figure 2

ment). Read a book just for pleasure. Take a short walk every day. According to Robert Thayer of California State University, Long Beach, short brisk walks are a natural antidepressant.[5] Watch a comedy, meditate, sit quietly looking at a tree, or play with a pet or a child.

Although stress is commonly cited as a negative factor in the disease process, both as a causative agent and as a factor in prolonging an illness or even contributing to death, current studies suggest that stress itself is not the problem. It's our response to stress that can depress our immune system and negatively affect our health. A sense of helplessness, hopelessness, or lack of control in the face of stress can lead to illness.

Dr. Bernie Siegel is a popular speaker and writer who has

brought the importance of the mind-body connection to the public. As he says, in his book *Love, Medicine, and Miracles*, "We don't yet understand all the ways in which brain chemicals are related to emotions and thoughts, but the salient point is that our state of mind has an immediate and direct effect on our state of body. We can change the body by dealing with how we feel. If we ignore our despair, the body receives a 'die' message. If we deal with our pain and seek help, then the message is 'Living is difficult but desirable,' and the immune system works to keep us alive."[6]

To make one generalization at this point, I would say we may need to have more fun in our lives. If you fill your "mind bucket" with more pleasurable activities on a daily basis, you will have less time for things that suppress your immune system. You will benefit in body and mind from these activities.

The healthy life is made of such small and simple things, just as the conditions that spawn illnesses are built up day by day, little by little. It may be possible for you to have a miraculous healing, and I believe it is. In the meantime, provide your own healing whispers to the body. Health will surely follow.

Inner and Outer Feedback

There is an internal mind-body dance, a complex communication network connecting the central nervous system, the immune system, and the endocrine system. Of course, all body systems are involved and affected. But this complex internal feedback system is not insulated within the body.

Just as these three body systems interact with one another, so do the mind, body, and life experiences (which I'll call "world") communicate constantly. Imagine a triangle with the nervous system, immune system, and endocrine system at the three points. (See Figure 3.) The lines of the triangle represent paths of two-way communication in which each system communicates with the other two. Now imagine the same triangle with mind, body, and world at the three points. The same two-way communication exists here.

Following is a more detailed look at the Universal Feedback System, demonstrating the two-way feedback among mind, body, and world.

The Mind-Body Dance

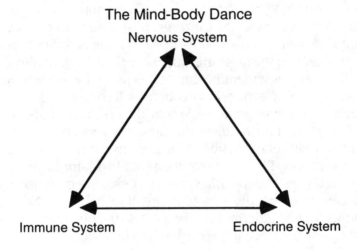

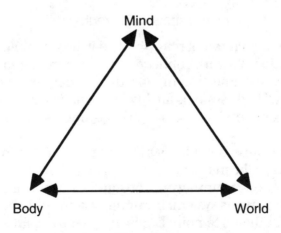

Figure 3

Mind-Body Communication

Every thought or feeling we experience affects our body. It's easy to see how negative thoughts and feelings can, over time, wear down our body's resistance to disease—things like worry, anxiety, and depression. The body, however, also "talks back" to the mind. The messages may take the form of fatigue, aches and pains, allergies, and illnesses.

Pay attention to worry-thoughts, guilt-thoughts, doubt-thoughts, and thoughts of self-deprecation. Notice feelings of fear, jealousy, depression, and chronic anger. Watch for positive and happy thoughts as well. Try to enhance and increase those thoughts and feelings that are life affirming.

Every thought and feeling you have affects your body. As you notice your thoughts and feelings throughout the day, ask yourself, "Is this thought or feeling contributing to my good health or to illness?" Try to immediately change negative thoughts and feelings into positives.

Every ache and pain is a body message to the mind. Of course, the message is a request for you to do something. It's a call for help. Are you fatigued? Are your muscles tight? Is your body in pain or upset in any way? These are all body messages to the mind, as are the first signs of illness or ongoing problems with digestion or sleep. What is your body telling you?

Is there some action you can take to alleviate what your body is feeling? Do you need more sleep, more exercise, a change in diet? Some body therapies are based on sensitivity to subtle feedback from the body. Try to notice such subtle feedback in your own body. Is it related to something you were thinking or worrying about? Is it related to some current life stress? Can you do something to alleviate that stress?

Mind-World Communication

The mind also affects our life experiences, how we relate to the world. Our beliefs and attitudes affect our world, both in the way we perceive it and literally in terms of the experiences we create. Our experiences in the world then feed information back to the mind. They say, "Here's what you've created. Is there anything you'd like to change or enhance?"

Many of the messages your mind sends to your body are also sent into the world. Other people are affected by your mood, attitude, and state of mind. Your self-image, sense of self-worth, and self-esteem are significant ongoing messages to other people. What you think and feel about yourself is often very evident to others, and they will respond accordingly. Obviously the choices you make with your mind and the actions you take as a result have a profound effect on your world and on the kind of feedback the world gives back to you.

How are your thoughts and feelings—expressed in mood, attitude, and energy level—affecting other people? Notice that the messages your mind sends to other people changes the quality of the messages that come back to you.

Of course, all of our waking experiences represent messages from the world to the mind. Look for redundancies. Certain messages will be repeated in many different ways. Also, pay attention to persons and experiences which have a strong emotional impact on you.

Body-World Communication

The body and the world communicate with one another as well. Body language sends messages to others, and we may respond to body messages from others without consciously being aware of it. The circulatory system is involved in blushing, for example—a bodily expression that communicates a rather specific message to others.

The world communicates with the body according to the activities we engage in. One of the most obvious ways in which the world impinges on our body is through what we put into it in terms of food and drugs. Our body is also affected by the weather. Some individuals experience rather serious winter depressions, and in spring we say a man's fancies turn to love. One of the most significant ways in which the world communicates with the body (and mind) is through our interactions with other people, from those close to us to the most casual encounters. Every sensation we experience has an internal electrochemical counterpart. When someone speaks to us the tone, content, and body language of the speaker affects our biochemistry. If *we* speak, our blood pressure goes up noticeably. If we hear a sudden noise, our body responds. Anything in the world that impinges on any of our senses affects the body.

Traumatic life experiences affect the body more severely. The death of someone close to us directly affects the immune system. Many surviving spouses do not live very long beyond their lost mates. On the other hand, close family or social ties enhance the immune system, as does active participation in a religion.

What is your body language saying to others? How does it invite them to respond to you? Aside from body language, we actually send chemical messages to one another. We know that dogs and other animals recognize and respond to a variety of odors. They recognize relatives by smell alone. They use scents, called pheromones, as sexual attractants. A single molecule of the female moth pheromone bombykol will attract a male miles away. Even more interesting, for our purposes, is the fact that humans are far more sensitive to scent—at least subliminally—than most of us realize.

Studies have revealed that human mothers can identify their baby's clothing by smell alone after only two weeks together. Close family members are usually able to identify one another by the smell on clothes they've worn. While human pheromones, as such, have not been discovered, males and females are influenced by body scents. Androstenol, a musky compound related to male sex hormones, repels males and attracts females below the level of awareness. A scent women give off helps synchronize the menstrual cycles of women living together. Weekly sexual contact between a man and a woman helps regularize the woman's menstrual cycle through chemicals passed through the male's skin. A chapter in *Healthy Pleasures* by Robert Ornstein and David Sobel goes into some detail on the importance of the sense of smell, including its healing uses in aromatherapy.

Just because we're not consciously aware of such messages does not mean we don't send and receive them *and* act on them. All of your external experiences affect your body. One of the skills you can work on as you progress through the book is body sensitivity. Learn to notice how your body is responding to different food, people, and experiences throughout the day. Your reactions to others is a message for you.

Be aware of what you're putting into your body. Aside from paying attention to your diet and use of drugs, practice eating more slowly and consciously.

A relatively recently diagnosed disorder related to weather and the body is called seasonal affective disorder (SAD). This is a form of depression brought on by winter. It is treated with large doses of full-spectrum lighting, special lights which most accurately reflect the spectrum of sunlight. By using these lights, the days are effectively lengthened as far as the body is concerned. You can purchase full spectrum lights for your home or office. They're similar to lights used for growing plants indoors. A classic book by full-spectrum lighting pioneer John Ott, *Health and Light*, goes into depth on the benefits of sunlight and full spectrum lighting, not just for mood alteration, but for preventing and healing illnesses.[7]

You may not be so strongly affected by the weather but all of us are affected to some degree. If you can't change the weather, you can take advantage of nice weather, and you can be more conscious about the environment inside your home. Do you live in a pleasant environment? Do you have pictures you love on your walls? Do you have beautiful and meaningful objects around you? Get out in nature more and bring more of nature indoors. Nature is one of the most powerful healers and immune system boosters available to us.

Spend more time with people you love. If you don't have a circle of loving and supportive friends, create one or join one. Become active in a religious or service organization. Volunteer an hour or two a week. Deliberately make decisions and take actions that will place you among people who are nourishing to you.

The communications among our internal bodily systems are pretty much below the threshold of consciousness. We *can* be more aware, however, of the messages among mind, body, and world. They can be read, interpreted, and acted upon for the sake of your health and wholeness.

Read Your Messages!

Perhaps you have already begun writing down or just paying attention to your thoughts and feelings. You are paying attention to the feedback from the world and from your body. From the mind-body-world triangle you have three arenas in which to check for messages. Notice and write down the ones that seem significant to you. As Bernie Siegel said, some of your messages are "die" messages and some are "live" messages. Your "live" messages need to be energized and increased. Your "die" messages need to be de-energized and eliminated or transformed.

As you learn this three-way communication system, you can consciously insert positive messages into any part of the system and remove or modify unhealthy messages. You can increase your conscious awareness and control of the mind-body-world system, and the mind-body will dance more to the tune of your choosing.

But how much can the mind affect the body? What are the outer possibilities of the mind-body?

3

The Outer Possibilities of the Mind-Body

Jesus said, "All things are possible to him who believes." (Mark 9:23) If we're to take "all things" literally, there may be no limits to what the mind can do through belief. In the Gospel of John, Jesus suggests that we can do even greater things than He did! (John 14:12)

Jesus' suggestion means that most of us are operating well below our potential. What would we be capable of should we begin to open up to that potential? Healing ourselves is only one possibility. It would also be possible to live a healing and fulfilling life and become a healing presence for others. One of our purposes on earth may be to learn how to consciously use our minds and the spiritual energy flowing through them to create a more satisfying and fulfilling life experience.

Clearly the mind is creative, but many of our creations seem to be out of our conscious control. Some of them, including serious illnesses, are harmful to us. We can experience more healing and love and less illness and fear by becoming more conscious of what our minds are creating on a daily basis and letting the Spirit flow through us more freely.

Many believe that we can create miracles with our thoughts. In trying to create a healing miracle, it will be helpful to explore the outer possibilities of the mind-body dance. The examples in this chapter may help you to overcome some of the limiting ideas you may hold concerning the ability of your mind to heal your body and your life.

Hypnosis

A familiar method for influencing the body through the mind is hypnosis. Reminiscent of Cayce's throat paralysis cure, recent studies have shown that blood flow can be increased, reduced, or stopped with hypnosis. Hypnosis is frequently used to help people lose weight, stop smoking, or overcome phobias. Some of these changes are only temporary, of course. If our self-hypnotic suggestions oppose those of the hypnotist strongly enough, the problem will reassert itself.

But hypnosis has also been used as an anesthetic in hundreds of operations, including dental surgery. Hypnosis as a method of anesthesia goes back at least to the 1840s and the operations performed have included amputations, cardiac surgery, and tumor extractions. Hypnosis has been used to improve agility and strength and to create hallucinations, illusions, color blindness, and deafness.

In *The Holographic Universe,* Michael Talbot notes that "under hypnosis a person can influence processes usually considered unconscious. For instance . . . deeply hypnotized persons can control allergic reactions, blood flow patterns, and nearsightedness. In addition they can control heart rate, pain, body temperature, and even will away some kinds of birthmarks."[1]

The common factor in all of these examples is belief. Hypnosis is effective only when the subject believes what the hypnotist tells him or her. Your self-hypnotic power works the same way, whether conscious or unconscious, to influence your health. Pay attention to the negative suggestions you give yourself, and make an effort to give yourself positive suggestions whenever possible. You don't have to be in a hypnotic trance for these suggestions to be effective.

Biofeedback

Biofeedback technology makes it possible for us to perceive internal body processes that are normally below conscious perception. One of the oldest and most common biofeedback devices is a stethoscope. Modern biofeedback machines give us auditory and/or visual representations of bodily processes such as heart rate, brain-wave patterns, skin conductivity, and even muscle tension. Using visual or auditory feedback, an individual can attempt to relax by "willing" the feedback to change in the direction representing relaxation. With time and practice, an individual can usually learn how to reach a relaxed state without the mechanical feedback.

Biofeedback has been used primarily for relaxation training and has proven useful in some cases for reducing blood pressure and muscle tension. Children suffering from Attention-Deficit Hyperactivity Disorder (ADHD) have also benefited from biofeedback training. Alyce and Elmer Green of the Menninger Foundation, pioneers in biofeedback research, write, "It may be possible to bring under some degree of voluntary control any physiological process that can continuously be monitored, amplified, and displayed."[2]

Of course, it's possible to learn to relax through meditation, self-hypnosis, and other relaxation techniques. Biofeedback is important because it demonstrates the possibility of bringing under conscious control many bodily functions that were assumed to be unconscious.

Yoga

The Greens and their colleagues at the Menninger Foundation also studied the ability of yogis to control autonomic functions. What others could do with biofeedback, yogis could accomplish through meditation, diet, breath work, and other forms of yoga. Yoga means *union* or *joining* and includes disciplines which lead to a balance of body, mind, and spirit.

One of their subjects, Swami Rama, was able to increase his heart rate to 306 beats per minute for sixteen seconds without pain or heart damage. Simultaneously, he was also able to create a temperature difference of eleven degrees between the left and right sides of his right palm.

Yogis can slow their heart rate, respiration, and other bodily functions to such an extent that some have been buried without oxygen, water, or food for as long as six weeks and were released unharmed.[3] In one case, a yogi was buried for eight days with an electrocardiograph (EKG) in the box with him. After twenty-nine hours his EKG showed a flat line (normally indicating death). Because of the abruptness of the cessation of a heartbeat, the researchers suspected equipment malfunction rather than heart failure and continued the experiment. Heart failure would have been preceded by heartbeat irregularities. About half an hour before disinterment on the eighth day, the EKG once again began recording the man's heartbeat. The researchers were unable to find any malfunction in their equipment and they could not simulate the removal and reattachment of the electrodes without disturbing the EKG trace.[4]

Again, these abilities show us what is possible. One man, who had no training of any kind, could stop his heart and show no EKG trace by, as he put it, "allowing everything to stop." Just before passing out he would take a deep breath and his heart would restart.[5]

In terms of self-healing, the abilities of yogis and others demonstrate the possibility of influencing bodily functions with our minds, functions previously believed to be beyond conscious control.

Athletic and Crisis Functioning

In our best athletes we see some of the heights which human functioning can reach. Although training and natural ability are big factors in athletic excellence, the role of belief and desire are being taken more seriously, and visualization techniques are increasingly being utilized in sports.

The four-minute mile is one example of the power of belief. Most people in the athletic and scientific communities believed that no one would ever run a mile in less than four minutes. Some scientists at that time even said it was physically impossible. British runner Roger Bannister did not accept that limit and believed he could break the four-minute mile—and he did, in 1954. This was clearly a limit of belief, not of physical ability, for within the same year that Bannister ran the mile in under four minutes, *fifty-two other men broke the record as well.*

Most of us are not interested in breaking world track records, but I want to emphasize the fact that the four-minute mile for a human was primarily a mind barrier, a barrier of belief. It's possible that the human body has always been capable of that accomplishment. The barriers to healing and living a healed life are also mind barriers. What you believe about your ability to heal yourself is far more important than what statistics or experts say.

While such feats—as with the feats of yogis—require years of training and discipline, ordinary people sometimes accomplish extraordinary physical feats in crisis situations. You may have heard stories about a mother lifting a car to rescue a trapped child and others performing amazing feats of strength, speed, or endurance in a crisis. If a woman is capable of lifting a car in a crisis, she has the potential to lift a car any time.

I had one such crisis experience as a boy. I was playing in the foothills near my home with three or four friends. We were about eleven or twelve years old. In the late forties and early fifties you could still find, near my home in Southern California, things left behind by the "forty-niners"—gold sluices, cradles, and the like.

We came across a small boarded-up shack. To us, it presented a challenge. We saw a good-sized hole in the low roof, climbed on top of the old shack, and dropped down inside.

We all dropped to the floor safely except the last boy. He dropped close to the wall and landed on a large nail that was sticking out of the wall at an angle. It caught him in the fatty area just above the hip. He hung there, his feet inches from the floor. I was small but strong. The boy on the nail was nearly a head taller than me and that much heavier. He was solid but not fat.

Had I gotten as close to him as possible and lifted him with my arms supported by my body, I probably could have lifted him high enough to get him off the nail. Certainly two or more of us could have lifted him without any trouble. That isn't what happened, however. As soon as he landed on the nail, we all froze. Then I stepped forward, without thinking, extended my arms straight out, and lifted him off the nail. As an adult in my prime I couldn't have lifted a boy his size with my arms straight out, yet he felt as light as a rag doll. Fortunately the boy wasn't badly hurt.

The key to that experience, as I've thought about it over the years, is that *I didn't think about what I was doing*. If I had hesitated for even a moment, if I had thought about whether I could lift him, I wouldn't have been able to do it. I had the strength and ability to do what I did all along and still have it now. The only reason I haven't exercised it before or since is that I don't believe I can. I have always thought of this as a feat of strength, but it occurs to me that it could as easily have been an experience of levitation or psychokinesis. I didn't really experience myself as strong; I experienced him as extremely light.

In crisis, limiting beliefs and ideas are often bypassed, as sometimes happens in hypnosis and other altered states. The body is able to perform at phenomenal levels. What the body is capable of in crisis, it is theoretically capable of at any time. All the crisis does is bypass the intellect which says, "You can't do that." From the point of view of the Cayce formula—Spirit is the life; mind is the builder; physical is the result, crisis experiences can be seen as the work of Spirit unsuppressed by the mind's limiting beliefs.

I had a game I used to play with my baby brother Alan. I'm eight years his senior, and I used to ride him around on my bike when he was three or four years old. He rode on the crossbar and held on to the handlebars near the middle. I held on to the grips at the ends of the handlebars and steered.

I discovered that Alan had a pretty strong grip; furthermore, I could feel him steering the bike along with me. What I would do, once in a while, is let go of the handlebars and let my brother do the steering. I found he was able to do it quite competently, even going up and down driveways and around corners—until, that is, he discovered he was steering. At that point he would scream and yell at me to grab the handlebars.

My brother, long before he would be riding a bicycle of his own, was quite capable of steering a full-sized bicycle. But he couldn't do it consciously because he didn't believe he could. As long as he didn't know he was doing it, he could do it. The limits we place upon our bodies and upon our abilities are mind- or intellect-generated. We limit our healing capabilities in the same way.

Extraordinary Abilities of Individuals and Groups

Extraordinary abilities are sometimes exhibited by individuals or groups under special circumstances. One of those individuals, Jack Schwarz, has been studied by researchers all over the United States. He is able to stick large needles completely through his arms without bleeding, flinching, or producing the beta brain waves which indicate pain. When the needles are removed, Schwarz does not bleed, and the puncture holes close tightly.

Schwarz acquired his abilities while he was in a Nazi concentration camp, where he endured terrible beatings. How did this happen? Apparently Schwarz passed out during a beating and had a vision of Christ. "Filled with love from the image, he said to his torturer, '*Ich liebe dich* [I love you].' The guard was so shocked that he stopped, and he was even more astounded when he saw right before his eyes the prisoner's wounds healing within moments."[6]

A similar feat was performed annually by an Indian community as reported in *Scientific American* in 1967. In this case, a different individual was chosen each year and was prepared, through a long period of ritual, to play an important community role. At the end of the ceremonial preparations, the chosen had two large hooks buried in his back, ropes were passed through the eyes of the hooks, attached to a boom on an ox cart, and then the individual was taken to the fields were he was swung in arcs over the fields to insure the success of the crops. At the end of the ceremony, when the hooks were removed, there was no blood and no puncture wounds to be seen.[7]

These two experiences demonstrate that such abilities can come about through a single or ongoing traumatic experience to an individual or through the ritual support of a community of believers backed by years of repetition. In 1947, another man, a Dutchman, performed an even more incredible feat with no explanation of how he was able to do so.

Mirin Dajo performed before audiences in Zurich, Switzerland, and elsewhere. He would have an assistant plunge a fencing foil completely through his body. After a time the foil would be removed and there would be no blood, just a thin red line to show where the foil had entered and exited the body. After one audience member suffered a heart attack, his performances were banned.

Doctors at the Zurich cantonal hospital, however, decided to study this ability as scientifically as possible. When Dajo had his assistant pierce Dajo's body, in full view of doctors, students, and journalists, all were stunned by what they were seeing. Shocked by seeing a foil pass through a man's body, knowing it had to pass through vital organs, the doctors asked if Dajo would submit to an X-ray. The X-ray showed that the foil did indeed pass through Dajo's body. When the foil was finally removed, some twenty minutes later, two faint scars were all that could be seen.

The elements of prayer, chanting, and dancing—or even traumatic life experiences—help produce altered states which make this kind of physical performance possible. Walking on hot coals, control of "involuntary" bodily functions, stigmata, and other extraordinary physical phenomena are often associated with meditation, prayer, singing, chanting, drumming, and dancing, activities that, over time, can bring on states of trance and/or ecstasy. Such altered states are another way of overcoming the intellect that says, "This isn't possible."

Stigmatics

Stigmatics seem to imitate the wounds experienced by Jesus on the day He was crucified. A few individuals experience all of the wounds, including the stripes of Jesus' whipping. Others experience only the bleeding of hands and feet. Some have the experience only at Easter and some weekly. The stigmata are often preceded by religious ecstasy. An eighteenth-century stigmatic, St. Veronica Giuliani of Umbria, Italy, was able to open and close a large wound in her side on command. It was also said that a beautiful perfume, sometimes called the odor of sanctity, emanated from her wounds and from the blood itself.

The wounds closely imitate paintings or crucifixes the stigmatics are familiar with, rather than the actual wounds of Jesus. In the time of Christ, the Romans placed crucifixion nails through the victims' wrists, not their hands, as the hands cannot support a body's weight. Although religious conviction and identification with the suffering of Jesus usually bring about the stigmata, belief is still what steers the phenomenon.

Hysterical stigmatics re-create on their bodies traumatic wounds received when they were children. One thirteen-year-old girl's father once ran his fingernails down her back, causing bleeding and leaving scars. She moved out four years later. Within a year after she had moved, her father called and said he was going to visit. The old wounds on her back opened up and began bleeding.[8]

Clearly, whether the wounds come from religious ecstasy or childhood trauma, they demonstrate the power of belief on our bodies. We have to wonder what kinds of wounds we're holding in our bodies and what old hurts, angers, or guilt may be turned loose to bring about an illness that seems to come from nowhere.

Multiple Personality Disorder

In Multiple Personality Disorder (MPD), two or more personalities exist within the same body. The average number of personalities is between eight and thirteen, but it can be over a hundred.[9] Until recently, most cases of MPD were misdiagnosed as schizophrenia, manic-depressive, or other mental disorders.

The precipitating factors in MPD are almost always severe child abuse, including incest, torture, and emotional or psychological abuse. This was the case in ninety-seven of one hundred multiples surveyed by Dr. Frank Putnam of the National Institute of Mental Health.[10] The symptoms are loss of memory and loss of time (blackouts) and the presentation of different distinct personalities (called *alters* or *subpersonalities*). A personality can be switched in seconds, or it may take hours. Some alters can consciously take over the body, while others are simply shoved "on stage."

The changes that occur from one personality to another are startling. They represent further evidence of the incredible plasticity of the physical body and personality, and the power of the human mind. Different personalities experience themselves as having different ages, sexes, nationalities, and even sexual preferences. They have different memories and histories, races, behavior patterns, and philosophies.

They may speak and write different languages, have different physical abilities (like karate or dance), fields of expertise such as knowledge of electronics or medicine, artistic abilities in different media, and different interpersonal skills.

Multiples have different brain-wave patterns, voice patterns, blood-flow patterns, muscle tone, heart rates, posture, allergies, susceptibility to drugs, different scars, burn marks, cysts, handedness, visual acuity (including color blindness), and *different eye color.* Aside from having different physical problems such as allergies or skin sensitivities, multiples have different diseases! Diabetes, epilepsy, and even tumors come and go as personalities switch. There is evidence that multiples heal faster, and Dr. Cornelia Wilbur, therapist in the well-known "Sybil" case, believes that multiples actually age more slowly.[11]

I want you to read the last paragraph again and take a few moments to let it sink in. We are talking about scars and cysts coming and going with a simple change in personality. Serious diseases are switched on and off, depending on the mind in charge. Multiple Personality Disorder is a terrible illness, brought on by overwhelming physical and emotional stress. What it teaches us, however, can save lives and may eventually change the face of medicine.

All of us are multifaceted beings—multiple personalities. Some of our personalities are created through stress and fear, as are true multiples, and some are created through hope and love. If you look at the characters in your dreams as parts of yourself (as I do), you are presented with a wealth of personalities, as well as animals, places, and objects. If you look at all of those around you in your waking life as parts of yourself—projections—you become a multiple indeed. If you open the arena of reincarnation, you can begin to see yourself not just as a multiple, but as a multitude of multiples!

While some of our personalities undoubtedly block and sabotage us, others represent a rich resource for expanding our abilities, our knowledge, our consciousness, and our capacity for healing ourselves. Therapist John Beahrs came to this conclusion through working with multiples: "In a very real way we may all be covert multiple personalities . . . Our obliviousness of these selves, not the multiplicity itself, is the problem. We defeat ourselves without knowing why.

"Our component selves may have conflicting beliefs."[12] I had a dream in which I met a character who was angrily diametrically opposed to my philosophy of life. I was shocked to find such a self in my dreams. As much as we may want something in our lives, including a healing, there may be parts of ourselves that have their own reasons for staying sick or even wanting to die. Part of the healing process and part of using the feedback system involves uncovering and dealing with these negative personalities, as well as with the host of helping and healing personalities we all have within.

Imagine that you already have a healed personality

within you. This self is not just disease free but is healthy in a much broader sense, healthy in attitude and outlook, spiritually healthy. There are two ways to try to contact this healthy personality. You can seek to make contact in a meditation or ask to meet your healthy self in a dream. The other approach is to create a healthy personality on paper in your journal.

Begin with the physical body and just describe what your healthy body would be like. Try not to use negatives. Think of how you want your body to be, not how you *don't* want it to be. For example, don't say, "My body isn't fat." Say, "My body is slim" or "My body is the perfect weight and shape." Also think in terms of what your body can do. What do you want to be able to do with your healthy body?

Next list the beliefs, attitudes, and feelings of a healthy mind or personality. How would a healthy personality act in the world? What would you do? How would you interact with other people? How would a healthy personality be different from your current personality? Again, do not list items in terms of negatives—what you *wouldn't* be like—but in terms of positives.

You may add to the qualities of the healthy personality over a period of days or weeks. Make that personality as real and attainable as possible, and then periodically "pretend" that you *are* that personality. See if you're able to feel differently about yourself and others. See if you can't actually interact differently with others from that healthy perspective. In order to live the healed life, we need to become the healed personality, to allow ourselves to change into someone different, someone closer to our true selves, closer to our spiritual ideal.

The Placebo Effect

The word *placebo* is from the Latin for "I shall please." The placebo effect has slowly and grudgingly been accepted by the medical and pharmaceutical professions. It is now routinely taken into account in any drug study, because it is known that the placebo will work on as many as thirty to forty percent of the subjects tested. New drugs must be significantly more effective than a placebo.

A placebo, in its simplest form, is a sugar pill that the patient believes is something else, a drug which is presumed to be effective for the problem. The placebo has taught us that if a patient believes in the effectiveness of a medication, treatment, or healer, that medication, treatment, or healer will often work. Studies have shown that placebos are sometimes effective *even when the subjects are told they're taking placebos!*

While most placebos take the form of a pill or an injection, the placebo effect operates in many different ways. For example, in *The Future of the Body,* Michael Murphy tells of an experiment done with angina pectoris patients. The original operation involved ligation or tying off the internal mammary artery to improve coronary blood flow. Further studies, however, suggested the process wasn't as effective as first believed. An experiment was carried out with a number of patients in which the incisions were made and then closed *without doing the ligation.* It turned out to be as effective or *more effective* than actually performing the operation.[13]

The body can heal itself, regardless of the problem. If there's something inside our body that needs to be cut out, the mind can eliminate it. If there's something that needs to be repaired, the mind can tell the body to repair it. If there's something broken that needs to be replaced, the body can replace it.

Faith Healing

Faith healing has existed in many different times, cultures, and religions, representing a wide range of sometimes conflicting beliefs. This suggests it isn't *what* you believe or *who* you believe in that heals; it's belief itself.

A faith healing is usually one that occurs without medical intervention. What is common to all forms of faith healing is the existence of one or more focal points which allow individuals to direct their energy toward a healing. These focal points are believed to have healing efficacy, whether they are a potion, person, place, ritual, or holy object.

A focal point or focusing agent is anything that serves to focus healing energy, something into which you can pour your hope, desire, and faith. Anything can be a focusing agent, whether it be a medication, operation, healing ritual, or treatment of any kind. It could be a person, dead or alive, a god, goddess, or other religious figure. Healing prayer and meditation can be focusing agents, as can the laying on of hands or various forms of bodywork. A holy place or a holy ceremony can be a focal point, or a psychic or faith healer can be the focus for healing.

How do focusing agents work? I would like to go back to the Cayce formula for creation. If health is our natural state, the power of the Spirit coming through our minds is constantly giving us a health or "live" message, constantly pulling us toward wholeness. Focusing agents help us align our intentions with the intentions of Spirit. They help us remove energy from habitual Spirit-suppression devices. They help focus the mind in a healing direction.

Miracles are the result of Spirit flowing through us unsuppressed. Experiences which help us focus and activate our faith and belief open us to the miraculous. Traditionally, an individual seeks divine healing through prayer, fasting, ritual, or through a healer who acts as a mediator between God and the petitioner.

Sometimes it seems that the image of God in this situation is that of a king or dictator, giving or withholding favors. God becomes an arbitrary being who may or may not be swayed by our petitions. If we believe that God heals us or fails to heal us as a result of our actions or words, we have given up our most important gift in life—our free will and our ability to form our own experience with our minds.

The Cayce formula shows a very different picture. The Spirit continually pours its energy into us and into all of creation. Spirit is what we are made of. Healing energy from God is always and everywhere present. We need not seek healing from God, although such seeking itself can act as a focusing action. We need only accept the healing that is always present. Whatever ways we can find to remove our blocks to growth and healing we should use. Anything that can focus our healing intent, our intent to live and grow spiritually, should be used.

This is not to say that prayer is ineffective, but prayer doesn't sway God, doesn't convince the Creative Forces to heal us. Prayer focuses our desire and intent, whether for ourselves or another, and can open us to the possibility of receiving a healing which is ever present.

The Power of Faith in Groups

Two stories taken from *The Holographic Universe* by Michael Talbot exemplify the most extraordinary abilities of the human mind-body. They come from two heretical groups that both the Catholic church and the French state tried to wipe out.

The first group was an offshoot of the Protestant Huguenots called the Camisards. They were active in the late 1600s in the valley of the Cévennes. One of their persecutors, a prior named Abbé du Chayla, complained to Rome that he was unable to kill or even harm these heretics. "When he ordered them shot, the musket balls would be found flattened between their clothing and their skin. When he closed their hands upon burning coals, they were not harmed, and when he wrapped them head to toe in cotton soaked with oil and set them on fire, they did not burn."[14]

Another sect, the Jansenists, were also hounded by church and state, but the movement was very popular in Paris because of the ability of Jansenist leaders to perform miraculous healings. Upon the death of a revered deacon, François de Paris, an astounding mass phenomenon began which was to last for over two decades and be witnessed by thousands.

Worshipers flocked to François de Paris's tomb where many miraculous healings occurred, including the healing of: " . . . ulcerous sores, persistent fevers, prolonged hemorrhaging, and blindness . . . The mourners also started to experience strange involuntary spasms or convulsions and to undergo the most amazing contortions of their limbs. These seizures quickly proved contagious, spreading like a brush fire until the streets were packed with men, women, and children, all twisting and writhing as if caught up in a surreal enchantment."[15]

These individuals were called *convulsionaires*, and while in their convulsive trance state they could endure incredible physical tortures. "These included severe beatings, blows from both heavy and sharp objects, strangulation— *all with no sign of injury, or even the slightest trace of wounds or bruises*."[16]

The tortures put to the convulsionaires did not come at the hands of church or state, however. They came from bystanders and other convulsionaires and they themselves asked to be tortured, often yelling at their torturers to hit them harder. The blows actually alleviated the pain of their convulsions. Levitation was also demonstrated by at least one convulsionaire.

It is almost certain that we have not yet discovered the farthest reaches of physical functioning. The examples in this chapter demonstrate the tremendous control that is possible over our bodies, control mediated by the mind, by belief or faith, and by expectation. I believe it is possible, by understanding the meaning of our illness, to direct the powerful forces of the mind in the direction of health.

But first it will be helpful to understand how the mind creates an illness. By understanding how illnesses are born in our bodies, we may be able to catch the early warning signs, the whispers, and prevent illnesses or heal them more quickly.

4

Birth Choices

If thoughts, attitudes, and emotions help give birth to an illness, what gives birth to our thoughts, attitudes, and emotions? Most psychological theories view early childhood experiences as the primary contributors to attitudes, beliefs, and emotional makeup. Most world religions, however, accept and teach some form of reincarnation, including some sects of Judaism (Hasidic Jews) and some Christian mystics. The process of reincarnation assumes that the soul has many earth experiences, and our former lives are influential in our current life. It also assumes the possibility of some input and choosing on our part before we enter a life experience.

From a strictly scientific point of view, the great diversity of birth experiences is a matter of chance. Fate determines parentage and other factors accompanying birth. If you are born with a defect, a physical limitation, or even a social and/or economic limitation, it's just chance. And you only have this one life in which to improve your condition or simply suffer the consequences of your birth situation.

As a traditional Christian, you would have only this one life to make it into heaven or suffer eternal damnation in hell. According to most Christians, the individual born in a non-Christian nation of non-Christian parents would be judged by the same criteria as one born into a Christian family.

As a Presbyterian minister, I struggled with the conflict of a loving God who still judged everyone by the same standards, regardless of one's birth situation. Eventually the idea of reincarnation made more sense to me. It explained the vast differences in individual birth circumstances and made it clear that we are not judged by the experiences and actions of a single lifetime. To speak of birth choices, of course, assumes an existence prior to birth, if not multiple existences.

In order to understand how illnesses are formed and how they can be healed or prevented, we will look at these two areas—past lives and childhood—as sources of information on our current ideas about ourselves, others, and the world. One of the central beliefs of reincarnation is that our past lives influence the circumstances of our birth. We will therefore look at the relationship between past lives and current physical problems before we look at childhood experiences and their influence.

Reincarnation

The idea that we live many lives pervades most world cultures, both past and present. In the predominantly Christian West, reincarnation is, for the most part, considered incompatible with Christian teachings and is pretty much ignored. After some twenty years of doing primarily health readings, Edgar Cayce, a committed Christian in his waking life, was surprised to find his inner source talking about reincarnation at the end of a reading on astrology, another topic the waking Cayce knew nothing about.

Because Cayce was a religious man, he did not accept this reading without questioning and investigation, including reading the Bible (a book he read cover to cover once for every year of his life). He was finally satisfied that reincarnation was compatible with Christianity, and a new type of reading was born that produced some nineteen hundred past-life readings or "life readings," as they were called.

Just like our current lives, past lives are also meaningful and are meaningfully related to our present life. According to the Cayce readings, "our very reason for being is to be 'companions' and 'co-creators' with God."[1] We *are* companions and co-creators now, but we have the potential to evolve in those roles and participate even more consciously. Our different physical experiences give us opportunities to learn the art of conscious co-creation and can help us gradually overcome our various Spirit-suppression devices, leading to healthier, more spiritually enriched lives.

We may choose to take many lifetimes to accomplish this. Whatever we can do to grow spiritually in this lifetime, to come into closer alignment with our fundamental spiritual nature, will contribute to our overall soul growth. Reincarnation gives us plenty of time and opportunities to accomplish soul growth within a physical setting.

All of our experiences in all of our lives contribute to the makeup of our soul. Through multiple lives, we are able to experience both sexes, as well as different races, nationalities, socioeconomic states, religions, and roles. The spiritual law of Spirit moving through mind to create the physical operates in each life. In each life we see the consequences of our thoughts and attitudes, whether or not we are consciously aware of it.

Karma represents the consequences of thoughts and attitudes *among* lives and not just *within* a life. In Sanskrit, karma means *action* or *reaction*. The Hindu concept includes the idea of *work* or *labor.* In Cayce's terms, karma is described as "meeting self," an expression he used frequently.

We meet ourselves in our relationships, in our illnesses, in our dreams, in our childhood memories, and in our past lives. But what self is being met? It is the current self with all of its beliefs, ideas, and feelings. Of course, we often don't recognize ourselves in these various mirrors because the self we see is often the denied or rejected self, a self we don't wish to recognize. Part of the healing process involves recognizing and accepting, owning, or integrating these various selves.

Our past-life experiences create patterns that are set in the soul. These patterns reside in the mind-body of our current self. We have experiences in our current life, including illnesses, which are related to specific past lives. The past-life experience is like a dream or metaphor, not in the sense of being unreal, but in the sense of containing emotional energy and information about certain current beliefs or feelings.

Past-life experiences can be used as one arena for healing. The emotional energy in these experiences can help bring about changes in thought and feeling, including the healing of a serious illness. One can, however, also work on the same issues through dreams, in visualizations and meditations, or through waking-life actions, including working directly on the illness itself as a metaphor.

Karma is not about being punished for something we did in another life. Karma is part of the feedback system. It tells us of patterns we created in other lives with our thoughts and feelings, patterns we have *chosen* to work on in this life.

It isn't *necessary* to work with past lives because the past-life patterns will be expressed in every aspect of our present life. However, from my own experiences in leading both individual and group past-life regressions, I have found they can offer a powerful emotional experience that can help change beliefs and attitudes and move emotional energy in the direction of healing.

Frances, a woman disabled by multiple allergies, was able to heal them, partly with the help of past-life recall. She recalled having been killed by men on horses in a glade filled with dust raised by the horses' hooves. She recalled another life where she was seriously ill, was taken into town in a hay wagon, and died on the way. In still another experience she dropped a cat down an open well as a little girl and then fell in trying to rescue the cat. Rather than retrieve her body and bury her, the family just filled in the well. In this life she was allergic to dust, hay, and cats.

The issue or pattern her allergies were associated with was fear of death. The allergies simply represented sensory associations with different unpleasant ways she had died in past lives. Frances used the past-life experiences to understand her current physical problems but also confronted and dealt with the larger issue of being afraid of death. It should be noted that her allergies served to protect her from her core fear. She was so sickly from her allergies that she couldn't go out much. She had to stay home a lot, which she presumed was safer—death was less likely to find her.

Frances's past-life memories, along with homeopathic and other remedies, helped her heal the allergies. Overcoming her debilitating fear of death helped her go out into the world and live a fuller life.

Through karma we meet self, but it is always the current self we are meeting, even when a pattern may have been generated in a past life or several past lives. And we don't have karma *with* someone else. We may choose to relate to someone we wronged or who wronged us in a previous life, and it *can* be helpful if we can work out these issues with that person. The issue, however, is an attitude or belief within the self, not between us and someone else. Sometimes it isn't possible to make amends with the person we wronged, or vice versa. It doesn't matter. It is the attitude or emotion within us that needs healing, not the specific relationship or past experience. We can create karma by stealing from one person in a previous life and heal it by being generous with another in this life. Or we can heal it by forgiving ourselves.

If I kill someone, it doesn't mean that I have to be killed in another life in the same way (although I may choose to experience that), and it doesn't mean that the person I killed is going to kill me in another life. Someone who kills people in one life may choose to save lives in another, as a healer, for example. Edgar Cayce recalled a life as a Mississippi riverboat gambler who used his psychic abilities to cheat at cards. Some of the people who came to Cayce and were helped for little or no money were those he had harmed with his gifts in that previous experience.

If we are guilty of hatred in one life, we can heal it with love in another. We don't necessarily have to experience being hated. Our past-life experiences are designed to let us know that our thoughts and feelings, and the actions they generate, have consequences. In that sense, no matter what else you might have chosen to learn or focus on in any life, those lessons are a part of every life. Our thoughts create our reality. We are free to create crimes or miracles. Crimes, however, represent distortions of the Spirit that flows through us. They represent distortions of who we most truly are, companions and co-creators with the Creator.

Past-life information can help us recognize thoughts and feelings that tend to create barriers or injuries to ourselves and others. By recognizing these thoughts and patterns, we can change them. There's no such thing as bad karma or a bad life experience. Every experience and every life contains within it the seeds of healing and spiritual growth.

It is important to note that past lives also represent an incredible storehouse of helpful abilities, useful knowledge, and positive personality characteristics. They are a source for life-changing and life-healing qualities and attitudes. Any area in your life where you feel some lack, or any ability you would like to develop, can probably be found in one or more of your past lives. If you decide to work with past lives or are doing so already, don't forget that past lives are sources of positive as well as negative experiences and feelings.

How can we get in touch with our past lives? You can get past-life information from a psychic. As with any information derived from a psychic source, you need to use discretion. A strong emotional reaction to the information you receive may indicate that it is genuine. The test of any past-life information is whether it's helpful to you. I don't advise spending a lot of time and energy trying to confirm past-life information. It is the meaning and emotional energy of the life that's important, not whether it really happened.

You can be regressed by a hypnotist or regression therapist either in a private session or in a group. I have done many past-life regressions without hypnosis with individuals and groups. The advantage of individual work is that I can question the client about what's happening during his or her visualization and make suggestions. In group work, the individual has a past-life experience on his or her own after a brief period of relaxation and a lead-in visualization.

Some dreams contain past-life information. You might find that you look different in a dream, or perhaps you're in a period costume and/or location. You may be a different sex or race. Some past-life information is disguised, and only the pattern or energy of the experience will find its way into the dream. Dreams operate in an arena where space and time are more fluid. You can have current people and places mixed up with people and places from the past.

I had a dream in which I experienced being a young woman in Old West garb in the desert or prairie. But it wasn't a "pure" past-life dream, because there was a modern house trailer present. The dream was mixing up a past-life experience with something more current. In another Old West dream I was a gunfighter, looking very different from my waking self. I was going to have a shootout with a former comrade. I was fast on the draw and a good shot and we both knew I was going to kill him.

The gunfighter is a good example of positive and negative material being mixed together. Far from being a gunfighter in this life, I'm a pacifist and opposed to killing for any reason. But the gunfighter had qualities which I could use in this life. He was supremely self-confident and sure of his abilities. I can use those positive qualities in this life without killing anyone.

Waking life is another source of past-life information. You may find yourself attracted to certain times and places, certain cultures. This may change at different times in your life, as you deal with different patterns. These attractions often represent past-life information.

As a small boy, I was familiar with many of the planes used in World War II. I lived in Southern California near an air force base and saw them fly over frequently. I was no more interested in such things than any boy my age. In my early thirties, however, I suddenly developed a fascination for biplanes, the planes of World War I. The interest seemed to come out of nowhere. I assumed I had had a past life during WWI and was probably a pilot. This demonstrates another feature of past-life information. Past-life experiences seem to be more relevant at certain points in our life and that's when they're most likely to come to our attention.

Past-life information surfacing in this life may be as simple as loving certain foods, clothing, or artifacts from some country and/or time period. One client periodically had a craving for Indian food, along with dreams about that country. You also might have a strong aversion to a particular country or time period. Some people have traveled abroad and recognized buildings and countrysides they had never seen before. You may have strong emotional reactions to times, places, or cultures, positive or negative, without a known cause. One woman, for example, felt wonderful when she visited castles in Europe, especially in Germany. She would touch the stone walls and feel very much at home and filled with positive feelings.

You are given past-life information every day if you're open to seeing it. It may come in the form of a movie, a book, or a program on TV. You can ask your dreams for past-life information. (I'll discuss this in a later chapter.) You can ask for past-life information any time during the day. I created a past-life game that's fun and enlightening. It involves synchronicity and trusting the universe or inner self to give specific feedback when asked.

Try this game periodically, and write your experiences in your journal. The game can be used to receive information about anything, not just past lives. While going for a walk, driving in your car, or even sitting at home, make a request or pose a question to the universe: "Give me some past-life information that is relevant in my life right now (or relevant to my illness)."

Trust the universe to respond. The next thing that catches your attention will be a clue to the past life. If you're driving or at home you might turn on the radio. The first thing you hear on the radio will be a clue to a currently meaningful past life.

The first time I played this game I was taking a walk while visiting my family in Southern California. I decided to find out about a past life by just asking questions and letting my surroundings provide the answers. I started by asking what year it was. I immediately saw the license number of a truck. It was a three-digit number. Because of the low number I asked whether it was B.C. or A.D. I saw a gas station sign with prices for leaded and unleaded gas. The "ad" in "lead" stood out and answered my question.

Not too impressive so far. Then I asked for the country, and the next thing my eyes landed on was a pizza place. So the country was Italy. I was feeling pretty good about the process by this time and decided to push for more information. I asked what city I lived in. At that point the answer came to me, not in my surroundings, but in my mind. I recalled a dream I had had that morning, which I had previously not recalled at all.

In the dream I was in a round room with my father and a young dark-haired woman. The room had a wall in the middle like a hub. The outer and inner walls of the room were all bookshelves filled with books. I don't recall the conversation, but the young woman spoke Italian, a language I don't speak. There was some mention of Palermo in the dream. I later found out that Palermo is in Sicily, not Italy, but I was still impressed with that cooperative effort between my morning dream and the game I decided to play in the afternoon.

I followed the information up with a meditation/visualization on that experience and got more details which I was able to utilize. The information had to do with my leadership role in some political and military adventures. Essentially it was about my misuse of power in that experience.

Another time I was walking in the parking lot of a shopping center and thought, "Give me some past-life information." The first thing I saw was a Jeep Cherokee. Then I heard squawking overhead and looked up to see some crows. I believe this indicated I was a Native American in one or more lives, possibly Cherokee in one and Crow in another. I supposedly have Cherokee blood in this life. Of course, such information needs to be followed up by a meditation or other type of regression. What's the significance of those lives? Do I need to get in touch with certain qualities I associate with Native Americans? Are there specific past-life incidents or abilities that are relevant in my life now? I think that's always true. Essentially, as with any other endeavor, the more effort you put into seeking out such information, the more value you will get.

Put your intention to get past-life information out into the world, and then watch for the feedback. Expect to get information, and you will. The information will help you understand your current thoughts and attitudes, your current Spirit-suppression devices. You can call upon past lives that will help you with a particular illness, problem, or gift.

Whatever you're working on, whether it's specifically past life related or not, remember the bias of the universe. The Creator is present in all times and all places. Spirit-divine energy-love flows through your life, through all of your lives. That bias can be called grace. We don't choose lives of suffering. We choose challenges and gifts. They can be met with suffering and struggle, or they can be met with the ever-present assistance of Spirit, with grace and acceptance.

The Starting Line

How do our choices manifest? We don't start life with a blank slate. We start life with a very particular set of circumstances. It could be called your personal birth ecosystem, an interdependent complex of things, people, and circumstances. I call it the "starting line."

Aside from our genetic makeup, which might predispose us to some physical problems or actually cause us to be born with some congenital defect, we are also born into a complete setting, a specific stage filled with props and characters. We are characters ourselves, with certain predispositions which determine some of our life challenges and gifts. We are born into a time period, country, and city, an economic class, a race, a religion. We are male or female. In the context of reincarnation, these are all choices we make before birth.

Our parents determine our race, religion, and socioeconomic status. They are our primary early models, our source or lack of physical and emotional sustenance. Most of our fundamental ideas about ourselves, others, and the world at large come from these important relationships. Our parents represent the world in our early years.

And, of course, there may be siblings and the issues relating to our position in the family relative to them. In our culture, the family is the most important group or unit. Other family members play greater or lesser roles in our formative years. Obviously, if we're raised by a grandmother or aunt or are adopted, a different dynamic is created. Whether this is the result of a parental death or other circumstances, a particular challenge is set up.

In terms of reincarnation, we may or may not choose parents based on past associations. We *will* tend to meet many people from past lives, sometimes in groups. Many people believe that group or national karma exists.

We don't simply choose our parents; our parents have the same free will and right to choose as we. These are agreements made in dream states or other nonbody states. We also have teachers and guides in the spirit state who talk to us about our choices, like school counselors helping us with our curriculum, a curriculum which must be consistent with our larger goals.

Take out your healing journal, sit down, and meditate for a few minutes in order to clear your mind. Then write out a description of your starting line, listing the factors mentioned above. By looking at all of the circumstances surrounding your birth, it's possible to get a pretty good idea of what challenges you chose to deal with in this life. You may also see some of the gifts you had from the beginning. This process can help you stop blaming your parents and other birth circumstances for the problems in your life and start trying to understand what you intended to learn from these experiences.

What attitudes did your parents have toward life? What expectations did they have for you? In what ways are you currently a product of your starting line, and in what ways have you broken out of that opening scene?

What important current issues are the result of starting line choices? For example, does being a male or a female represent a significant issue in your life? If you were born into a working-class family, is that important in your life now? Is your race or religion a meaningful factor in your daily life? If you look at all of these things as choices, rather than accidents or fate, what purpose might they serve in your growth as a spiritual being? Do you hold attitudes and beliefs from your starting line that may be interfering with spiritual growth and with living a healed life? Is there anything from your starting line that may be relevant to a current illness?

Our current feelings are not the result of our childhood experiences or our past-life experiences. They are the result of how we respond to those experiences. We can continue to carry our childhood and past-life wounds or we can heal them. The choice is ours.

Life Challenges

Just as we choose classes in school, a mate, a career, and other life challenges and goals, so do we choose our major life challenges before birth. Our starting line is perfectly designed to set them in motion. You may get a sense of your challenges just by looking at the circumstances of your birth.

For example, being female may be a large part of your life challenge. Being African-American, Jewish, being born into poverty or wealth, or being adopted may be a challenge. If you were born with some physical disability, there's a good chance it represents a challenge. It's important to understand your own attitude toward these aspects of your starting line because each individual's situation is different. Not everyone born poor has poverty as a major life issue. Money may not turn out to be a problem or an issue at all. Trust your own intuitions about what is important and what is not. Look at the issues that you know are problems in your life right now.

Now try changing your point of view. Instead of looking at your birth situation as something that happened *to* you, a cosmic accident, imagine that you are writer, director, and star of your own play. When you were born, the stage was set, but for what? What does the setting suggest about the challenges your heroine or hero will have to meet? Get out your journal and write down any challenges that seem to be suggested by your birth choices. Are those challenges active in your life right now? Those challenges will also suggest some possible meanings for any present or future illness.

Life Metaphors

According to Seth, an "energy essence personality" channeled by the late Jane Roberts, "core beliefs [are] strong ideas about your own existence . . . It is the core belief which is strong enough to so focus your perception that you perceive from the physical world only those events that correlate with it."[2] I call core beliefs *life metaphors,* in keeping with the idea of looking at illnesses and other life experiences as meaningful, as metaphors.

The life metaphor can be seen as a framework for, or picture of, our major life challenges. The metaphor itself is a highly charged and highly compact scene from childhood, which sets in motion major life challenges in the form of beliefs. It will also probably be found in one or more past-life experiences. The childhood experience or metaphor represents a significant life challenge. I see it as acting as a trigger for the challenge you have already chosen, not as a cause. In many cases, as you'll see, the precipitating experience doesn't seem to be that powerful or dramatic.

The life metaphor creates colored glasses that we slip on at an early age, from two to four years old. From that time on, we perceive ourselves, others, and the world through these glasses. Looking through the glasses becomes so habitual that we don't know we have them on. These powerful, life-focusing beliefs are virtually invisible, so we take our perceptions of the world to be truths, rather than ideas or beliefs created by the glasses.

Life metaphors represent patterns or themes we choose to deal with in a particular life. They represent challenges chosen in our prebirth state. It's important to understand that the childhood experience or scene does not *cause* the life challenge. The experience often involves a parent but not always. If a parent is involved, he or she does not cause the life metaphor. A parent cooperates with you in setting it in motion. It's very likely that your life metaphor will relate to important adult challenges and crises such as a serious illness.

Another way to look at the life metaphor is as your personal myth. If the life metaphor is a concentrated image or expression of your life challenges, your personal myth is the unfolding of that image, a telling of your story. The idea of life myths was formulated by Carl Jung. "Jung came to the conclusion that every human being had a story, or to put [it] in its most evolved form, a myth of its own."[3]

In the next section I will give some examples of life metaphors and the core beliefs or life challenges they triggered. For now, I want you to do a writing exercise in which you "tell your story." Starting with your birth, write down the major experiences in your life, positive and negative. What scenes, from your childhood to the present, stand out in your mind? What are the highlights? You might fill out your story over two or three days.

Now look at your story as if it were about someone else. Get some distance from it. Starting with your birth circumstances, what are the major patterns and themes that have run through your life? What kinds of experiences tend to get repeated? What are the problem areas in your life? Are they to be found, in seed form, in your starting line? Are there repeating themes in your relationships, in your work life, with your health, with money, with your religious or spiritual life?

One important aspect of healing is a willingness to give up parts of our story or myth, to write a different story. In order to do that, we have to honestly look at how the old myth may have served us and how it may still be serving us. Some people get stuck telling their story over and over again in order to explain their present difficulties, but they never attempt to change their story, to create a new myth. Healing may require us to change our story and give up myths and life metaphors that no longer serve us in a positive way.

It can be very empowering to look back at the circumstances of your birth and early childhood from a totally different perspective. See yourself as the creator of the opening scene. Even though you were a child, you can change yourself from victim to star. You can say, "Now I see the challenges I set for the little girl or little boy that I was." It is hoped that you can also see the gifts and potentials you had as a child, gifts and potentials which still reside within you. Try to recognize that, regardless of the difficulties inherent in your starting line, your story/myth/life was meant to have a happy outcome. You were meant to become a fulfilled individual. That's the divine bias that runs through all of life. A serious illness, among other things, may be telling you to change your story.

Examples of Life Metaphors and Life Challenges

I have done life metaphor exercises with individual clients and in groups, with some powerful results. I will give you some examples of life metaphors and the life challenges they represent as well as some techniques for finding your own life metaphors.

My client Grace was adopted as a baby. In the course of

our work before doing the life metaphor exercise, Grace often said, "I think something's wrong with me," or "Do you think something's wrong with me?" Such self-hypnotic disaffirmations hold clues to our primary life issues. It was clear that one of Grace's primary life challenges was to overcome the idea that something was fundamentally wrong with her.

I did a guided visualization with Grace to find her life metaphor. In this visualization I ask individuals (or the group) to go back in time to age two to four. I tell them to get in touch with an incident that occurred at that time which had an impact on the rest of their life. The recalled incident is a life metaphor. Out of that experience-as-metaphor will come a life challenge in the form of a belief about themselves, others, and the world.

Grace did not go back to a remembered childhood experience but instead remembered something she had been told about her birth. When the nurse asked Grace's birth mother if she wanted to hold her baby, the mother said "no." It is understandable that this young mother did not want to bond with the baby she was giving up for adoption. But for Grace this scene was a metaphor for the core belief, "Something must be wrong with me. Even my mother didn't want me."

As I worked with Grace, it became obvious how this scene of being given away by her mother and not being held set up many of her life challenges, challenges that revolved around the issue of feeling somehow flawed and also the fear of abandonment. Her self-image, her relationships with others, and her interactions with the world were all colored by this core belief. Feeling that her friends didn't care for her as a teenager, as shown by Grace's dream interpretation in chapter 1, is in keeping with this core belief.

In a group visualization, Janet, a woman in her sixties, recalled an incident in which her mother had a pan of boiling water in the bathroom. Somehow the pan of water spilled on the little girl, giving her a painful burn. That experience was a metaphor for the core belief, "Those you love hurt you (or those who love you hurt you)." In this case, the triggering incident was an accident. No harm was intended. In Grace's instance, she was not given up for adoption because something was wrong with her. We're not dealing with reality or "truths" in these metaphors, but experiences that set powerful beliefs into motion. Our first challenge is to see them *as* beliefs about reality, not reality itself.

Another woman, Muriel, saw herself in the visualization swinging with a girlfriend on a playground. They swung higher and higher and her little friend suddenly let go and went flying. She ended up breaking both arms. That metaphorical scene triggered the core belief, "If you swing too high, you'll get hurt," or "If you try to fly, you'll get hurt." In this case the woman, through her own growth and spiritual work, had already recognized and was healing her blocks to being too successful (flying too high). The metaphor simply encapsulated for her an issue she had already been working on.

Exercise: Life Metaphors

Make yourself comfortable, sitting in a chair or lying down. Take a few deep breaths and allow your body to relax. Hold firmly in your mind an intention to experience a life metaphor.

Imagine yourself drifting backward in time to about age three. (It might be helpful to first try to recall an experience from an older age such as thirteen and then perhaps eight or nine.) Try to remember an incident or something someone said that might represent one of your life metaphors. Let the incident come up spontaneously, if possible. (Because these represent life challenges, it isn't likely that you will have more than two or three. There may be only one that's your central life challenge.)

If you're unable to recall such an incident in this exercise, you can still uncover your life metaphors by looking at themes and patterns in your life. The triggering metaphorical scene is played out over and over again in your life. You can find it in emotional incidents throughout your life. Life metaphors are the predominant themes in your life story.

Life metaphors are childhood experiences which can trigger negative beliefs in later life such as: "The world is not a safe place." "People can't be trusted." "I'm a bad person." "I'm stupid or too emotional or too sensitive," etc. However, not all life metaphors are completely negative. One woman recalled being in a flood and being held by her mother. That metaphor led to this belief: "There are scary and dangerous things in the world, but I'll be safe."

One of the things you can do with your life metaphor and the corresponding belief is to search for an antidote. It may be an affirmation. Grace, the woman who believed "Something's wrong with me," could affirm "Something's right with me." It's better not to say, "Nothing's wrong with me," because the negative word "wrong" is still there. She might just affirm, "I'm OK."

Janet, who believed "Those you love hurt you" could affirm "Those you love, love (or help) you." Create affirmations as healing antidotes to your life metaphors. Put them in your healing journal and place them in prominent places where you'll see them frequently. Be aware of incidents in which you find yourself playing out a negative life metaphor, and recall and repeat your affirming antidote.

Another advantage of seeing the childhood incident as a metaphor is that you can treat it like a dream and change the experience. I did another visualization with Grace. We were dealing with physical symptoms at the time. She was feeling nauseated and faint during our session and was experiencing lower back pain.

We did a visualization in which Grace spontaneously found herself present at her own birth. When the nurse asked the mother if she wanted to hold the baby, Grace stepped forward and said, "I'll hold her." She took the baby and experienced holding and giving suck to herself as a newborn. Her physical symptoms immediately went away. It was only afterward that we both realized her symptoms were among those associated with pregnancy.

Such reenactments can be very powerful, and I'll write more about them when I discuss dreamwork in a later chapter. Grace experienced a powerful healing of her belief that something was wrong with her through this metaphorical act of self-acceptance and self-nurturing.

Our life challenges are contained in our life metaphors. Our challenge is to uncover and change the beliefs triggered by the life metaphors. But life metaphors and challenges have a purpose beyond healing. Our challenges always contain gifts. Part of your healing and spiritual growth will involve looking for the gifts contained in your challenges. For those with serious illnesses, it will mean looking for the gifts within the illness.

Life Gifts

Our primary life gifts are contained in our life metaphors and core beliefs. Through understanding her life metaphor, for example, Grace began to learn about and accept the things that are *right* with her. She has decided to become a counselor and transform her own difficult life experiences into compassion for others. She will help others find out what is right with them.

I spoke of Melinda, the woman who had had two strokes, in chapter 1. She was not projecting or imagining her life beyond her illness and its limitations. Her strokes protected her from going out into a world that she perceived as dangerous. Healing for her would involve finding the courage to enter that world. Beyond that, the gift in her illness might be to help others who are afraid to go out into the world.

If you have a sense of some of your life challenges at this point, see if there aren't some specific gifts hidden in those challenges. Janet, who was scalded as a child, and believed that love hurts, is spreading love in her work for a spiritually oriented organization. Ask for your gifts in a quiet meditative state, or ask for a dream to reveal your gifts to you. If you are dealing with a specific illness, ask yourself for the gifts contained in the illness.

If you turn your life challenge into a positive affirmation, the affirmation itself may suggest the gift contained in your challenge. For example, many public performers are actually shy. In facing and overcoming their shyness, they also share their gifts with the world. If a person believes he or she is fundamentally unlovable, healing would be found in learning to love himself or herself. Beyond that, however, that person might find a gift in loving others and helping others to love themselves.

Every problem has a solution, but every problem also has a gift. Every illness contains more than the possibility of healing your symptoms. It contains the gift of the possibility of healing your life. It also contains the gift of the possibility of your being a healing influence for others.

The most challenging life issues may contain the greatest gifts, gifts we have prepared for ourselves from before our birth, gifts waiting to be activated through the process of changing our life metaphors and meeting our life challenges. Your greatest growth may come about through moving in the direction of your greatest fear and greatest risk. It is there that you may find your greatest gifts.

PART 2

THE WAYS WE USE ILLNESS

5

Negative Uses

Illnesses are meaningful. They are purposeful, just as dream experiences and symbols have meaning and purpose. The purpose of a dream image is always positive, always carries within it the seeds of healing and growth, however negative the dream may seem. All illnesses, large or small, represent opportunities for positive change, opportunities for deeper healing.

You can ignore the messages from your dreams. You can also ignore the messages from your illness. It's possible to avoid using these messages for your greater healing. It's also possible to use them in negative ways, ways that can be harmful to yourself and others.

In this chapter I will share some of the avoidant or negative ways an individual can use an illness. In the next, I will speak of positive ways that individuals use illnesses, ways that you can consciously cultivate. It's important to understand that, while I have neatly separated the negative and positive uses of illness into two chapters, the reality is more complex. Most people use their illnesses in both positive and negative ways.

Do not judge yourself if you recognize tendencies to use your illness in some of the negative ways listed in this chapter. Some negative uses are natural stages in the process of dealing with an illness. They become harmful only if you remain stuck in them, unable to move into healthier uses. Ironically, you are more likely to remain stuck if you *do* judge yourself.

Is your illness leading you to greater health in terms of your relationships, your values and ideals, your sense of self, and your relationship with your community? If not, you may not be taking advantage of the hidden potential within it.

Feelings of anger, frustration, self-pity, or denial are normal responses to illness. To deny such feelings would be countertherapeutic. To stay stuck in such feelings for too long, however, can serve to prolong an illness unnecessarily and in some cases can become a negative, ongoing life focus. As with many of the negative uses of illness, it will take some honesty and a certain level of self-awareness to know when you are stuck in these feelings. Sometimes a second party, someone you trust, can help you clarify things.

Being Ill Versus Being the Illness

One of the dangers of a serious illness is identifying with it too strongly. Instead of being a person who *has* an illness you *become* the illness. You experience yourself and your life through the lens of the illness. Even medical terminology sometimes identifies the person with an illness. An individual *is* schizophrenic or diabetic. The person and the illness can become one, essentially creating a sick personality.

For people who identify with their illnesses, the illness becomes the primary avenue for relating to others. Most conversations revolve around their pain, medication, and treatment. It's difficult to get them to talk about anything else. If you fall into this habit, you can become more important in your own eyes because of your illness. The illness becomes a dramatic happening that makes you a more interesting person and your life more interesting. An illness *can* be a vehicle for changing your life and making you and your life more interesting. The illness itself does not make you more interesting.

Doctors sometimes use labels which affirm their belief in the permanency of some disorders, as do the rest of us. Regarding persons with physical disabilities that we consider permanent, for example, we say, "She is blind," or "He is lame."

I have worked with mentally ill adults, and I have seen them get well and go back into the world. Some people with blindness *do* regain their sight, and some who have lameness walk again.

I'm not trying to instill false hope in those with irreversible disabilities or illnesses. Some physical problems are for life. Even if you have a "permanent" disability, it isn't healthy to let your disability become your identity. You don't deny your physical limitation; you don't pretend it isn't a daily reality for you. You also don't limit your sense of self. No matter how limited you may be physically, the *limitation* is not who you are.

There is also a danger of identifying with your illness even if it isn't considered permanent or life-threatening. The least that can happen through this identification is an unnecessary prolongation of the illness. The worst is that the illness could become life threatening or a life-threatening illness might be contracted. Focusing on the illness gives it emotional energy. It is an ongoing form of negative self-hypnosis. If the illness *is* life threatening, you may be damaging the quality of whatever life remains to you by narrowing the focus of your life to your illness.

In Roberto Assagioli's process of psychosynthesis, he speaks of dis-identification. You would dis-identify from your body by saying, "I have a body. I am not my body," and from your feelings with, "I have feelings. I am not my feelings." I would like you to begin dis-identifying with your illness by saying, "I *have* an illness (or disability). I am *not* my illness (or disability)."

Self-Punishment

You can use an illness as a way to punish yourself for real or imagined sins. If you have actually done something to feel guilty about, it would be far better to put your energy into trying to reconcile with the injured party, if that's relevant or possible, and to forgive yourself. Self-forgiveness can be difficult, and for some of you it may be an ongoing part of your life healing. It's well worth the effort.

Punishing yourself through illness is counterproductive and counter to spiritual growth. It's not good for you. It's not good for anyone. It doesn't change anything for the better. It would be far better to try to understand why you feel guilty and work on forgiving yourself instead of harming your own body. Guilt and ongoing self-punishment are ways to stay stuck. They do nothing positive for the injured party, and they do nothing positive for you.

One of Edgar Cayce's physical readings was done for a woman who was suffering from shaking and paralysis. Her husband had exhausted all medical avenues and turned to Cayce out of desperation.

From hundreds of miles away, with no information except the couple's name and address, Cayce put himself into a trance. Aside from apparently having access to individuals' bodies, Cayce sometimes remarked on the surroundings he "saw." In this case he saw a woman in a wheelchair with two nurses in attendance. This was exactly correct. He continued with his observations: "She is as rigid as a piece of marble. She can look neither to the right nor the left."[1]

Cayce's diagnosis was that the woman was suffering from guilt over a secret sin. The secret sin was masturbation, which the woman had engaged in from the ages of eighteen to thirty-nine, at which time she married. Cayce prescribed certain drugs for this woman, but the revelation of her "sin" and being able to talk about it were the primary cure.

It's amazing how quickly the power of a painful and secret sin can be dissipated just by sharing it with someone. If you have a guilty secret, find a rabbi, priest, minister, therapist, counselor, or trusted friend and share your secret *before* it makes you ill. The relief of just talking about something can be enormous. As soon as it's shared, your secret suddenly becomes much smaller. You may still need to go through a process of self-forgiveness, but sharing can help you see your "sin" through the eyes of others. In most cases, others will see it as being far less serious than you do.

If you have no one you feel comfortable talking to, use your healing journal. Confessing in writing, even if no one else reads it, can be healing. These confessions can be about things that happened to *you*, as well as things you might have done to others. Confession can turn the negative use of punishment into a positive.

Recent studies show that confession is not just good for the soul; it's good for the body. Holding onto something from the past and making yourself sick over it can be worse than the original "sin."

Sacrifice

Using an illness as a sacrifice is one way to pay for your sins. In the Judaic tradition, sacrifice was a regular part of religious practice. In many ancient religions, sacrifice played some part. It was believed that there was purification in the shedding of blood, especially innocent blood.

The closest we come to religious sacrifice in modern Western culture is in the ritual of surgery. In operations, we sometimes sacrifice parts of our bodies in imitation of ancient blood sacrifices. I'm certainly not suggesting that every operation is a sacrifice for sins. I *am* saying that surgery can sometimes be misused in this way.

There have been many studies which have shown that many more surgeries are performed in this country than are necessary. This is partly an example of the medical profession practicing good economics but bad medicine. Surgery may also be a safer course for the doctor who fears malpractice suits as may happen in some Caesarean sections. Many people acquiesce too readily to surgery. It should be a decision that is made with great care.

If your doctor tells you surgery is a necessary part of your treatment, you certainly should take the recommendation seriously. Doctors are fallible, and a second opinion is always a good idea. Whether surgery is part of your treatment or not, I recommend that you ask yourself if self-punishment or sacrifice is involved in your illness or treatment. The problem with sacrifice is that it usually doesn't work. The guilt doesn't go away, and you may have to look for new sacrifices or other ways to deal with it, each more harmful than the last.

Martyrdom

Illness can be the handmaiden of martyrdom. There is a stereotype of the individual who uses physical problems to act the martyr, always talking about aches and pains and the latest operation. You never want to ask how these people are, because they're likely to tell you in vivid and gory detail. Martyrs use physical problems to manipulate others.

Although this is a stereotype, we all know people who are

like this. When you talk to them, you know you're going find out about the latest bodily crisis. Some people seem to live from one illness to the next and seem most "alive" when they have something wrong to talk about.

We can laugh at the stereotype, but it's not very funny in reality. Using an illness to play the martyr is not uncommon, and it can be played out far more subtly than our loudly complaining caricature does. The symptoms of martyrdom are self-pity, manipulation, and seeking pity from others. A little bit of self-pity is understandable in a serious illness. As a lifestyle, it's deadly.

It's OK and even important to let others know when you're scared or in pain and need their support. Some individuals with serious illnesses tend to protect family and friends from their pain and fear because they don't want to alarm them or make them feel bad. That's as counterproductive as playing the martyr.

When we use our illness to control others, we are doing something very unhealthy to ourselves and our loved ones. There are healthy ways to gain power in one's life, and illness can open some of them to us, as I'll discuss in the next chapter. Martyrdom and manipulation are toxic to all involved. As with other negative uses of illness, this can be a difficult one to recognize if you're in it up to your neck. Again, honesty, self-examination, and a trusted friend can help.

Revenge

Ernest was a client who had serious physical and emotional problems. Because of them, he quit his profession and worked at various less physically, emotionally, and mentally demanding jobs.

I saw Ernest at least twice a week for several months. We talked about his issues and did a lot of visualization work. We uncovered some important material. He spent a lot of time talking about what his parents had done to him and complaining about his ex-wife.

He was receiving acupuncture, taking Chinese herbs, and watching his diet very carefully. He was apparently doing everything a person could do who really wanted to be healed and get on with his life. He spoke of wanting to get married again, have a family, and get back to the profession he loved.

In spite of everything he was doing to heal himself, Ernest had no intention of being healed. I'm not saying this was conscious. After all, he *was* doing everything possible to be healed. There was a genuine part of him that *wanted* to be healed. The greater part, unfortunately, did not.

He was using me as a witness to the wrongs done to him in the past. The focus of his life was to affirm himself as a victim. His problems were the evidence of past wrongdoing by others. If Ernest allowed himself to heal, the evidence would be gone, and the guilty would go unpunished.

Recognizing this negative use of illness requires extreme honesty on your part. Are you holding someone else responsible for your illness or other life problems? Are you determined to keep your illness to punish them?

Life Avoidance

A chronic illness can be used to protect you from the things you claim to want in life. In the case above, Ernest was not just keeping his problems to use as evidence against the perceived perpetrators. He was also using his problems to avoid fulfilling his own stated desires—to marry, have children, and go back to his chosen profession.

His problems were keeping him from the life he desired. I don't doubt that some part of him *did* desire the life he described, but it wasn't a big enough part. My assessment is this: if that's what he really wanted, he would have had it or would certainly be moving toward it.

His illness protected him from failure in work and relationships and it protected him from success as well. If his life was not one of fulfillment, he was at least clear about whom to blame.

Melinda, the woman who had had the strokes, who was not projecting her life beyond her illness, is another example of life avoidance. Because her life as a child was so painful, she came to believe the world was not safe. It wasn't safe to go out among people. In the course of our workshop, she came to realize how her strokes protected her from contact with people. Healing would require facing her fear of being out in the world. But there's still a more drastic way of avoiding life in the world.

The ultimate life avoidance is death, but death can also be a positive resolution to illness, as I discuss in the next section. Mental illnesses are a close second to death as life avoidance. I call schizophrenia "living suicide." It allows one to be in the world but not of the world. Schizophrenia used to be called dementia praecox because it primarily strikes in adolescence. I believe the age group may have more meaning in terms of choice than in terms of biochemistry or genetics.

I have worked in a number of residential facilities for adults with various mental illnesses, mostly schizophrenia. Schizophrenia may be a decision not to deal with life. Adolescents stand at the brink of adulthood. They face marriage, family, and possibly a job or career. For many, that's a frightening prospect. It was frightening for many of us who went ahead in spite of our fears and our sense of not being prepared.

Some, however, just say, "No, thank you" and use mental illnesses to avoid the challenges and responsibilities of life. I will write about this more in chapter 10 when I discuss the question, "Do you want to be healed?" You can use physical illnesses to say "no" to life. The reason schizophrenia is so difficult to treat is that the individuals cannot be healed without changing that initial antilife decision. Unless something happens to convince them that life is not as frightening or difficult as they initially perceived it to be, there's no reason for them to change that decision. If your physical illness exists primarily to help you avoid life, you may have to face the fears that caused that life avoidance choice.

Death

Death is a good issue to discuss to make the transition from negative to positive uses of an illness. Death is not necessarily a failure, not necessarily a negative use for an illness. We all die, and in some cases death can be seen as the healing for a life. There *are* some instances, including suicide, in which an individual dies in order to escape from life. It is beyond the scope of this book to discuss suicide or the complex ethical issues surrounding euthanasia. Each individual needs to ask if his or her life-threatening illness is a "sickness unto death" as a way of simply leaving physical life or if it is an escape from life because the challenges seem too great.

I would like those of you in life-threatening situations to honestly look at your attitude toward your life, not just toward your illness and its possible consequences. In your healing journal create two columns. At the top of one column write "Reasons to Live" and at the top of the other, "Reasons to Die." The exercise will be most valuable if you are able to be completely honest.

It is not enough to simply see which list is longest. Some who have only one or two items in their "Reasons to Die" list may nevertheless be in great danger if those reasons are strong enough. The items in the "Reasons to Live" list should perhaps be turned into affirmations that can be repeated or put up around the house where you can see them. The items in the "Reasons to Die" list should be dealt with. Is there an antidote or a positive polarity to the item? Is there

an action you can take in terms of a relationship reconcilia-
tion, forgiving another, or forgiving yourself? Is there a
change that can be made in terms of your work or some
other negative life circumstance? Do you see negative attitudes or beliefs that you might work on changing? Work on
the "Reasons to Die" list could be the most significant healing work you do.

Even those with a non-life-threatening illness or no illness at all might benefit from this exercise. Grace had multiple physical problems, none of them life threatening.
Nevertheless, she discovered a large part of her that wanted
to die. It wasn't because her life was so terrible. It was because she believed life after death would be so much better
and easier than physical life.

She saw herself as constantly struggling and was tired of
the struggle. She needed to see that life-as-struggle was just
a belief (like "life is difficult") and that she could change that
belief. In instances like this one, death is not the answer—
but death of the old self *may* be, death of the self that believes in struggle.

If you find no redeeming value in your illness, no opportunity for positive changes in your life, no change of values
that could give your life new meaning, I suggest you might
be missing something, and I would ask you, for your own
sake, to look for the possible gifts in your illness.

If you find yourself thinking of death as a positive alternative, at least consider some other alternatives. Consider
the possibility of letting the old *self* die instead of the body.
You may need to change your values or your self-image. You
may need to change some of your relationships. It doesn't
matter how old you are or how set in your ways you think
you are. You have the right and the opportunity to throw off
the yoke of your old beliefs and the expectations of others
and completely re-create yourself!

Just as your mind-body contains images and patterns
from your childhood and past lives, so does it contain im-

ages and patterns of a healthier, happier version of your present self. If you do not see those healthy, happy images within your own body and life right now, remember the feedback system. All around you, as well as in your dreams, you can see healthier, happier versions of yourself—if you take the time to look.

You can change your thoughts. You can let the Divine flow through you unsuppressed. You can *allow* yourself to become whole. You're never too old or too sick to dream and never too old or too sick to make your dreams come true— unless you *believe* you are.

Some individuals who are told they have only months to live find the illness has made such a positive difference in their life that they are actually grateful for it. They say they would rather have only months of living the quality of life that their illness helped them discover than to live for many years as the old self. Ideally, of course, they would like to be healed and live many more years with their new quality of life.

As Linda Ellerbee discovered, illness *may* be the best thing that happens to you if you take advantage of the gifts it brings. When it comes to living and dying, it's not how many days we have in our life that matters, it's how much life we have in our days.

Negative uses of illness can be difficult to recognize and require a great deal of honesty and courage to face. The rewards can be well worth it and can result in physical healing and a less restricted and negatively focused life.

In every case of illness, whether mild or serious, you can ask the questions, "How is this illness serving me?" and "What is this illness protecting me from?" If the illness is serving you in a negative way, such as giving you the opportunity for martyrdom or revenge, you have a choice to make. Negative uses of illness can be uncovered and released with honesty, courage, and self-awareness. In the next chapter we'll look at some of the positive uses for illness and the gifts contained in every illness.

6

Positive Uses: The Gifts of Illness

When I speak of the positive uses of an illness, I am speaking of the potential contained in every illness. You can find the positive uses your illness contains, and utilize its gift to improve your life. I also wish to help those of you who are not experiencing a serious illness or other life crisis to prevent that possibility by uncovering imbalances and dis-eases in your life and correcting them before they develop into a crisis.

There are as many meanings for a specific illness as there are people who have the illness. Dreaming of a cat means something different for different people. Having cancer, even the same cancer, has a unique meaning for every individual. Just as no one can tell you what your dream means, no one can tell you what your illness means. At some level of your being, however, hidden from you by the thinnest of veils, you know exactly what your illness means. Instead of saying to yourself, "I don't know why I have this illness, but I will try to find out," say, "I know *exactly* why I have this illness, and I will allow myself to bring that knowledge into my awareness."

Whatever the specific meaning of your illness, the purpose of your illness, whether it comes from your unconscious or your superconscious, is to bring about a greater healing in your life. One way to understand the meaning of your illness is to honestly look at aspects of your life that need healing, whether in the area of relationships, work, values, lifestyle, money, habits, feelings, spirituality, or other parts of your life.

Whatever area of life your illness primarily relates to, a serious illness almost always brings up an awareness of mortality. One of the positive uses of a serious illness is to make peace with death, to accept the fact that life is limited by time. Ironically, it is possible to experience being more alive when you're able to come to terms with death. When death becomes a more imminent possibility, life can become more precious, and the way we spend our time and with whom becomes much more important.

Illness for Change

The purpose of every illness is to help an individual change in some way. That's a general positive meaning for every illness. Death represents one end of a spectrum of change. Other changes are smaller and more easily made. Some changes involve a lifetime of struggle or the need to overcome years of habit. Look for a part of your life that is out of balance or stagnated. The illness calls attention to the imbalances and presents an opportunity to make healing changes. There are a number of different ways an illness can be seen as an agent for positive change. Illnesses can actually energize you if you're feeling stuck and help you get your life moving and on a positive path again.

Path Correction

One of the images I use to describe movement and growth in an individual's life is that of paths. We are all on many different paths. Our physical body and its health is one path, our work another, family and other relationships another, and religion-spirituality still another. We could be on a healthy path with our work, but our relationship or family path might be a little rocky. I see illness as one natural form of path correction. An illness can tell us we're on a wrong path somewhere in our lives. We must decide what path or paths our illness is trying to correct. Ironically, an illness doesn't necessarily tell us we have a problem in our physical path, a problem with our health habits or diet. It may be more related to our relationship or spiritual path than to our bodies.

Julie used her breast cancer to make two major path changes. She divorced her husband and quit her job. She didn't change her career path entirely, but found a way to work within her chosen field that was much more satisfying. Ruth also used her cancer for both a work and relationship path change. She cut back on her work hours and allowed her adult children to be more responsible. Frances's allergies were so severe at their height that she was essentially an invalid and was unable to participate much in life at all. She not only healed herself physically, with past-life work and homeopathy, but she also started on a path that included doing past-life workshops to help others. Grace left a high-paying corporate job to go back to school to become a therapist.

Illnesses tell us we need to make some path changes. Serious illnesses can be life shattering, altering or permanently changing many of our life paths. They can make it impossible to continue business-as-usual in many areas of our lives. They give us the opportunity to create and walk an entirely new path, to build, with our minds, a healthier, more joyful path than the one we were on. Most of us know, without a serious illness, which paths in our life are not as smooth and straight as they could be.

Open your healing journal. Take a few moments to think about each of your major life paths. This would include your most important relationships, work or career, money and/or possessions, body—diet, exercise, and habits—religion and/or spirituality, and recreation. Think about each path in terms of both positive and negative aspects. Write down what you consider to be obstacles for each path, areas of anxiety, unhappiness, anger, guilt, or helplessness.

In terms of the negative aspects of a path, are there external actions you can take to improve the path, such as honestly sharing your feelings with someone, seeing a counselor or therapist, or leaving a stressful situation? Are there internal actions you can take in terms of changing beliefs, attitudes or expectations? It will require courage to take these actions, and they will likely be both external and internal. Here's a big clue: if your obstacles are other people, your place of employment, the economy, the government, or some accident of birth, you have some inner work to do. You are externalizing your obstacles, as we all do.

What if those obstacles were just metaphors telling you something about your own beliefs, attitudes, and expectations? If your path obstacles are the result of your beliefs, what beliefs do they represent? If you feel unappreciated at work, it is because you expect to be unappreciated. You can tell me a hundred stories of how your hard work has gone unappreciated and you might tell me that no one has ever appreciated you as you deserve. If the lack of appreciation goes back far enough, you may be dealing with a core belief. There may be a life metaphor from your childhood relating to not being appreciated. Any of your path obstacles could turn out to be connected to core beliefs and may be life obstacles, not just work obstacles. The more powerful the obstacle, the more important the healing.

Look at the positive aspects of your paths and see if

there's some way you can feed and nurture them. Just acknowledging and giving more time and attention to the positive aspects can help them grow. If individuals are part of the positive aspects of a path, you would do well to acknowledge them in some way as well. What can you do to change the negative aspects of a path and enhance the positive in order to prevent a serious illness or other crisis and get you back on a more healing life path?

Initiation and Rites of Passage

There are other models that can help us visualize change as a healing process. Two are initiations and rites of passage. In many ancient or "primitive" cultures, initiations and rites of passage were supported by the entire community and were highly structured and ritualized. Modern Western cultures have very little in the way of such formalized, culturally supported rituals. We often have to make important life transitions without such community support, and it can be very difficult.

Illnesses can act as an initiation or rite of passage, sometimes a trial by fire, presenting us with challenges to be met and overcome. The purpose of such rites and ceremonies is to move an individual from one stage of life to another. For adolescents, it was a passage from childhood to adulthood. For adults, it might be an initiation into a particular role. It almost always meant a change in privileges and responsibilities. Most important, it always meant the death of the former self and the resurrection of a new self. The girl or boy goes through a rite of passage ceremony and comes out a woman or a man. A woman goes through an initiation experience and becomes a medicine woman or shaman. In many cultures, shamanic initiations often involved images of dismemberment and reassembly. The individual woman or man comes back as an entirely new being, sometimes forgetting significant people from their former life. Ilpailurkna, an Australian aboriginal magician, told of his death and dismemberment at the hands of a very old doctor. At the conclusion of the initiation "Ilpailurkna had completely forgotten who he was and all about his past life. After a time the old man led him back to his camp and showed it to him, and told him that the woman there was his *lubra*, for he had forgotten all about her."[1]

For many of us, change is not easy. We resist it because it represents upheaval and dislocation. It represents the unknown. The more change is resisted, the more difficult it becomes. Resistance builds up like a dammed river, and sometimes an explosion is needed to destroy the dam and allow life to flow again in a pattern of healthy growth. Serious illnesses can blow up the dam. Less serious illnesses give us the opportunity to create a spillway, to make changes before the backup is too great.

In a sense, all changes, however small, represent little deaths and resurrections. To the extent that we are open to these changes, allowing ourselves to be in a process of becoming, these deaths and resurrections will hardly be noticed. It is only when we try to freeze ourselves in time, to stay the same person beyond the time of natural change, that a wiser part of ourselves steps in and gives us an opportunity to get unstuck, to move forward, to move toward the healthy and joy-filled life which is the birthright of us all.

Relationships

One of the most common changes for those who have near-death experiences is a heightened appreciation for relationships and an understanding of the importance of the impact of their lives on other people. The same is true for those with life-threatening illnesses. When faced with our own mortality, family and friends suddenly become much more important. Our hierarchy of values can be turned upside down. A serious illness can be a vehicle for healing old relationships, ending unhealthy or toxic relationships, and creating new, more nourishing friendships.

One of the most important things you can do in terms of illness prevention and healing is to take an honest look at your current relationships as well as any past relationships that still have an emotional charge for you. It is impossible to live a balanced life, to have the Spirit flowing through the mind unsuppressed, when our relationships are out of balance.

Lucille came to me with a repeating dream about rushing to get on a plane on time. Once on board, she realized she had forgotten something important. She was in conflict between staying on the plane and getting to her destination on time or going back to retrieve the forgotten item. One simple question to ask about such dream situations is, "What is happening in your life that feels like this?"

In this case it didn't take long for Lucille to realize the dream represented the conflict she felt between her career and her home and family. The plane represented taking off in her career. Her family was the something important she had forgotten. As is often the case, this was a conflict she was already very aware of. The dream served to tell her that it was important to try to resolve it.

While this is not an easy problem to resolve, it's easier to make changes when the shouting is just in the dream state. If she should continue in this stressful situation long enough, it could shout at her in the form of a serious illness or a breakdown in her marriage. The positive use of your illness or dream "shouts" of potential illness is not likely to fall neatly into any one category. This situation involves relationships as well as the issues of work and values. Julie's breast cancer and Ruth's cancer of the throat both involved relationships as well as work. Both of these areas will be covered in following sections.

Get out your healing journal and spend a few minutes getting quiet. Think about the people closest to you. Does everything feel clean and clear between you? Is there something you need to say to or ask of anyone? Sometimes love is taken for granted between those who are close, and the words aren't said often enough. Do you need to tell some people you love them or appreciate having them in your life? Do you need to tell others you're angry at them or upset because of something they did or said? Write down the names of specific people with whom you may be out of balance. Write down possible corrective actions you could take.

If you need to tell some people you love them or you're angry with them, try to do it in person. If that's not possible, as in the case of someone who has died, an imaginary conversation can have a healing outcome that is far more than imaginary. It isn't always necessary to confront people. Sometimes you can heal a relationship by talking to someone in a visualization. Imagine speaking to the individual, and imagine him or her responding to you. Or write down a conversation between the two of you in your journal. You may be surprised to find the conversation and the other individual taking on their own life.

Now repeat the process with people you work with or with neighbors, those with whom you are less close. You might even search your feelings for unfinished business with those you no longer relate to. Some people hold on to old injuries and real or imagined wrongs, thinking they can do nothing about them because the other person is no longer in their life. You can have the same kind of conversation with someone who is no longer part of your life as you can with someone who has died.

Finally, take a few moments to see how you feel about yourself. The relationship you have with yourself is the most important and affects all others. It's very difficult to be in positive relationships with others if you are not in a positive relationship with yourself. I suspect every serious illness contains the challenge to improve our relationship to ourselves. Using an illness to learn to love yourself more is one of the most positive uses to which an illness can be put; self-love is one of its greatest gifts.

Work/Career/Vocation

Our work is important on many levels. Most jobs take up more than half of an individual's waking weekday hours. What happens at our work, how we feel about the work itself and about our co-workers, are going to have a significant effect on the other hours of our life and on our health.

I think the number of people who are unhappy in their work for one reason or another is probably very high in this country. Many people feel they have no choice but to stay at a job they hate, especially during times of economic uncertainty. Some who feel trapped in their jobs also feel there's nothing they can do to improve their current situation.

Although it may be difficult to change jobs or change the situation at your current job, there is no job or career that's worth dying or getting seriously ill for. For example, among the primary indicators for heart disease are things like cigarette smoking, diabetes, high serum cholesterol, and high blood pressure. Studies have shown that, among those who have their first heart attack below the age of fifty, however, the majority of them exhibited *none* of these indicators. Instead, heart attacks in this age group occurred most frequently on Monday and they clustered between eight and nine in the morning. Job dissatisfaction is the most dependable predictor of heart problems in this age group. If your heart is not in your work, metaphorically speaking, your health may be at risk.

Look at your own work situation and see if you're getting a whisper or even louder feedback that's telling you your health is at risk. Leaving a job or a marriage is an extreme solution that is sometimes necessary. Other avenues, however, should always be explored first.

Are there relationship problems at work that can be improved with the healing journal exercise previously mentioned? One of the problems in relationships is that we sometimes attribute motives to individuals that are inaccurate. One woman I'll call Shirley was extremely frustrated because her supervisor was always critical of her work. She felt the woman just didn't like her, and nothing she could do would please her.

Instead of quitting or continuing to suffer, Shirley changed her approach to her supervisor. Instead of being defensive and expecting the worst, she treated her boss with warmth and respect, the way she wanted to be treated. After a short time, the supervisor called Shirley into her office. She said she was sorry for the way she'd been treating Shirley. The supervisor had some serious personal problems at home and was in a lot of emotional pain. She shared her pain with Shirley, and not only did she stop being critical of Shirley, they became close friends.

We tend to be rather egocentric and think everything is about us. Sometimes it's not. Try being nice to someone you don't like at work or whom you think doesn't like you. Such behavior, over a period of time, can be pattern shattering. Your change in behavior can change *your* attitudes and beliefs as well as those of the other individual.

Sometimes the only thing needed to change an intolerable situation at work is to talk to the parties involved and tell them how you feel. Grace repeatedly complained about her boss and conditions at work. She would tell me what was wrong and what needed to be changed. I asked her if she said these things to her boss. She said she hadn't. She was afraid of getting fired for being too honest with her boss; she ended up quitting the job because it became intolerable. She never tested whether honest feedback would have gotten her fired. The good news is that this experience helped convince Grace to go back to school to work toward becoming a therapist. It's important to try to understand whether a bad work experience is telling you to heal that situation or is meant to get you to leave as an important life path correction. I recommend you always try to heal a situation first.

A work relationship, like any other, represents a feedback loop. You receive certain information from the other party, and you feed certain information back. By not feeding back accurate information on how you really feel, or withholding information, you help perpetuate a negative feedback loop. If your feedback is accurate and truthful, the negative feedback loop can be broken and the boss has an opportunity to make changes. In a very real sense, Grace was keeping her expertise, her professional observations from her boss.

If you feel you really need to quit your job to protect your health, begin creating a new and better job in your mind before you give your notice. Write down the specifics of the new job you want in your healing journal. Be open to something better coming along. Affirm the healthiness of your choice, and trust the Spirit flowing through you to help create it.

Money and Possessions

It's certainly possible to be concerned about money and possessions enough to get sick over it, especially if money is connected to concerns about security. A serious illness can help put such things back into perspective. One of the most common outcomes of a serious illness is a re-evaluation of one's life. Things that seemed so important before the illness seem silly when one's life is threatened. It can be helpful to look at your relationship to money and material possessions and see if it is healthy. Are you out of balance or in dis-ease around money? Do you worry about money a lot? Is that the meaning and gift of your illness? What choices and actions can you follow to come into a better relationship with money and possessions?

Ironically, those who struggle with money problems may not have to struggle with health problems. Money and possessions may be the main arena they have chosen to work out their life issues. If you have money problems *and* health problems, look for an underlying theme. (I realize that health problems can cause money problems with today's health-care costs. It is still helpful to look for a common meaning in the illness and financial crisis.)

Ruth didn't have money problems but she believed she couldn't quit her nursing job and look for another one without putting her finances in jeopardy. As her children became more responsible, mediated by her illness, they became less of a financial burden. She was also able to cut back her work hours without jeopardizing her benefits or seriously reducing her income. Many people could live quite comfortably on a reduced income by simply changing their values. Serious illnesses can help us change our values in many areas, including money and possessions.

The Physical Body

Within the medical model, all illnesses are related to the body. Whether a disease is the result of germs, genes, diet, lifestyle, or any number of other causes, it is seen as a physical problem with either a physical solution or no solution. From a metaphorical or meaning standpoint, illnesses are seldom just related to the body. They are more often related to other areas of life, the body simply acting as the vehicle of expression, a metaphorical vehicle.

Some illnesses, however, *do* call attention to the body and its needs. They are a wakeup call to do something about physical habits and/or an out-of-balance lifestyle. Less serious illnesses can be a warning to change some aspect of your body habits before something more serious occurs. The meaning of these illnesses is "Change what you're doing with your body or what you're putting into it." The gift is the possibility of a more vigorous and robust life.

Perhaps the most common category relating to the need for body changes is physical addictions such as to alcohol or drugs. The illnesses associated with addictions are often side effects of the addiction, cirrhosis of the liver, in the case of alcohol, and susceptibility to a variety of diseases because of a lowered immune system, in the case of many drug addictions. In the case of addictions, however, it is often the social and interpersonal consequences of addiction that lead individuals to seek help in changing their lives and physical habits.

Those with heart problems often confront the necessity of making diet and other physical changes. As popular as heart bypass operations seem to be, what they actually do is bypass the problem. Many individuals need multiple bypass operations. Those who use blocked arteries as a call to change their lives on the physical level find that they can bypass the bypass surgery altogether with simple changes in diet, learning relaxation techniques, and getting involved in a mild exercise program, a program championed by Dr. Dean Ornish.

Religion and Spirituality

An illness can be a call to re-examine your spiritual life. I believe that every aspect of life is spiritual. There are spiritual practices which can enhance life and bring you closer to your spiritual origins. Prayer and meditation, chanting and movement, or just spending time in nature are often the first to be put aside in the pressures of modern life.

An illness can mean that you've forgotten what is important. Reclaiming your spiritual life or seeking it for the first time can be the gift in your illness and part of the healing process as well. You may or may not want to pursue or express your spirituality through organized religion, but there is evidence that participation in a close-knit religious organization is good for your health.

I met Melinda at a healing workshop I gave for a spiritual organization in Southern California. Her strokes led her into a spiritual quest which involved private and inner work as well as venturing out into the world. Churches and spiritual organizations represented safe places where she could be in the world while seeking spiritual answers to her physical problems.

Self-Image and Roles

Every illness is about changing the self. It doesn't matter if the illness primarily concerns your relationships or your work. Changing yourself really means changing your ideas about yourself, changing beliefs, attitudes, and expectations. One gift in every illness can be a new self, a changed self. A great deal of the resistance to healing that people sometimes experience is really resistance to change, to the transformation of the self.

An important aspect of self-image is the roles we play. Many of us, unfortunately, define ourselves by our roles. In our culture we highly value what people do, what they have accomplished, or what they possess. It is common in Western society for men to die shortly after retirement. If an individual's self-image is primarily tied up in his or her work, when that work is gone an identity crisis will ensue.

One of the meanings of an illness can be, "You are not your role." Each of us is more than what we do, more than what we have accomplished, more than what we possess. An illness can help us find that "more." The gift can be "You are loved for who you are, and you can love yourself for who you are."

Julie, the nurse with breast cancer, was very sick from her treatment and was bedridden for long periods of time. On Valentine's Day her two daughters were downstairs in the kitchen making cookies, a family tradition. As the mother, it was Julie's role to be downstairs with her daughters, participating in this tradition. Not being able to be with them made her feel very sad and helpless. She was not able to fulfill one of the roles for which she valued herself.

She was crying when her four-year-old daughter came into the room. "Why are you crying, Mommy?" she asked. "I feel bad because I can't be downstairs helping you make the Valentine's Day cookies," Julie replied. With the wisdom of a four year old, the daughter said, "We love you because you're our mommy, not because you make cookies for us."

If our self-image is too tied up in our roles, a serious illness can help us re-evaluate what's important. We may find that we're loved just for being who we are. Are you valuable just because you exist? Are you loved and lovable just for being? If a disease can help you learn this about yourself, it will be a gift indeed.

Values, Priorities, and Ideals

Illnesses present opportunities to examine all of our values, not just self-valuing. When life is threatened, the things that are important immediately begin shifting. Whether one does it consciously or unconsciously, priorities are rearranged. What was very important yesterday may be unimportant today. A low priority yesterday may be at the top of the list today.

An illness may mean you need to look at your values, priorities, and ideals. What do you value in other people? What do you value in life? What are your priorities? If you knew you had only months or a few years to live, would your priorities change? What would you do differently? Why not change your priorities now? Why not decide what's important to you, what you value, and pursue those things now while you're in good health? Or if you're ill now, what things can you change, what can you do that's important to you, even with your illness?

You may simply want to spend more time with certain people or spend more time alone. You may do more things that bring you pleasure, activities you now put off because of other things you "should" be doing. All of us will leave this physical existence at some point. When you look back on your life, will you regret not doing certain things, not spending more time with certain people, not having more fun?

While I have divided the gifts of illness into neat categories, the examples I've already given demonstrate that one can benefit from an illness in many areas of life. A dear friend of mine I'll call Ted found out he had cancer when he went to the doctor for a different complaint. On the weekend he received his diagnosis, he had brought home from work an application for a supervisorial position. The position would mean more money and prestige and more hours. Knowing Ted as well as I did, I asked him if he really wanted to become a supervisor. He felt that he *should* apply because he and his wife could use the extra money and also because it is expected that you move up as high in the company hierarchy as you can.

As you can see, this experience involves work, money, and role. It also involved relationships and self-valuing. As a result of the illness, he became closer to his wife and other family members and he also found out how important he was to his friends and relatives. To his credit, Ted, a man with a strong scientific background, accepted the possibility that he actually contracted cancer to help him avoid becoming a supervisor. He was operating on the values of others—or what he believed others valued—including society's values, and not his own. The illness brought what was really important in his life to the fore, both in terms of work and money and in terms of relationships.

Am I saying that it was no coincidence that he brought home those forms on the same weekend he was "accidentally" diagnosed as having cancer? That's exactly what I'm saying and it's an excellent example of how powerful we are in our ability to create situations with such precision. If the forms and the diagnosis hadn't coincided so perfectly, my very rational friend might not have even considered any relationship between the two. As it was, it really got his attention.

The gift in changing your values and priorities can be more joy and satisfaction in your life. Don't wait for a serious illness, as Ted did, to look at the things you value, to see where your time and energy are going. Make some different choices now, and begin to bring your life back into balance.

Use your healing journal to make a list of the things you value. If you had unlimited time and money, what would you do? What activities bring you pleasure and satisfaction? Are there things on your list that don't actually take much time or money, activities you could do more often in your life right now? Begin to do some of the things you value. Give them a higher priority than you have in the past.

What are your priorities? List your priorities in terms of how you are actually spending your time now. Examine your list and see if this is really how you want to spend your time and energy. What would you add or change in terms of raising or lowering some of your priorities?

Related to values and priorities is the idea of ideals. Ideals are more long term and not necessarily attainable. They are usually goals with a spiritual dimension. Ideals are meant to stretch you spiritually. They can become a framework for your values and priorities. Your values and priorities should always be in alignment with your ideals.

An ideal might be creating peace on earth or bringing more love into the world. It could be a desire to be of service to humankind, or it might be more specific, such as an ideal of being a healer. Any imbalance or dis-ease in your life is moving you away from your ideals. On the simplest level, our worries and stresses take our time and energy. To the extent that your time and energy is going into your obstacles; fear, doubt, anger, guilt, etc., the less time and energy is available to focus on higher endeavors. On the other hand, an illness can bring you back into alignment with your ideals or even help you discover them. It can help you question what is important in terms of your use of time and emotional energy.

Open your healing journal. Quiet yourself and let your awareness move to your heart or to your spiritual center, wherever you conceive that to be. Ask for your guiding ideal or ideals. Be still and see what comes into your awareness. You may already be aware of such an ideal. Write it down in your journal and perhaps in a prominent place in your house. Seeking daily alignment with your ideal can itself be healing and prevent disease as well.

Beliefs

Whatever the meaning of your illness, you can be sure it means you need to change some beliefs. "Thoughts are things." It is the mind that creates the illness and the mind that creates the life situation the illness is meant to correct. Ultimately, the meaning of an illness will be found in beliefs, attitudes, expectations, feelings, and desires. As part of the Universal Feedback System, illnesses always point back to the beliefs that gave them birth. The most positive use of an illness is to uncover the beliefs and ideas that brought you to a point of imbalance and dis-ease. Changing those beliefs and ideas can result in more than good health. It can lead to a fuller more meaningful life, a daily experience of Spirit unsuppressed by doubts and fears.

Power

In the previous chapter I wrote about the negative use of an illness for feeling powerful, such as trying to manipulate others through martyrdom. Can illnesses be used in a positive way to feel more powerful in our lives? In a very important way, helping you to feel more powerful and more in control of your lives is one of the primary purposes of this book. As you begin to see yourself less as a victim of illness and more as the creator, your sense of power in your life should increase. As you begin to take conscious steps to understand the meaning of your illness and take healing actions to change your life, I believe you will receive feedback that will further confirm your power as co-creator of your life experiences.

I had a remarkable experience that showed me that I had the power to heal myself any time I was willing to set aside my limiting beliefs. I led a weekly group for over fifteen years which involved the phenomenon known as channeling. I helped individuals get in touch with inner guidance and channel that guidance if they chose. I did some channeling myself but had (and have) a healthy scepticism about the process and was most sceptical about my own channeling.

One evening I was suffering from hay fever, an on-again, off-again annoyance of many years. My congestion got worse as the evening wore on until I was pretty miserable. Someone in the group asked me what I thought the hay fever was about, feeding my own teachings back to me. I think my hay fever has many meanings, but at that time I said, "I think it has to do with me blocking my channeling." Someone else said, quite reasonably, "Well, why don't you channel?"

So I did. As soon as I began to speak for my guide, my sinuses immediately began to clear. And remained clear the entire five minutes or so that I channeled. That was remarkable enough. More remarkable for me, however, was the fact that, as soon as I finished channeling, my nose and sinuses immediately became stuffed up again! I had an experience of what must happen with a multiple personality, except I was fully conscious in both states.

I wish I could report that, from that time forward, I have

been able to heal myself instantly of any physical problem. Unfortunately, that isn't the case. I still sometimes give myself physical messages that I must try to understand in order to continue on or correct my spiritual path. The experience did make it very clear to me, however, that it is my mind that gets sick, not my body, and I do feel more powerful because of that experience.

Try a brief meditation in which you imagine yourself becoming your healed self, whether you have a physical illness or not, putting on the mind of the healed self. Imagine this self as a completely different personality with different assumptions, attitudes, beliefs, expectations, and feelings. You don't have to channel this self, as I did, but you could if you wanted to, speaking aloud or in your mind or writing down the words of the healed self in your journal. The important thing is to see if you can actually feel different as the healed self, both physically and emotionally.

Notice if there is any reduction in symptoms and write your experience down in your healing journal. Open yourself to this healed self often and feel the positive power of that being.

Another way to uncover unhealthy beliefs, to discover the meaning of your illness, *and* the positive uses and gifts it contains is through that aspect of the Universal Feedback System known as dreams.

PART 3

UNDERSTANDING YOUR ILLNESS

7

Doing Dreamwork with Your Illness

Thoughts are things. Dreams are also things, both in the sense of being creations of mind and in the sense of being experiences, as real to the body and emotions as any waking experience. While dreams come from the mind, they do not come from the waking conscious mind. Waking consciousness is present to some degree, of course, or we wouldn't be able to recall our dreams. But in dreams the unconscious and superconscious mind pretty much have the stage to themselves. Spirit has access to our dreams while our Spirit-suppression devices are temporarily on hold.

We get the same feedback in our dreams as in our waking life, but in the dream state there is more fluidity of time and space and a greater range of images and experiences to draw from. Our emotions are given freer rein. The issues we're dealing with in our waking life can be played out with high drama on the big inner screen.

The techniques in this chapter can be used to do dreamwork on your dreams, on your illness, or on any waking-life experience. There are at least three different ways in which dreams can help with your illness and life issues:

Dreams give us experiences that can change us. People are changed by waking-life experiences. Serious illnesses certainly change us. We make choices and take actions in our waking life that have life-changing consequences, both large and small. We can also be changed by our dream experiences. Our choices and actions in the dream state are real to our mind and emotions. They're real to our bodies as well. Dream fear is real fear; dream courage is also real courage.

Dreams give us information about what the mind is building. We meet ourselves in our dreams as well as in every other part of our life. Dreams exaggerate some of those selves in order to get our attention. We receive both explicit and symbolic information. Any issue that is important to you will be dealt with nightly in your dreams.

Dreams affect us physiologically. It is possible to be healed directly in a dream because dreaming is a highly charged physiological state. Actions and feelings in the dream produce electrochemical responses in the body. People also wake up sick from a dream or in pain, such as being shot in the stomach in the dream and waking up with a stomachache.

I'm still asked, "If you hit the ground in a falling dream, will you die?" The answer is no. One man who called me on a radio talk show said he let himself hit the ground in a falling dream. "What happened?" I asked. "I bounced," he replied. I've been killed at least a couple of times in my dreams, and I feel fine.

You can ask for a healing dream. A woman with a severe backache asked for such a dream. She dreamed that a bodyworker friend of hers worked on her back in the dream, and she woke up relieved of her back pain.

Dreams are a great source of whispers. They will always give you information about imbalances in your life before they show up physically, either in your body or in other areas of your life. As you learn to hear the dream whispers, you will be able to prevent waking-life shouts. Dreams shout at us in the form of nightmares and other emotionally disturbing dreams. Dream shouts are preferable to waking-life shouts. It's better to have an automobile accident in your dreams than in your waking life.

One of the great benefits of dreams, whether they whisper or shout, is that they have a high level of body sensitivity that we can only "dream" of in our waking life. The dreaming self "knows" of impending illnesses long before they begin to manifest in the body. While the conscious self may never have that level of body sensitivity, it *can* elicit that information from dreams.

Dream Physiology and Cycles

There are certain important physiological accompaniments to dreaming. Although we have thoughts, images, and dreamlike experiences at other times of the night, a state of sleep called Rapid Eye Movement or REM sleep is particularly associated with dreaming.

Rapid movement of the eyes is one correlate of the dream state and was the behavior which called researchers' attention to the phenomenon. Other physiological correlates to the dream state are a brain-wave pattern similar to a waking pattern, rapid respiration and heart rate, fluctuations in blood pressure and galvanic skin response, and penile erection in men and clitoral erection and vaginal lubrication in women, regardless of age or dream content.

One of the most important physiological responses in the REM state is the relaxation of the large muscles. Except for this relaxation, the physiology of dreaming is very much like the adrenaline surge in the classic fight/flight syndrome. If the large muscles were not relaxed during dreaming, our dreaming would look like an epileptic seizure. Cats, with this muscle relaxation response disabled, jumped up during REM sleep, arched their backs, hissed, and ran around the room, presumably chasing dream mice.

We dream in a regular cycle. We dream every night, whether we remember any dreams or not. The sleep cycle is broken down into four stages, each classified by fairly distinct brain-wave patterns. We move through these four stages of sleep in roughly a ninety-minute cycle.

When we first fall asleep we enter a distinct Stage One sleep called hypnogogia. Children experience hypnogogic imagery more frequently than adults. In this state we may have visual or auditory hallucinations. We are most likely to experience this state when we take an afternoon nap or are bedridden with an illness and drift in and out of sleep.

From this initial Stage One sleep we move down into deeper states of sleep—Stages Two and Three—until we reach Stage Four or deep sleep. We stay in Stage Four for half an hour to forty-five minutes and then "rise" back up through Stages Three, Two, and back to One. This Stage One sleep is different from hypnogogia. This is the dream state. In this first dreaming period we may dream for only five to ten minutes and then we repeat the cycle through the stages.

The ninety-minute cycle remains relatively constant through the night, but the percentage of time spent within the stages changes. In each succeeding ninety-minute cycle we spend less time in deep sleep and more time in dream sleep. As morning approaches we will not go into deep sleep at all, and our last REM period of the night may last half an hour to an hour. Most of the dreams you recall in the morning are from this last Stage One sleep. Although you may have some long dreams, it's far more common to have several different dreams in this last dreaming period.

Dream Recall

You can't work with your dreams if you don't recall them. For those who don't recall dreams and would like to or those who would like to recall more dreams, here are some simple techniques.

The simplest and most effective dream recall technique is suggestion. Just before going to sleep, give yourself the suggestion, "I will remember a dream tomorrow morning." You might repeat it three times. You can give yourself the suggestion during the day as well. To show your psyche that you're serious about this, place a pen and a writing pad or your healing journal by your bedside.

There are also some less simple techniques. One old technique involves making a dream pillow filled with the herb mugwort. A colleague who tried this said it worked very well because the smell kept waking her up! It doesn't guarantee you'll wake up in a REM state, however. Others recommend setting your alarm to try to wake up during a REM period. This can work also, but it requires dedication. Another colleague wears socks to bed. During the night her feet get too warm and she wakes up. Some have actually gone so far as to put some noxious-smelling substance in an ice cube near the bed. When the ice cube melts, the smell will awaken you (or create a dream about something smelly!).

When working on an illness, the illness itself is the dream symbol or image you will be trying to interpret. In order to get a little distance from your illness so you can work on it as a dream, you might write about your illness as if it were a dream: "I dreamed I had a cancer in my neck, and I had to go through radiation treatments." Fill in as many details and feelings as you like.

Dream Recording

It's important, when you first begin recording your dreams, to *write everything down.* If you wake up with just a feeling, write it down. If you remember dreaming about your mate, write it down. Don't prejudge the importance of a dream. I have found over the years that some seemingly mundane or insignificant dreams can be loaded with emotion and significance once they're opened through dreamwork. Honor all of your dreams.

Date your dream. Some people date their dreams on the night of the dream. I date mine from the next morning, because most if not all of my dreams occur after midnight. The date will help you associate the dream with important waking-life happenings when you look back at it later.

Title your dreams. A dream title can be an important part of your dreamwork. Pull together the important elements of the dream or find a theme and make that your title.

Write the dream down in the present tense. This helps to keep the dream alive and present, instead of treating it like a memory. Always record your feelings in the dream, not just the images and actions. In your healing journal or dream journal, write down the significant events, interactions, and images from the day before. By comparing these to your dreams, you can find significant redundancies and synchronicities of image or theme.

It can be helpful to immediately *draw simple representations of certain dream images or locations.* More elaborate drawings or paintings can be done later as part of your dreamwork. Also write down whatever spontaneous associations you have to dream characters, images, and locations.

As you begin recalling and writing your dreams down, look for dreams that seem related to your illness. Many of your dreams *will* be related to your illness, even some that may not seem relevant at all. Remember, the symbols in your dreams and the symptoms and location of the illness are pointing to a common inner issue, a mind or belief issue.

Dream Programming and Incubation

Dream programming, in its simplest form, is speaking or writing a request to your dreams. It is a form of suggestion, another example of a focusing agent. When you tell yourself you will remember your dreams, that's dream programming. You can specifically ask for a healing dream or ask for a dream about the underlying meaning of your illness. When I suggested asking for a past-life dream earlier, that was an example of dream programming.

A dream suggestion can be spoken aloud or in your mind just before you go to sleep. Some programmers repeat the suggestion periodically during the day. You can also write out your request or suggestion and put it in your healing journal or write it on a piece of paper, perhaps in the form of a letter to your dreams, and put it under your pillow. Put the programming in the form of an affirmation: "I will have a healing dream tonight." Always honor your dream programming by writing down whatever dreams or fragments you remember the next morning.

Incubation is a more complex form of programming. Incubation suggests a ritual which takes place over time. You could do an incubation just before you go to bed, setting up candles and incense, meditating, and repeating your dream programming over and over again. But a true incubation takes place over a period of at least a couple of days. The amount of time taken in incubating a dream helps to build up the energy around the programming and strengthens intention.

Ancient Greek dream temples, dedicated to the god Asklepios, represented a powerful form of dream incubation. Patricia Garfield's book, *The Healing Power of Dreams*, has a rather elaborate healing dream incubation based on the Asklepion temple rituals. You may want to try that, revise it, or devise your own.[1]

Traveling to healing places like Lourdes, France, mimics

ancient incubation rituals. The time, energy, and actions which lead to arriving at such a healing place, added to the energy and mystique of the place itself, serve to focus healing intent very strongly.

A simple incubation would involve setting a date, a week or less in advance, on a day when you are able to sleep late. Each day leading up to the incubation night you could light a candle and repeat your dream affirmation or program. You might drink a special tea or eat a special fruit. Take a ritual cleansing bath or shower. Anything you can do to enhance your expectation and affirm your intentions can be helpful in incubating a healing dream.

Dreamwork

All of the following techniques and suggestions can be applied to dreams or to your illness. At some level of consciousness you know exactly what your dreams mean. You also know exactly what your illness means. This is a process of uncovering what part of you already knows. Ultimately you are the expert on your own dreams and on your own illness. Let your feelings guide you as to the accuracy of your dreamwork.

Dreams are so deep and multilayered that no one interpretation will ever do justice to a dream. The purpose of dreamwork is to come up with information that's useful, that can be immediately applied to your life. Dreams are reflections of waking thoughts, ideas, beliefs, attitudes, and emotions. They will faithfully reflect our fears and doubts, loves and hates, our guilt and shame, and our highest aspirations and ideals. Dreams don't just tell us what's wrong with our thinking. They also tell us what's right, and they present transcendent images that draw us forward into greater realms of spiritual fulfillment. Remember, if you see a negative or frightening image in your dream, it is: (1) bearing a gift for you and (2) telling you about what you believe or fear, not what is true.

Dream Dictionaries. It might seem that dream dictionaries would be perfect for new dream explorers. The opposite is true. If you're new at dreamwork, I believe that you should stay as far away from dream dictionaries as possible. No dream dictionary knows the meaning of the symbols in your dreams. Our dreams, like ourselves, are absolutely unique. Even so-called universal symbols such as water and fire do not mean the same thing in every case.

A cat means something different to someone who hates cats, someone who loves cats, and someone who's allergic to cats. It makes a difference whether it's *your* cat or some unknown cat. Your own associations are far more meaningful than anything a dream dictionary might tell you.

The same is true for books which tell you what different body parts or diseases mean. Every individual's illness and symptoms mean something different. Garfield's *The Healing Power of Dreams* lists different individuals' dreams that are associated with specific physical problems. These examples demonstrate how dreams can relate to an injury, disease, or treatment.[2]

Louise Hay's book, *You Can Heal Your Life,* has a chapter in which she lists physical problems and body parts, giving a probable cause and a "New Thought Pattern" or affirmation for healing for each.[3] Such lists carry the same limitations as dream dictionaries, so you should use them, if at all, only for stimulating your own knowing, not as the definitive meaning for your illness.

Puns, Slips, Sayings, and Word Games. If you learned nothing more than the way your dreams use language, symbols, and metaphors, you would be a pretty good dream interpreter. If puns are the lowest form of humor, then dreams are shameless. Dreams find puns very useful. One of the reasons information is given to us in visual or symbolic form rather than straightforward conversations is that we tend to forget the words in our dreams but hold on to images.

Karen can be a pun on *caring.* A woman is given a gift of a ruler in her dream. It represented her need to be in control (rule). Do you dream of people from your past you weren't really close to? Look for a pun in their names, or just ask yourself what they represent to you. One woman dreamed of a childhood friend named Hershey. The dream was about her femininity (her-she). It might be good to dream about Bob *Hope,* or if you were seeking a positive change in your life you might dream of Paul *Newman.* I worked with a woman who dreamed of a dead lion in the street. She was waiting for a tow truck to arrive and take it away. I suggested her dream might be telling her she needed to tow the lion (toe the line).

I dreamed of stacks of new lumber lying on Third Street, making it difficult to get my car through. In typing up the dream I misspelled the word *lumber* several times, spelling it *lumbar.* I'm a good speller and an accurate typist. I knew that the word *lumbar* had something to do with the back, so I looked it up in the dictionary and found that it refers to the lower back region. This is an example of a slip that exposes a pun. I assumed the dream was telling me that I had a blockage in my third lumbar vertebra.

The body message was even more significant because I was seeing a friend that morning who was doing bodywork on me. I asked him if there was blockage in my third lumbar vertebra, and he concurred. The dream was very timely because I didn't know what to do with the dream information, but my bodyworker friend did.

Any dreamer would be happy to arrive at the understanding I had of this dream *and* to have a bodyworker present the same morning to make the adjustment. In my understanding, however, the dream was not just telling me about a physical problem. Both the dream *and* the physical problem were telling me about something else. It was a redundancy. A more significant message concerned the new lumber, which represented the potential for building something new. I was blocked in terms of something I needed to build in my life.

The symbol of new lumber was a redundancy. It existed in my waking life as well. Before I had the dream I had seen stacks of lumber on Third Street in my waking reality. They weren't in the street, but in an empty lot on a corner. It was only in my dream that the lumber was blocking my path.

Sigmund Freud wrote of the importance of slips of the tongue. Whether you write out your dreams by hand or type them on a typewriter or word processor, there will be opportunities to make meaningful mistakes like my lumber/ lumbar slip. Watch for meaningful slips when you read your dreams. Don't correct misspellings too quickly on your word processor.

Sayings are found frequently in dreams and can be important in understanding your illness. "Toe the line" is a saying revealed by a pun. Earlier in the book I spoke of Ruth saying, "This job is killing me." Part of your awareness program is to watch for those kinds of sayings in your own repertoire. Some of these sayings will relate to specific body parts:

He's a pain in the neck/butt; She will be the death of me; I'm so mad I can't see straight, I just don't see it (eyes); I can't stand it, I don't have a leg to stand on (legs); Get off my back, Back off, My back's against the wall, Getting back at someone, Back down, Stabbed in the back (back); He pisses me off (urinary); Getting something off your chest (chest or breast); She broke my heart, Have a heart, You're heartless (heart); Heading for trouble, I'm losing my head, I'd forget my head if it weren't attached, I can't get ahead, I'm out of my head with worry, Just thinking about it gives me a headache (head); I'm so busy I don't have time to breathe (respiratory); I just can't stomach that (digestion); I need to get my shit together, I can't take any more of this crap (elimination), etc.

There is often overlap in these categories of puns, slips,

sayings, and word games. I place won ton/not now in the word-game category. I've had quite a few meaningful word reversals. In one dream a woman friend and I were going to cross a wide river on a log. As we began to cross I saw English wolfhounds on the other side. The wolfhounds turned into wolves, and my friend decided crossing the river wasn't such a good idea.

I realized that *wolf* backward is *flow*. That fact alone wouldn't necessarily mean anything, but it created a redundancy with the river, which also flowed. A third redundancy could be found in the transformation of wolfhound into wolf. One could say the wolfhounds in my dream flowed into wolves. Log can be turned around to become *gol* (goal). The log was actually the bridge or means to a goal. Crossing the great water is a significant symbol for change in the Chinese oracle called the I Ching.

The mission was aborted because of fear of the wolves. That told me that I (or a female part of myself represented by my friend) was afraid of change, flow, transformation.

I had a dream about a jade triple-dragon figurine. I associate the dragon with power and with fire. A dragon can be seen as an amplification of the meaning of a snake. Though serpents have taken a bad rap in our culture—the devil in Genesis—they can be a symbol for healing, rejuvenation, and rebirth.

I turned the word *dragon* around and came up with *no gard* (no guard). This was interesting, because Western dragons are frequently depicted as guarding caves filled with treasure. I decided that the message was that I needed to stop guarding or hoarding my treasures, my talents, and abilities.

Sometimes a description of an action or situation in the dream encapsulates the meaning of the dream. A sentence in the dream represents a feeling or attitude the dreamer has about some part of his or her life. If you are backed into a corner in your dream, for example, you should ask yourself if some part of your life feels like that. In another dream you might be in a situation where you need to choose to go in one direction or another. In your dream journal you might write, "I don't know which way to go." What's happening in your life that feels like that?

That question was useful to Lucille, my client with the repeating airplane dream. Dreams often dramatize or exaggerate life situations in order to call our attention to their importance. You can also ask the question of your illness. An illness may also dramatize an aspect of your life. If an illness makes you angry or scares you, if you feel helpless or powerless, did you already feel that way in some part of your life before the illness? If so, changing those feelings is the challenge of the illness and the answer to healing your life.

Carl Jung saw dreams as projections of the self. One could theorize that all parts of the dream represent parts of the self. Fritz Perls turned this concept into an effective therapy and dreamwork tool, as we'll see in the next section. My friend and dream colleague Jeremy Taylor also uses a dreamwork technique which helps highlight this aspect of dreams.

He suggests you rewrite a dream adding the phrase "part(s) of me" to each of the images. Here's the example he gives in his book *Where People Fly and Water Runs Uphill*, with the phrase added: "I run through the dark forest part of me, chased by unknown parts of me. I hide from the unknown parts of me in an old dead hollow-log part of me and hear the unknown parts of me rush past. I can't tell if the unknown parts of me are even human parts of me."[4]

Dream Dialoguing. Fritz Perls developed the concept of having his clients dialogue with different parts of their dreams. They would sit in a chair or on a pillow and talk to a person or symbol from the dream, perhaps asking it a question. They would then move over to a facing chair or pillow and answer for the person or symbol in the dream. The dialoguing and moving back and forth would continue until some resolution occurred.

This is a very effective technique. You can carry on such a dialogue in a fantasy in your head or write it out in your healing journal. The various parts of the dream take on their own personalities fairly easily and often don't represent what you expected, nor are their intentions always what you assumed.

The dialogue technique is one of the best for working directly on your illness as a dream symbol. You can have this conversation imaginatively in a fantasy, or you might want to write it in your journal. If you have cancer, you can speak directly to your tumor if you have one at the present. You will then answer on behalf of the tumor. Continue the conversation for at least five or ten minutes. You may be surprised to find the "tumor" telling you things you were consciously unaware of. Or you can speak to the body part affected. You may feel silly doing this at first, but the results can be very enlightening.

In such a conversation, your tumor might remind you that it's a growth. It may tell you that it's growing inside your body because of your resistance to growing in some area of your life, and you're creating the growth in your physical body instead of in the appropriate place. A man might learn that the growth of a tumor represents repression of the feminine, the tumor representing the creativity associated with giving birth. This would all depend on the location of the tumor and the beliefs of the individuals involved. These are just examples of possible meanings.

You might find that you can enlist your tumor or other diseased system or disease symptom as an ally in your healing. Assume the tumor or disease "wants" to be healed as much as you do. Allow it to give you healing information.

Free Association. Freud's technique of free association is still an effective dreamwork tool. Take any dream symbol, including your illness. Write down every word that comes to your mind when you think of the symbol. Let the associations take you where they will. You may find yourself far afield from your original symbol, but that's the value of the process. You may find that your illness is related to an issue you weren't even conscious of.

I did an exercise in a dream workshop that involved meditating on a dream symbol and allowing it to speak or transform. The symbol I was curious about was a turtle. I imagined holding a small turtle in my hand as I simply went into a state of relaxation. A kind of free association occurred in which I thought that a turtle might actually be a tortoise. In my relaxed state, however, I quickly went from tortoise to porpoise. As soon as I thought of porpoise, I realized the symbol had to do with purpose, my life purpose.

As I mentioned, I rarely use dream dictionaries but I find my regular dictionary to be helpful sometimes. I will often look up objects or words whose meaning I already know, only to find some additional meaning I wasn't aware of. My dictionary has the meanings of a number of common names, and I will sometimes look them up as well. Baby name books can be helpful in this regard.

Dream Groups. Doing dreamwork in a group can be very rewarding. Aside from having so much additional input to help you understand your dream, you have a ready-made support group for your growth and healing. See if you can find a local dream group, or consider putting one together yourself. It isn't necessary to have a professional leader, although it might be helpful to have someone familiar with dreamwork to help get you started.

Jeremy Taylor is a great booster of dream groups. His book, *Dream Work: Techniques for Discovering the Creative Power in Dreams,* has two chapters on group dreamwork, as well as an excellent annotated bibliography on dreams. His more recent book, *Where People Fly and Water Runs Uphill,* has even more information on dream groups.

In *Dream Work* Jeremy gives twenty-one basic hints for group dreamwork. Space doesn't allow for more than a few rules for dream groups here. Following are some of the more important ones:

Always respect the dream and the dreamer. The dreamer is always the expert when it comes to his or her own dream. Sometimes an individual may want to just share a dream but not work on it. Respect the dreamer's wishes and the limits he or she sets.

Two rules help keep the integrity of the dream and the dreamer intact. *Always say, "If this were my dream..."* when giving suggestions about the meaning of someone else's dream. This phrase acknowledges that anything you say about someone else's dream will be your projection. It may or may not be "correct." It may or may not be helpful to the dreamer. The second rule is to *trust your own response to suggestions made by others.* Jeremy calls this the "aha." If you don't resonate with a group member's suggestion or interpretation, it may not be correct. The "aha" is a gut feeling of rightness. Follow your own "aha" and don't let yourself be overwhelmed by the opinions of others, even the experts.

The Association for Research and Enlightenment, Inc. (A.R.E.), studies, tests, and propagates the teachings found in the Edgar Cayce readings. There are study groups throughout the country, many of which share and work with dreams as well as meditating and following a course of study. If you're interested in exploring a local group, you can find more information at the back of this book, as well as addresses of other healing groups and organizations.

The techniques above are far from exhaustive. Some books on dreamwork methods are listed in the bibliography and reading list. In the next chapter I'll share some simple and effective methods I've developed that don't require dream interpretation at all!

8

Noninterpretive Dreamwork

Noninterpretive dreamwork techniques can be used to understand your dreams, your illness, or any other life issue you're dealing with. These methods can and often do lead to interpretation, to the meaning of your dream or illness. Sometimes they do not. Even when they don't lead to interpretation or understanding, they can still be used to change your life.

One theory on dreams held by the Hindus and some esoteric traditions is that the dream state is actually an out-of-body state in which we travel to other dimensions or realities. These dream experiences are holistic emotional experiences that do not involve words or images. Such experiences cannot be fully expressed in words or images.

The dream we remember, according to this tradition, is a translation of a nonverbal, nonimaginal experience. When we write down what we remember of the dream, a further translation is involved. The purpose of noninterpretive dreamwork is to try to stay closer to the original emotional energy and intention of the dream experience, to deal more directly with the language of the dream.

Dreams Can Change Us

One of the assumptions of noninterpretive dreamwork is that dreams can change us. Dream symbols and experiences can have a direct effect on the body itself and/or on our attitudes and beliefs. The ancient Greeks, through the rituals connected with their dream temples, were often healed directly in a dream. Since REM sleep is a highly charged physiological state, images and actions in our dreams affect the body directly through the nervous, immune, and endocrine systems and can lead to healing.

On a psychological or emotional level, a dream will sometimes bring about a change just because of the actions in the dream. You may have experienced dreams in which you were faced with a problem or a challenge and in which you took some action and resolved the problem in the dream state. Any dream can be interpreted and can provide insight and understanding. A dream that contains a resolution, however, has already accomplished something of value.

The feelings and actions in a dream are real to the body and to the mind; therefore, we can be changed by what happens to us and by what we do in a dream. If we're aware of our fears or blocks, we can ask for a dream that will give us an opportunity to face our fears. A simple noninterpretive technique is to tell yourself, in the form of an affirmation, that you will be brave enough to confront your fear in a dream. The fear can be related to your disease, whether it is the fear of death or other fears associated with the illness or treatment.

The Senoi

The Senoi is a group of tribes who lived in the central highlands of Malaysia. Today, many of them have been assimilated into modern Malaysian society. In the past, as with many other native peoples, dreams played a central role in their daily life. Dreams were consulted before any major decision was made, decisions such as where to hunt or when and where to move a village. The same is true of many Native American peoples as well. Kilton Stewart, an early researcher into Senoi life, claimed that their method of dreamwork made them a peaceful people, respected by neighboring tribes.

The Senoi always tried to move their dreams toward pleasure, but they always faced what was frightening in a dream. They taught their children to stay asleep when they had nightmares and turn to fight their nightmare figures. They believed this action would transform the frightening figure and turn it into a friend, even if the dreamer had killed it.

The new ally would then be asked for a gift, which could be a new toy, a song, a poem, or a game. Dreams would be shared with the family at breakfast. Dreams and dream gifts, from children and adults, would also be shared with the entire community. A dream song, dance, or poem would be performed. A dream game would be played. A dream object would be created. A dream message would be shared and discussed.

The Senoi believed their children were changed through successful confrontations with nightmare figures, not only receiving creative gifts, but becoming less afraid because of their dream courage.

Of Tigers and Horned Alligators

I was fascinated by the possibility that an individual might be changed by a dream experience without ever knowing what fear he or she was confronting. This would confirm the idea that we're always dealing with current beliefs and attitudes. Even if our fears come from our childhood or our past lives, we can overcome them by confronting present symbolic representations.

I have spoken to hundreds of children of all ages in schools and churches and have done a guided "nightmare" with them so they could have an opportunity to face some fear. There is no question that facing a nightmare figure changes our dreams. I have heard dozens of stories from children and adults about confronting a frightening figure from a recurring dream and never having the dream again.

My cousin Denis, when he was seven years old, had a rather typical dream of being chased by a tiger. He had the dream so frequently that he became afraid to go to sleep. Finally he decided he was tired of running from the tiger, and the tiger could just eat him if it wanted to. Denis wasn't going to run any more. He knew nothing about the Senoi method of facing nightmare figures. His young wisdom came from frustration.

That night the tiger showed up right on schedule, and my cousin, true to his decision, just stood there. The tiger, much to Denis's surprise and relief, also just stood there. He never had the dream again.

Such dream confrontations almost always end with a positive resolution, usually without the necessity of actually doing battle. I believe it's because the nightmare figure never intended harm in the first place. These nightmares represent our own energy tied up in fears and doubts. They represent our own power and are, in reality, always potential gifts from the Spirit.

But does such a successful dream confrontation change the individual? I believe we *are* changed by our dream decisions and dream actions, as the following example demonstrates:

I taught a college extension class to adults called "Interpersonal Communication." In the class I taught the Senoi method of confronting nightmares. Not long after that, one young mother from the class was awakened in the middle of the night by her seven-year-old daughter. The girl told her mother that she dreamed about a big alligator that had a big horn on its nose. If it opened its mouth it would eat her. If its mouth was closed, it would stab her with its horn. It was clearly a lose-lose situation for the little girl.

The half-asleep mother remembered only part of what I had said about the Senoi. She didn't tell her daughter to face the alligator and fight it. She just remembered the part about the gift, so she told her daughter to ask it for a gift. The little girl was dubious, but trusted Mommy and went back to bed.

The Senoi taught their children to fight and possibly kill their nightmare figures. That wasn't necessary in Denis's case, and I have found that confronting our fears is sufficient. Certainly, in dealing with children, there's enough fighting and killing on TV and in the movies. I don't think we want them to believe that overcoming their fears requires hurting or killing someone else, even a monster or scary animal. Overcoming their fears simply requires the courage to face them.

The little girl didn't fight her alligator either. She faced it and asked it for a gift. From the mother's description, I don't know if the little girl went back into the dream (which many children are able to do) or if she did it as a waking fantasy, a noninterpretive technique I'll discuss later.

The next morning the mother asked her daughter what happened. The girl said the alligator gave her three gifts. The first gift was a whole bunch of pets. This was simple wish fulfillment because the girl wasn't allowed to have any pets. The second gift was a scary mask. The purpose of this mask, she explained, was to scare adults in her dreams so they wouldn't scare her. Now we have a gift with some power! The third gift was even more abstract and symbolic. She told her mother the alligator gave her "Hands, hands, hands." As she said this the little girl put her hands out in front of her, palms forward, and opened and closed them three times.

I assumed the little girl was changed by her experience, so I asked the mother if she had noticed anything different in her daughter's behavior since the dream. The mother said the girl was fighting back against her older brother, who tended to bully her—fighting hands. She also said her daughter was helping out around the house more—helping hands. We never discovered the meaning of the third "hands," but it is evident that the little girl's daily behavior, along with her self-image, was changed by the experience.

I believe that noninterpretive dreamwork can help us change ourselves if we accept and utilize the power of our dream and waking-life symbols, allowing them to work on us and possibly even heal us.

Your illness is the monster that is threatening you in your waking life. You can program yourself to confront that monster in your dreams and/or do a visualization in which you confront your illness while awake. You can confront your illness in a realistic form, as a tumor, a virus, a blocked artery, or a damaged heart. Or use your imagination to give a more symbolic form to your illness and then confront it in that form. Do battle with the "monster," or just confront it verbally and ask it why it wants to harm you.

Lucid Dreamwork

One noninterpretive way to work with dreams is to take actions within the dream itself. This can be done by programming oneself to do so in advance, such as programming to face a fear or a repeating nightmare figure. Another way to do this is by taking conscious action within the dream.

This method assumes that you are lucid in the dream, knowing that you are dreaming while the dream is happening. Those of you who are already lucid dreamers have an opportunity to choose to confront the attitudes and emotions that led to your illness. You can ask for a symbolic scenario in which you can confront the issues related to your illness and take actions which will change your mind and thereby change your life.

If you're not a lucid dreamer, you can ask to become lucid by suggesting to yourself that you will have a lucid dream. You can do this just before going to sleep and throughout the day as well. Because I look at waking life as a dream, I use lucidity as a model for enlightenment. The object of waking life is to "wake up" to a higher level of consciousness, to become lucid in our waking life. I often say to myself, over the course of my day, "This a dream. What's this dream telling me about myself?"

It's beyond the scope of this book to go into lucid dreaming in any detail. *Lucid Dreaming Tips,* a book of tips on becoming lucid and what to do with lucidity, was put together by Jill Gregory, director of the Novato Center for Dreams, and can be found in the suggested reading list. As you'll see later in this chapter, it's possible to imagine that you're lucid by going over a dream as a visualization, making desired changes, and trying out different scenarios.

Symbol Manifestation

This simple technique can be very effective for getting in touch with denied energies, whether they represent fears or positive characteristics. Some Native Americans and other indigenous peoples manifested their dream and visionary symbols. They painted them on their bodies, clothing, horses, and homes. Some tribes painted on skins and with sand. They made dolls and other figures to represent characters and energies from their dreams, visions, and mythologies. They utilized teeth, claws, feathers, heads, and hides from various animals and birds to represent the energy of these creatures.

Such physical symbols not only represented certain characteristics associated with the animal, tree, or stone; they contained the energy of the dream or visionary symbols. By putting symbols where they can be seen or touched, by wearing them close to your body or on your body, the emotional energy or power of those symbols can be activated and incorporated.

Carl Jung wrote of projection, the idea that we project denied and rejected parts of ourselves onto other people, animals, objects, and places. We then react to them as if separate from ourselves. While many psychologies seem to focus on negative projections, it's important to recognize that we project our power, beauty, and even our divinity outside ourselves as well.

Symbol manifestation can help us to acknowledge or "own" our negative projections as well as our positive ones. As Cayce said, we are always meeting self. Symbol manifestation puts portions of the self out where we can see them, accept them, and allow them to change us and, if they seem negative, allow them to be transformed.

Drawing or painting our dream symbols or our physical symptoms is the most obvious and simplest form of symbol manifestation. Such drawings need not be accurate or artistic. In fact, you may want to draw the *feeling* of the symbol or symptom, to capture its emotional power in an abstract representation, rather than attempting an accurate or photographic depiction.

In some cases you can cut your symbol out of a magazine or go buy it in a toy store or hobby shop. The point is to put the symbol out where you can see it and allow it to work on you. During the day you might try to understand how you're like that symbol, even if it's a symptom of your illness. Try to accept it as part of yourself, even if it's very negative. Acceptance precedes transformation. We become what we reject and deny. We can transform what we accept and incorporate.

If you are unable to create or find a representation of your symbol or your illness, you can always invest the energy in an object. Take a stone or crystal, a small piece of driftwood or other object, charge it with the energy of your symbol or illness, and carry that object around with you or put it where you can see it until you feel that you have accepted or transformed the energy of the symbol.

It can be very healing to create a collage of powerful positive symbols, whether they're from your dreams, meditations and visualizations, or just meaningful figures from religion, fantasy, or mythology. You can put them in a circular or mandala arrangement to represent wholeness. These are sometimes called dream shields and are associated with some tribes of Native Americans.

Edgar Cayce suggested something similar, which he called life seals. Unlike a dream shield, the life seal dealt more with images containing energies that were relevant for a lifetime. Such images might include symbols from past lives. You might begin to think about which of your meaningful symbols might be life symbols as well as being current healing or transformative symbols. Once you have enough life symbols, you can draw, paint, or make a collage of these symbols as a life seal or mandala.

You might also consider working with wood or clay in manifesting your symbols. The more your hands get involved in the creation of the symbol, the more energy you can invest in it. Again, even if the object is abstract, it can be charged with the energy of the symbol or your illness.

When you feel you have incorporated or transformed the energy of the symbol/illness, you can take it down and work on another one. If a symbol seems very important, it may be a life symbol and you may want to leave it up permanently.

Dream Completion or Rescripting

When you confront a nightmare figure in a dream or a waking fantasy, as in the Senoi method, you are rescripting the dream, changing the outcome. You can do this with any dream or waking-life situation by re-entering the dream in a visualization. Because it's a visualization and you are awake, you are now conscious in the dream—lucid. You can do anything you want. How would you change the dream? How might you act differently? Can you practice feeling different? Maybe instead of being afraid, you can get angry.

Any dream or waking-life situation can be changed in a fantasy or meditation. The purpose of changing it in fantasy is to try to change the attitudes and beliefs represented by the dream or situation. You may need to repeat the fantasy a number of times until you feel there's a real shift in your feelings or beliefs. If you do it too casually, the exercise won't bring about any changes.

If you are suffering side effects from your cancer treatment, for example, you can imagine a scenario in which the chemicals or radiation are highly effective in destroying the cancer cells but have little or no negative side effects. You might couple the imagery with positive suggestions to that effect. It may help to do this while actually undergoing the treatment.

Doctors' negative suggestions about the side effects of radiation or chemotherapy treatment have caused some individuals to become nauseated and even begin losing their hair *before* their treatment! Others, through positive suggestions and visualizations, have gone through radiation or chemotherapy with little or no negative side effects. When you look at your treatment as a dream, you can visualize a more positive outcome.

Most of us have repeated, in our heads, experiences in which we have acted in less than an ideal manner. We think of things we could have said differently, different actions we could have taken. None of this seems to do much to change the past. We can, however, visualize different endings to our dreams and waking-life experiences in order to change the future. Aside from rescripting, we can also script or rehearse a future event, such as a treatment or the outcome of an illness, to help focus our energy and intention on a positive outcome.

Dream completion or rescripting is simply making conscious an activity that goes on unconsciously all the time. We are constantly following some kind of script. That script has an ending or completion already built in. Many of these unconscious scripts are written by our fears or our lack of self-worth. Our illness is itself following a script written at some time in the past. By looking at our illness and the life experiences preceding it, perhaps we can make some healing changes in our script and write a happier ending.

Symbol Transformation and Activation

I have spoken of focusing agents as well as the concepts of mind as pipe and mind as bucket. The way we create our physical experiences is simple, regardless of how much we may feel out of control of that process. "Mind is the builder." "Thoughts are things." *The things we give time and energy to in our minds are manifested in our lives.* One of the fundamental precepts for positive change, for growth on the physical, mental, emotional, and spiritual levels, for healing on every level, is to withdraw emotional energy from negative thoughts and feelings and give time and emotional energy to the positive.

One of the difficulties inherent in healing an illness is the fact that we automatically give time and energy to the illness and its symptoms rather than focusing on the healing. The more serious the illness, the more time and energy it receives. Unfortunately, we end up feeding the illness. Working on a problem, however sincere we may be, can simply reinforce the problem. At some point we need to focus time and emotional energy on the solution, the desired outcome.

If you are not likely to recover from your illness, you can focus on the quality of your remaining time. You can even focus on the quality of your dying. If you are permanently disabled, you can try to shift your focus away from your limitations, what you can no longer do, and instead focus on what you can do and on the highest quality of life you can possibly experience.

Remember Melinda, the woman who had had two strokes? She was working very hard on her rehabilitation. What she wasn't doing is focusing on or putting energy into the outcome—being healed. Symbol transformation is a method for refocusing energy and attention away from the problem and toward the resolution. This can be done in a number of different ways.

If you draw a picture of a negative dream symbol or of your illness, whether realistic or abstract, draw a second picture which represents the change or resolution. A child can do this with a nightmare, rather than redoing the dream in his or her imagination. Give time and energy to the new drawing, the image of the resolution.

Exercise: Symbol Transformation

In this exercise you begin with a negative symbol from your dreams or waking life, or you can use a physical symptom or the illness itself as the symbol. You can also begin the exercise by creating a symbol in your mind to represent the illness or whatever it is you want to change. If you already have a symbol you want to transform, you can go right to the second part of the exercise.

Part I— Getting a Symbol to Transform. Get in a comfortable position, sitting or lying down. Take a few deep breaths and let your entire body relax. Imagine yourself releasing your Spirit-suppression devices for the duration of this exercise, and try to allow Spirit to flow freely through you. Think about the issue or illness you wish to characterize with a symbol. Feel its energy.

Allow a symbol to come into your consciousness, into your mind's eye, that will represent your issue or illness. It can be a person, animal, or object. It can be abstract. If you have trouble visualizing, you may use the feeling itself as your symbol or you can use a word or a sentence.

Part II — Transformation. Stay with your negative symbol for just a minute or two. Feel the energy of the symbol. Notice where it seems to be located in your body. When you're ready, you're going to transform your negative symbol into a positive. You can use any method that works for you. You can send it into space and blow it up, letting the pieces drift back down to earth where they will re-form into your new symbol. You can throw the negative symbol into a fire and let a new symbol rise up, phoenix-like, from the ashes. Touch the old symbol with a magic wand, sprinkle it with pixie dust, or pray for it.

Allow a new symbol to form. Visualize it as vividly as possible. Again, the symbol can be a feeling, word, sentence, or even a sound. What does the new symbol feel like? Where is it located in your body? How is the feeling different from the feeling of the old symbol? Forgive the old symbol and release it.

After a few minutes, if a new symbol does not come into your mind spontaneously, simply create a new symbol consciously, one that evokes positive feelings for you. The importance of the new symbol is that it directs your energy away from the problem and toward the solution. A made-up symbol can work just as effectively as a spontaneous symbol.

To show you the potential of this simple exercise, Susan, a woman in my Mind Development group, had a large lump on her shoulder caused by an accumulation of uric acid, a stress chemical. She went to her chiropractor for it, and he worked on it for some time. It was the most painful session she had ever had, and yet the lump was not completely reduced. He told her she would have to come back in a few days.

I led the symbol transformation exercise in the group, one we repeated frequently. Members of the group would choose their own issues or symbols to work on. She chose to work on the physical symptom of her painful lump. The negative symbol for the lump took the form of an egg. She imagined it flying into outer space, exploding, and pouring back down into her shoulder. It came back in the form of a golden liquid. At the end of the exercise, much to her surprise, the lump and the pain were completely gone. This demonstrates the power of attention and intention.

Steven, a young man hospitalized because of a serious motorcycle accident, suffered from constant pain in his back and was unable to take enough pain medication because of the nature of his injuries. A friend of mine, interning as a chaplain in the hospital, asked the young man to visualize the pain in his back. He said it felt like a nail was driven into his spine. She asked him what he needed to remove the nail. He was a religious young man, and he said he thought Jesus could remove the nail. She told him to imagine Jesus coming into the room and pulling the nail out. The young man did so, and the pain went away immediately.

If you don't experience an instant healing or relief, you can manifest the new symbol in some way, as discussed earlier in the symbol manifestation exercise. The point is to use the new symbol to redirect your energy when you find yourself focusing on and energizing the problem. The new symbol can help break a negative energy habit and create a new healing habit.

Symbol activation, on the one hand, just means giving energy to a positive symbol. On the other hand, it can be a powerful exercise designed to get you in touch with the denied positive aspects of yourself—what I call golden shadows.

Exercise: Symbol Activation

In this exercise you start with a positive symbol. It can be the symbol that resulted from the transformation exercise. It can be a powerful and meaningful symbol from your dreams, no matter how long ago you may have had the dream. It can be a symbol, image, or person from your waking life, from history, religion, fantasy, or myth. The important thing is that you ascribe to this symbol positive and perhaps healing properties.

Use the same relaxation as above. This time you will visualize the positive symbol. See it as vividly as possible. How do you feel as you look at it? Where is the feeling located in your body? Spend a minute or two seeing the symbol as separate from yourself.

When you're ready, I want you to *become* the positive symbol. Imagine yourself to be the symbol as completely as possible. Allow the symbol to expand you, break down your limitations, open you to greater possibilities of being. Feel yourself as this symbol. What does it feel like? Where is the feeling located in your body? Hold the feeling and the sense of oneness as long as you can. Come back when you feel completed.

You can go back into this exercise a number of times, allowing yourself to expand more and more into this positive representation of yourself. Of course you can also manifest this image in any of the ways mentioned before. You might create an image of your healed self and see what that self feels like. I am convinced that the biggest difference between the self we are now and the self we can become is simply the way we feel about ourselves.

My younger brother didn't need to gain skills or even

practice to be able to steer a bike. He needed to get to the point where he believed such a thing was possible for him. The self he was at three and four and the self who could ride a bike with confidence at eight and nine were not just separated by years, size, or strength. They were separated by self-image and belief.

If we can get in touch with the feelings of the self who is healed, the self who is no longer afraid, the self who has learned how to love self and others and how to receive love, we can more quickly become that self. This exercise can help you get in touch with that self.

Eat Your Dreams

At first glance this might seem frivolous. Yet for some of you, it can be a helpful symbolic gesture. It is an effective nightmare tool for children. Eating your dreams is based on the traditions of some Native American tribes and on other ancient magical concepts.

The idea is that when you eat a particular animal or part of an animal you partake of the characteristics of that animal or animal part. If you eat the heart of a lion, especially if you have killed it yourself, you incorporate the characteristics associated with the heart of a lion.

One of the important concepts in dreamwork is the idea of integration or what Jung called individuation. Another term for this is incorporation. Since our dreams represent parts of the self—often denied or rejected parts, healing comes when we acknowledge, accept, and re-own these parts. We need to incorporate our shadows, both dark and golden.

One way to dramatize this is to eat either dark or light shadows as a symbolic gesture of acceptance. If a child dreams about a tiger chasing him, as my cousin did, try giving the child an animal cracker depicting a tiger. You can tell the child that if he eats this tiger, he will be as strong and brave as a tiger.

Adults can do the same. You can find animal cookies or make your own symbols from cookie dough, bread dough, gelatin, or some other form of malleable food. Once again, the image doesn't have to be accurate; the important thing is that you invest it with the appropriate energy.

In fact, you can take any food or drink and, through ceremony and ritual, invest or energize the substance with the symbol-energy you need to incorporate, or simply invest food with the qualities you feel you need right now to deal with whatever illness or other issue you are confronting. Consume the energized food or drink with as much solemnity as you can muster. Feel it affecting your body. Feel where it goes in your body or where the feelings seem to be located. See if there's any difference between your feelings before and after the ceremony.

Some of you may want to ingest your illness or symptoms. This represents an acknowledgment and owning of the illness, not as a truth about you but as a meaningful symbol or feedback from the universe. When we own negative symbols or symptoms, we are more empowered to release them. We cannot release or give away what we have not first owned.

9

Illness as Spiritual Teacher

Your illness is *designed* to be your teacher. It represents a book to be read, a curriculum to be followed. The lessons found in your illness will not just help you to heal, they can restore your soul. Ultimately your illness can bring you to the Master Teacher, the Creator. We can begin to contact the Mind of God and practice aligning or attuning with it. We can experience the concept of the "will of God" in a personally meaningful way.

Think of the categories in this chapter as frameworks for utilizing the meaning you have discovered in your illness and for channeling and focusing your healing intentions. Certain frameworks may be more appealing than others, or you may find helpful elements for your healing process in all of them. These metaphorical frameworks may suggest others to you that are more personally meaningful.

Illness as Teacher

The teachings in your illness will, of course, relate to whatever meaning you have been able to uncover on your own or from the exercises in this book. Your illness can teach you new things about yourself as you experience new depths of courage, new ways of being in the world. Ultimately, the teaching contained in your illness and all other life feedback will lead you in the direction of unfolding, experiencing, and expressing your fundamental spiritual nature.

While our lives are affected by personal beliefs, such as those found in our life metaphors, we are also subject to family beliefs which include family rules, family secrets, and roles. Religious, political, and class beliefs are passed on by the family and the immediate social circle. In speaking of the "starting line" in chapter 4, I mentioned elements such as race, religion, and nationality. These contribute to larger core beliefs or cultural metaphors that so permeate our lives that they are virtually invisible, accepted as truths without examination.

Our illnesses can teach us about these beliefs as well as our more personal core beliefs. In choosing our starting line, we are not just part of a family but part of a culture which is itself steeped in beliefs and attitudes, many of which are not truths about reality. There are many different cultural metaphors, four of which I discuss in this section, which contribute to the challenge of opening to the spiritual self, metaphors which all devalue human beings. See if any of these limiting beliefs are operating in your life, if you have incorporated them into your self-image, affecting your sense of self-worth.

Original Sin.   You don't have to be a Catholic or even a Christian to believe in the fallen nature of human beings. The idea that the First Couple screwed up, and all of us are flawed as a result, permeates our culture. It is a part of many individuals' belief systems whether it is ever spoken of or consciously recognized.

It is difficult to get in touch with the Divine Self, to allow the Spirit of creation to flow through us unsuppressed, if we believe that our very nature is flawed. How can miracles come through a flawed self?

We have been given the gift of free will and the gift of creation. That means we can deny our spiritual heritage and create crimes as easily as miracles. We cannot, however, separate ourselves from that heritage in any real way. The Spirit that created us dwells within our beating hearts, flows through the rivers of our blood, moves in and out with our breath. While we can feel ourselves to be separated and fallen, such separation can never be real. God does not condemn or exile any portion of Itself.

Believing that you are flawed and separate is just as effective as the real thing, however. Ask yourself if you feel flawed or less spiritual because you dwell in a physical body. If you believe that the body is flawed, then illness is almost inevitable. Is it possible for you to love your body even in its diminished physical condition? Is it possible to see the body and the self as an expression of the Divine even when the body is sick? That is one of the challenges and teachings of illness.

The Id.   Although many people today discount some of Sigmund Freud's ideas, they still seem to have gotten under our skin and become part of our unconscious cultural beliefs. Freud's *id* is the ravenous and selfish part of ourselves that looks out for Number One. If it were not somewhat controlled by the *ego* and *superego*, we would all be out raping and pillaging on a daily basis. This concept of the self as a barely controlled beast is reflected in cultural beliefs about the necessity of laws and police forces to protect us from ourselves.

I would contend that no such beast exists. We are fundamentally spiritual beings, and therefore our primary motivation is to love and do good. There is no question that we act beastly at times, both individually and collectively. Such actions are aberrations of human nature, suppressions and distortions of Spirit, of love, not basic human nature breaking through the veneer of civilization.

A belief in a flawed self, whether because of original sin or the *id*, can cause a lot of unnecessary guilt and shame. These can lead to illness and operations—one of the negative uses of illness—and can prolong the course of an illness if one consciously or unconsciously believes they deserve to be sick. Self-punishment and repentance can rise out of a psychology of personal guilt.

How do you view your own nature? Are you basically a good person who sometimes makes mistakes and sometimes acts out of fear rather than love? Or are you basically a selfish beast which must be kept constantly under control lest it break through and express its true nature?

Survival of the Fittest. Our third cultural belief which devalues human beings also happens to devalue animals. In fact, it perceives the entire world as an arena for competition in which only the strong survive and good guys definitely finish last. "Survival of the fittest" doesn't necessarily mean that I can only survive by defeating you, " ... it merely suggests that creatures that adapt best to a changing environment are allowed to live and reproduce another day."[1] This quote from Alfie Kohn, author of *No Contest: The Case Against Competition,* is from a talk given at a symposium in Washington, D.C., in 1989. Kohn's position, arrived at as a result of an analysis of more than four hundred studies, is highly radical but is in keeping with the fundamental spiritual nature of human beings: "My position is that competition is destructive and counterproductive not merely in excess; it is destructive not merely because we are doing it the wrong way; it is destructive by its very nature."[2]

Those in the natural sciences explore nature and come to the conclusion that nature is characterized by competition. Though death is part of nature at every level, and certain animals act as predators and others as prey, the system can justifiably be seen as a cooperative dance rather than a deadly competition.

Scientists conclude that humans are basically competitive because of the behavior they observe in the wild. But they go into the field with their attitudes and beliefs about human nature already in place. What they observe in nature, then, is filtered through these beliefs. They meet themselves in nature.

Physical reality contains challenges of various kinds. It *is* filled with conflicts that need to be resolved. As for competition, however, and the need to struggle against a predatory nature, such may not exist at all. Remember that the feedback system helps us to meet our self. Anyone who seems to be in competition with us is really cooperating with our beliefs. Anyone who seems to be an enemy is cooperating with our fears. Our physical illnesses represent the body cooperating with our beliefs and attitudes.

Jesus said that we should love our enemies. Since the world is simply a reflection of our own thoughts and attitudes, the enemy is just a reflection of our fearful self. In that sense there are no external enemies. Loving our enemies means loving that fearful part of ourselves.

Soul Slumming. Finally, certain spiritual systems look on the body and physical reality as a place we're stuck in until we can become spiritual enough to get out. We are spirits trapped in vessels of clay. Physical reality is a kind of soul slumming.

When you perceive all of creation as being made of God stuff, there is no hierarchy of values placed on different kinds of experience. Physical reality is one way in which the spirit is expressed, one form of experiencing and learning. It is not inherently inferior to any other expression of the spirit. It's true that we may move on to other forms of being once we've learned all we need from physical experience.

We will still be students (and possibly teachers as well) just as we are now. We will still be learning, growing, experiencing, and creating, whether in a body or not.

An individual in a physical body may be more spiritually advanced than many individuals who are in the spirit realm. I like to say, "Just 'cause you're dead, don't mean you're smart." Edgar Cayce, as a matter of fact, used to have a number of invisible "students" attend his Sunday school classes. Although others could not see them, he was very aware of these "phantom" students standing at the back of his class, and they obviously thought they could learn something there.

Physical life is not slumming. It is not a degraded form of being. It is certainly not a place of punishment. It is a place for experiencing, and we can be as close to our spiritual roots in physical being as we can in some nonphysical states. See if you have a belief about being physical as a degraded or inferior state. Such a belief can interfere with healing and living the healing life. My client Grace was giving herself "die" messages because she thought life after death would be much easier and better than life on earth. She thought she would become instantly enlightened when she died and she would be taken care of there.

Illness as Initiation/Transformation

Another framework for examining the teachings of your illness is the concept of initiation and transformation. Initiation is a series of steps designed to help an individual change from one way of being to another. It is a transformative practice. Many of the stages individuals with serious illnesses go through are similar to primitive initiation rites. Our illnesses are designed to change us, to change our self-image, to transform us. Through the framework of initiation, we can consciously cooperate with that change.

In our culture, initiations and rites of passage, while they still exist, tend to be somewhat watered down, form without substance. Graduation, baptism, confirmation, bar and bat mitzvahs, as well as the rituals of many fraternal and service organizations, while they are sometimes deeply meaningful to some individuals, generally do not have the power that such rites had in the past.

"Primitive" initiations often involve an ordeal that prepares an individual for a special role: priest, priestess, shaman, medicine person, etc. The idea of death and resurrection is almost always involved. The rites of passage for boys and girls facilitate the dramatic change from child to adult.

Initiation changes us, transforms us. We come out of the experience a different person. Although specific teachings are often part of the initiation process, the experience itself is the real teacher. Elements of initiation include teachings from those already initiated and from the shaman, direct spirit communications, and usually separation from the tribe. There is almost always an element of solitude and sometimes of danger. Fasting is common as are altered states of consciousness, sometimes mediated by drugs, and the initiate may experience journeying to other worlds. Often the initiate will confront his or her own fears in the form of dreams or visions. In some cases physical mutilations occur.

In some traditions the initiate, in an alternate state of consciousness, imagines being stripped of his or her flesh, being dismembered, and having his or her internal organs removed. The initiate is given a new body and organs and becomes a new being. Among certain Eskimos, shamanic initiation sometimes begins because of a serious illness or accident. This is a sign of a spontaneous vocation.[3]

As I mentioned earlier, in the case of one Australian aboriginal magician, the ritual of dying, losing his organs, and the rest of the initiatory experience changed him so profoundly that he didn't know who he was when he came out of it. He couldn't remember any of his past and had to be introduced to his wife and other tribe members.[4]

A serious illness or other life-shattering experience can be seen and experienced as an initiation. Even the breakdown of the body through illness can be experienced as a symbolic removal of the old self. The different elements of the illness, from the first symptoms through diagnosis, treatment, and recuperation, can be seen as part of your initiatory journey. Even changes in friends, work, role, and identity can be seen as part of a positive transformation.

The important question the initiate must ask is, "Who will I become at the end of my journey?" or "Who do I wish to become?" The initiate must leave the old self, with all of its assumptions, beliefs, attitudes, and fears behind. The new self must be allowed its birth—a self with different values, different priorities, and perhaps a whole different reason for being.

Some initiations involved ritual death and resurrection. Cayce, in some of his life readings, claimed that John the Baptist and Jesus went through such initiation in Egypt. The Egyptian initiates were "buried" in a tomb or cave, usually for three days. This was echoed in the death, burial, and resurrection of Jesus. A number of sources suggest that the pyramid of Cheops in Egypt was not a burial pyramid but an initiation temple. The purpose of such initiations was to give the initiate the opportunity to face and do battle with his or her own demons or shadows. The successful initiate would come out of the experience completely reborn.

Mary, a friend of mine, contracted amoebic dysentery and was unable to care for herself. A strong, intelligent, and independent woman in her early forties, Mary went home to stay with her parents. She found the parents she never had as a child. She was there for three days, and they took care of her completely. She was totally helpless and dependent on them, like a small child.

Her mother read to Mary and told her stories of her own childhood. Mary's father spent time with her and told her the biblical story of creation. She was reborn by the experience. When she left the house, all of her senses were sharpened, and she felt more alive than she had before the illness.

Can we release or change our past? Can we allow ourselves to become new beings? Who will that new self be? How will that new self act in the world? What path will the new self take?

Path-Finding, Path-Making, and Prophecy

If one advances confidently in the direction of his dreams, and endeavors to live the life which he imagined, he will meet with a success unexpected in common hours. He will put something behind, will pass an invisible boundary; new, universal, and more liberal laws will begin to establish themselves around and within him, or the old laws will be expanded and interpreted in his favor in a more liberal sense; and he will live with the license of a higher order of beings.

— Henry David Thoreau[5]

The initiate begins life anew, sets out on a new path. The question is, what path will that be? When we allow ourselves to be transformed by our illness, new forces come into play, as Thoreau suggests. Healing our illness is an important part of our goal, but it may not be the final goal. Beyond illness lies a whole new path. What will your new path include, and who will you, as the person on this path, be?

A path can be described as the direction in which we are looking. Our attitudes and beliefs, dreams and expectations, fears and desires, point us in a certain direction. The self that we are or believe ourselves to be illuminates a particular path as if we were wearing a miner's cap with a light on top. Right beside that path are other equally legitimate paths that are simply not seen because of the direction in which we are looking.

A path can also be seen as a prophecy. Our current self is like a prophecy in the sense that our current thoughts and feelings project certain future outcomes. If we do not change, we continue to project more of the same. When we *do* change our thoughts and feelings, we change the path, we change the prophecy.

As W. W. Wagar says, "The function of prophecy is not to tell the future but to make it."[6] In the same way, we are not just seeking a new path but *creating* a new path. We can choose the path we wish to follow, choose the prophecy we wish to fulfill. If an illness does not take one's life, it can give one new life. Both your challenge and your gift is to project a new path, create a new prophecy, set before yourself new goals and ideals.

Earlier in this book I suggested that you write the story of your life, your personal myth. Have there been some changes since then? Read that story and see if you want to revise it or write a new story/myth.

Write a story about your new self, your new life. In this story you can use the imagery and metaphor of path or prophecy, or just tell your story as a new myth. How is your new self different from the old? What are the values and priorities of this new self? What does this self spend time doing, and with whom?

If you wish, you could create a character in a fantasy or meditation, a prophet who would be the bearer of the new prophecy, a guide on the new path. This prophet can be a source of guidance and encouragement. In meditation or through writing in your healing journal, you can dialogue with your prophet and see how you're doing. She or he can be a source of ongoing path correction.

Mind of God/Will of God

Mind is the builder, but what is the model for the mind? How would the ideal mind work? God, the Creative Force, is the original builder and is the model for us as life builders. Part of the way our minds work is "hard wired," that is they work automatically by converting our thoughts and feelings into our physical experience. No one is better at such creations than another, but some do create their experiences more consciously. Being on the healing path means creating our physical experiences more consciously, and that means being more aware of what is going on in our minds.

The other part of the model is not hard wired or automatic, although it exists in every mind as a potential and, from my point of view, represents part of the positive bias of the universe. The motivation for original creation, as well as the energy for that creation, was love. Love is the aspect or ingredient of mind which determines the kind of personal world we are creating. Love is polarized by fear. While I don't want to oversimplify a complex process, one could say that the experiences we create for ourselves come from a particular point on the fear/love continuum. As beings of spirit, then, we have as our happy task to practice creating more and more from love (love of self as well as love of others) and less and less from fear.

This last framework, a pattern for spiritual teaching and learning, is another way of looking at the natural flow of Spirit. When the Spirit flows through our life unsuppressed, we can be said to be in the Mind of God. From that position, miracles become almost commonplace.

One framework in which the development of Mind has been practiced for hundreds of years is the martial arts. Beyond the physical skills involved, many martial artists seek a harmonious blending with the universe, aspiring to shift functioning from the ordinary ego to their deeper nature.

According to Japanese swordsman Yagyu Tajima: "The Mind (*kokoro*) is Emptiness (*ku, k'ung, sunyata*) itself, but out of this Emptiness an infinity of acts is produced: in hands it grasps, in feet it walks, in eyes it sees . . . it is indeed very difficult to have this experience because we cannot get it from mere learning, from the mere listening to others talk about it. Swordsmanship consists in personally going through this experience. When this is done, one's words are sincerity itself, one's behavior comes right out of the Original Mind emptied of all ego-centered contents."[7]

As with many of the abilities mentioned earlier, such as those exhibited by yogis, athletes, and some spiritual leaders, this ability to contact and act from Original Mind involves years of meditation and other practices. But the Mind of God is not out of reach; it is not far away or hard to find. Mind is as close to us as our own mind is. It is simply a matter of removing our Spirit-suppression devices and allowing a harmonious blending with nature and with our own true natures.

Illness can open us to this Mind, give us glimpses and experiences of it. We can ask for openings to Mind, seek to make awareness of Mind part of our path, choose to practice co-creation with Mind. Jung puts it this way: "I cannot define for you what God is . . . I can only say that my work has proved empirically that the pattern of God exists in every man, and that this pattern has at its disposal the greatest of all his energies for transformation and transfiguration of his natural being. Not only the meaning of his life but his renewal and his institutions depend on his conscious relationship with this pattern in his collective unconscious."[8]

You can open to the Mind of God with the Spirit suppression device exercise or with the Mind of God meditation below. When our fears, doubts, worries, guilt, blame, and other shadows are put aside, Mind is what is left. Being in touch with Mind is our natural state, as is health and life fulfillment.

Exercise: Mind of God

You can use any terminology that is meaningful to you for this exercise. I call it the Mind of God meditation. Cayce called God the Creative Force or Forces. Seth called God All-That-Is. Lazaris uses the terms God, Goddess, All-That-Is. You may call it a Higher Self meditation. It is based on the understanding that we are in the Mind of God and God is in us, that we are, in fact, made out of God "stuff."

Get yourself into a receptive and meditative state. You can do this by sitting or lying down in a comfortable position and taking a few deep breaths, or you can use a more elaborate relaxation procedure if you wish. I have found it helpful to begin by imagining that every cell in my body is alive and alight with the love of God or the Spirit of God. Many near-death experiencers find light and love to be interchangeable expressions for the presence of the Divine. Use whatever image or word is best for you and imagine every cell in your body filled with divinity.

Take as much time as you need. Now think of yourself or your mind as being in attunement and alignment with the Mind of God. Imagine that your mind and the Mind of God are one. It can be helpful to speak aloud or to yourself and say, "My mind is coming into alignment with the Mind of God. My mind is attuning to the Mind of God. My mind is becoming one with the Mind of God." Repeat these phrases three times or more, and then be still and allow yourself to experience the Mind of God.

If you find your mind wandering, call it back with words or phrases. The word "one" is good, or simply "Mind of God," or you could use the three original sentences to get back on track. Simply allow yourself to experience the Mind of God as much as you can. This can be a very emotional experience. Allow the emotions to come up, and express them, with sound or tears, if you feel comfortable doing so. You may receive some helpful images or insights. Write your experience down in your healing journal. You should practice the Mind of God meditation and Spirit-suppression device exercises often. They can be very powerful and very healing.

Another way to think of the Mind of God is in terms of the will of God. This is not a matter of subjugating your will to the will of God. To do so is to think of yourself as God's puppet, and God doesn't need any puppets. God seeks companions and co-creators. The will of God is not even a particular life pattern or path; there are many patterns and paths that any individual can follow within the framework of the will of God.

The path of the will of God is a way of being in the world. It can be called attunement, something I'll discuss in greater detail in chapter 12. It is another way of being in the Mind of God. The will of God is for each of us to fulfill our potential. We are practicing the path of the will of God when we are in alignment with the positive bias of the universe, when we allow Spirit to move through us unsuppressed, when love and creativity are given full rein.

And now to the healing process itself and the question that must be asked, "Do you want to be healed?"

PART 4

HEALING AN ILLNESS

10

Do You Want to Be Healed?

"Now there is in Jerusalem by the Sheep Gate a pool, in Hebrew called Bethzatha, which has five porticoes. In these lay a multitude of invalids, blind, lame, paralyzed. One man was there, who had been ill for thirty-eight years.

"When Jesus saw him and knew that he had been lying there a long time, he said to him, 'Do you want to be healed?'

"The sick man answered him, 'Sir, I have no man to put me into the pool when the water is troubled, and while I am going another steps down before me.' Jesus said to him, 'Rise, take up your pallet, and walk.' And at once the man was healed, and he took up his pallet and walked." (John 5:2-9)

On the surface, one would have to say that Jesus' question is absurd. The man had been sick for thirty-eight years and had been lying around this pool for a long time. Because of his infirmities he was unable to get into the pool before others, and he had no one who would help him. To ask him if he wants to be healed shows either a twisted sense of humor, a severe lack of awareness, or—something else.

After many years of working with people with illnesses, trying to help them understand their meanings, I have learned that Jesus' question is neither mean nor thoughtless. In fact, it's one of the most important questions to be asked of any illness or other life issue. As we look at the many ways in which illnesses serve us, negatively and positively, it makes sense to confront ourselves with Jesus' question.

Sickness unto Death

In some cases people get serious illnesses in order to die. As I've already said, that isn't necessarily a bad thing. Physical life is terminal. Death of the body is a certainty. The only questions that remain about our deaths are "when?" and "how?" I think we choose our deaths, both the time and the means. These are unconscious choices, in most cases, but some yogis and other religious adepts have been able to consciously leave their bodies and die when they were ready.

Dying of an illness is just one choice, and a common one in our culture. Some would rather go out younger, while their bodies are in good health, possibly choosing to die with a bang in an accident. Even those who die of an illness have a range of possibilities, some dealing with lingering illnesses and possibly a lot of pain. Others die in peace after a short illness or abruptly with heart failure or some other instantly fatal bodily failure.

Because dying of an illness is just another way to die, there should be no judgment attached to such a death. In our culture, unfortunately, we tend to see serious illnesses as failures. Some people hide their illnesses from all but the closest family members and friends because of the embarrassment involved. The person with the illness may feel guilty or ashamed for having allowed such a thing to happen. Friends or family members may be embarrassed because they don't know how to deal with the possible death of a loved one. This is especially true with AIDS, even in those cases where the virus is not transmitted sexually or through tainted needles. AIDS is the leprosy of the twentieth century.

Early in Edgar Cayce's career, a group of supporters created a prayer group, following the directions of the Cayce readings. One of the first individuals they prayed for was a young man with a serious illness. They would pray for him, and Cayce would do a followup reading to see how the young man was doing.

The man improved at first and then got worse. Eventually he died. The group was devastated by his death. Over and above the grief over the loss of the young man, they were disappointed in their apparent failure to stay the course of his illness, to bring about a healing with their prayers. They had done everything the readings suggested, had prayed sincerely and with great hope. What had gone wrong?

Cayce did a final reading to determine the cause of the young man's death. In the reading Cayce said simply, "He is healed." Death is one form that healing takes. It is also a kind of birth.

A dear friend of mine, whom I'll call Betty, was diagnosed with liver cancer. She went through traditional therapies without success and was sent home to die. She traveled to Mexico and went through a cancer program that included a special diet. She returned home and continued her dietary regimen with the help of a circle of caring friends. We took turns during the day, staying with Betty and preparing her special meals. Her daughter was with her at night. It was a pleasure spending time with Betty, reminiscing about old times together, talking about her life, and sharing mementos from her past.

One rainy Thursday I arrived at the house to find Betty dying. Her daughter had stayed home from work because of Betty's condition and a strong premonition. We called Betty's mother, and she arrived within an hour or so. A nurse came by and checked Betty's vital signs. Another friend/helper stopped by.

Betty's daughter sat on one side of the bed and her mother on the other. Each held a hand and spoke to Betty. Both, with tears, told Betty they loved her and she could go if she wanted. They gave her loving permission to leave this life. I don't remember the passage of time. It may have been an hour or less that we five were gathered in the room with Betty.

I held Betty's feet. There was sadness and a sense of loss as I watched Betty die, but there was another feeling that didn't contradict, but mixed with the sadness. There was a growing feeling of joy, perhaps even a feeling of holiness. I felt privileged to be a witness and participant in this event. As the joy rose in me, I finally understood the source of my feelings. They were not the feelings of someone witnessing a death. I was witnessing a birth.

Betty's bedroom had French doors that led to a small garden. The rain had stopped, but the wind was blowing. I looked at Betty and knew she had died. I said, quietly, "She's gone." Just then the French doors blew open. We all looked at each other and laughed. She was gone indeed!

Polarities

Physical reality is characterized by polarities, life and death being one of the more obvious. Aside from such externalized polarities as male and female, positive and negative, black and white, and yin and yang, there are internal polarities. These internal polarities exist in our beliefs and attitudes, feelings and desires, and even in our values. In many cases we are only aware of one end of the polarity, the other being hidden in our psyche as a shadow.

When an individual says, "I want to be healed," there is often another voice, usually inaudible but not necessarily weak, that says, "I refuse to be healed," or "I'm afraid of being healed." These contrary voices are shadows, in Jung's terminology, parts of ourselves that we deny or repress. We normally project these aspects or qualities onto others and reject *them* or do battle with them. These shadows still reside within us, however, and they can cause a *lot* of trouble until we recognize and integrate them.

In chapter 3 I briefly mentioned meeting in a dream a version of myself who was *angrily* opposed to my philosophy of life. In that dream there were two distinct versions of myself having an argument. Bob One looked physically pretty much as I did at the time. Bob Two was an idealized version, taller, thinner, and younger. Bob One was crouching like a frightened or cornered animal, arguing with Bob Two. Bob One finally scuttled from the room as Bob Two shouted after him, "You *do* create your own world!"

I was shocked! Bob One was an aspect of myself who was diametrically opposed to my philosophy of life, a philosophy which I not only attempt to live on a daily basis, but one which I also share with others in my counseling, teaching, group work, and writing.

I have already discussed the idea that we are all multiple personalities, a multiplicity of selves, and that we are always meeting self, in our dreams and waking life as well as in our childhood and past lives. It may be difficult to accept, but our conscious beliefs and feelings, our attitudes and desires, the very things that make up our personality and self-image, are sometimes opposed by other personalities, shadow aspects of ourselves who seem to have their own agendas.

These polarized personalities are not all negative. Any qualities or attitudes we reject or suppress will become shadows. When we suppress our beauty and power and reject our divinity, those qualities still reside within us, hiding in the darkness of our psyches, becoming golden shadows. A complete healing, or healing process, requires that we bring as many of our polarities into the light of waking consciousness as possible .

When we become aware of dream characters that oppose our healing, we can do something about them. We will even find that most of them, as with any dream figures, have gifts for us. Because it takes energy—sometimes a great deal of energy—to maintain these shadow figures, we can retrieve that energy and use it for our own positive purposes by uncovering and integrating them.

Those with Multiple Personality Disorder create alternate personalities primarily to perform in some protective capacity. The same is true of many of our shadows. We give birth to inner selves to defend us against real or imagined foes and dangers.

I spoke to "Bob One" in a fantasy/meditation to find out who he was and why he was in such strong opposition to what was central in my life. What I discovered about this shadow—my philosophical polarity—is that I had *hired* him to do a job for me. I hired him to embody my doubts and fears, to contain my subconscious beliefs that my philosophy might be wrong. He was the bearer of my disappointments, those times when my philosophy didn't seem to work. By putting those feelings outside myself (or deep inside) I felt I could teach more positively, with more conviction.

He was angry because he didn't like his job. He had no power to do anything constructive. He was just a container for my denied doubts and fears. What he *could* do, and what many of our polarities do, in fact, is cause trouble. Ironically, his sabotage brought about the very failures and disappointments I sought to avoid. The more deeply we bury our polarities, the more energy they have. That energy is creative. Doubt and fear of failure were Bob One's only focus and his only avenue of action. When I denied those feelings, they only became unconscious, and from that place they created life experiences for me. The activity of my Spirit-suppression device was being shown to me in my daily experiences, so I had an opportunity to recognize it and get rid of it or transform it.

In order to integrate these shadows, it's necessary to take back the previously denied and repressed feelings and attitudes they embody. Once I owned the shadow's characteristics as my own, I could fire him or release him from his duties. However, it does no good to fire a polarized character if you continue to deny the qualities she or he has taken on for you. A new shadow will simply rise up (or sink down) to take its place.

Polarities or shadows can be difficult to uncover, because they represent the opposite of your conscious beliefs and feelings. It takes a great deal of courage to uncover and acknowledge these shadow selves. One clue to polarities is the phenomenon of protesting too much: individuals who boast of their accomplishments may be hiding a polarized shadow that feels insecure and incompetent. The bully hides the fearful and powerless self.

In the case of illnesses, the conscious self says, "I want to be healed," but there may be a polarity who says, "I'm terrified of being healed." Those parts that say "yes" to healing will have a very hard time without the cooperation of those parts that say "no." The woman in my workshop, Melinda, wanted to be healed and worked hard at getting her body functioning again. Her inner little girl, however, equated being healthy with being out in the world, being with people. To Melinda being with people meant being hurt and abused.

My client Grace was also working hard to be healed. Aside

from doing metaphorical healing work with me, Grace was following a healthy diet, taking vitamins and herbs, seeing a chiropractor, and attending spiritual workshops. In the session in which Grace told me she believed life after death was far more desirable than physical life, I realized there was a part of Grace which did not want to be healed. All other healing work would be ineffective until Grace confronted that shadow and made a decision to live out her physical life.

Our shadows and polarities are not our enemies. They are simply parts of ourselves which continue to protect us beyond our need for protection. We need to relieve them of that duty, to acknowledge our fears and doubts, and to make our life choices with as much awareness as possible.

Healing Choices

We *do* make choices. Although healing is something that happens naturally, something our bodies know how to do, the course of healing is guided by our choices. The course and timing of our illness are also guided by choice, as this reading by Edgar Cayce demonstrates. A woman asked him if there was a chance of ill health in March. He responded: "If you are looking for it you can have it in February! If you want to skip March, skip it—you'll have it in June! If you want to skip June, don't have it at all this year!" (3564-1)

This is an amusing exaggeration of what we do all the time. Both through conscious choices and less conscious expectations, we plot our life course, the path we will walk, and the body we will walk it in.

You create your illness over time with conscious choices, unconscious expectations, and with the assistance of polarized shadows. Illnesses may be protective like shadows, protecting you from something fearful, like the stroke victim's fear of going out into the world, or from the risk of success or failure. Part of the healing process is to find the courage to put the illness's false protection aside and face the fears that a healthy future may hold for you.

I worked with mentally ill adults in a number of residential settings performing individual, group, and family counseling. I learned a great deal from the residents, both about myself and about their illnesses. It seemed to me that many of the residents worked very hard to maintain their level of illness. They thought about their illness and gave it their time and emotional energy for most of their waking hours. The more seriously ill stayed focused on their illness almost constantly to maintain their level of malfunction.

I believe if they ever reduced this level of energizing their problems, they would begin to get well. In fact, one man diagnosed as catatonic just stopped being symptomatic one day. After observing this startling change in behavior for a couple of days, I asked him what was going on. He said, "Well, Bob, I just decided to put down my crazy act for a while." A couple of weeks later he picked up his "act" again. Years later he was still in the mental health system.

If there was a magic pill that would instantly heal the mentally ill, many of them would find a way to avoid taking it. The norm for residential facilities in the county I worked in was for clients to improve until they were nearly ready to leave the facility and go out on their own, at which point they would have some kind of breakdown or crisis and the process would start all over again. I think many people who are not considered mentally ill would also avoid such a pill, one that would heal our illnesses and/or solve our problems. Ernest left our counseling sessions just as we were about to make a breakthrough. Every other therapeutic relationship he had been in failed.

I believe that, because we *have* such a pill. We have the ability to heal ourselves, to make any healing changes in our life we desire. If we haven't taken the pill yet, there's a reason: life without our problems confronts us with an unknown future, a future where we will have to succeed or fail in terms of our life goals and ideals.

Cayce asks, "What would ye do with thy mind and thy body if they were wholly restored to normalcy in this experience?" (3684-1) We are not just talking about being healed, we are also talking about life after health. What will you do?

One of the most severely disturbed individuals in a residence where I worked taught me something about the dangers of life after health. I'll call her Margaret. Occasionally I was able to have lucid conversations with even the most disturbed residents. I had one such conversation with Margaret.

Margaret was diagnosed as having schizophrenia, having had her psychotic break at the age of sixteen. When I knew her, she had spent as many years suffering from her illness. I spoke to Margaret one morning about her illness. She referred to it as her "accident," placing it outside herself as all of us often do.

I told Margaret her illness was like a monster that followed her everywhere she went. No matter what she did, it never went away. "But," I said, "it's not following you. You have it on a leash and you're dragging it around with you. If you want to be healed, all you have to do is let go of the leash, turn around, and face the future."

I was younger then and still thought humans, including myself, were primarily rational beings. Margaret taught me that things weren't as simple as I had imagined. "What if there are monsters in the future?" she asked. Her question was perfectly reasonable. For me it was a revelation!

Like Margaret, we keep our monsters around because they protect us from the future. Sometimes they're large monsters in the form of a serious illness or accident, and sometimes they're a lot of small monsters in the form of troubles, worries, and fears. We focus on our monsters. We energize them with worry. We complain about them to our friends. We work on them, sometimes very hard.

What we're really doing is feeding them and taking good

care of them. They're like annoying pets, but pets nonetheless. They *do* annoy us. They harry and harass us. They seem to prevent us from growing, from fulfilling our potential, our destiny. In fact that *is* what they do, but they do so at our behest; they do it through our choices. It is precisely our growth, our potential, our destiny, our ideals from which our monsters protect us. Ultimately our monsters protect us from our own divinity.

We have choices. No matter what choices we have made in the past, we can make new choices now. Those new choices will require courage and determination. They require our willingness to let the old self go, to die to that self. New choices mean facing our future stripped of our protective Spirit-suppression devices. They require, ultimately, that we open ourselves to the fullness of our spiritual being, whatever form that may take for us.

> Within each of us is a spark. Call it a divine spark if you will, but it is there and can light the way to health. There are no incurable diseases, only incurable people.—Bernie Siegel[1]

> There are in truth no incurable conditions . . . The healing depends upon the individual, and the attitude taken toward conditions . . . (3744-2)

Attitudes, Emotions, and Other Monsters

All monsters are "thought" monsters. They are often formed by our attitudes and emotions. The way we feel about ourselves, others, and the world strongly influences how we perceive our life experiences. Our "monsters" also influence what illnesses we have and the course of our healing. Researchers, for example, study the "cancer personality" as well as personality and attitudinal characteristics of long-term cancer and AIDS survivors. Many studies have found that expression or suppression of feelings is a strong predictor of healing outcome.

Edgar Cayce said: "To be sure, the attitudes oft influence the physical conditions of the body. No one can hate his neighbor and not have stomach or liver trouble. No one can be jealous and allow the anger of same and not have upset digestion or heart disorder." (4021-1) Answering "yes" to the question, "Do you want to be healed?" requires more than a desire to be rid of your symptoms. It requires a willingness to change your life, a willingness to look inside and see what attitudes, emotions, and thoughts have led to this illness. You *can* uncover these thought and attitude monsters. Then you must be willing to let them go.

Open your healing journal, and then open your heart. Look into your heart and list all of the feelings you find there. Explore your entire body, because some of your feelings will be found in places other than your heart. You may feel a tightness in your chest or a lump in your throat. If you feel fears or anxieties, write them down as well as where you feel them in your body. Write down your positive emotions as well. When you're finished, go back over your list and give a "weight" to each feeling, or order the feelings according to which ones you experience the most often.

What are the dominant feelings in your life? Do these feelings serve you in a positive way, or are they monsters that prevent you from growing? Many people believe their feelings are as fixed as any genetic trait. "That's just the way I feel," they say. "I can't help it."

Feelings are not fixed. They are not a part of who we are. Our thoughts and beliefs give birth to our feelings. If I believe that women can't be trusted, I will feel nervous and perhaps fearful around women. That feeling has nothing to do with what women are really like, although I will surely have experiences with women that support my belief. The feeling comes from my belief. The experiences come from what beliefs lead me to expect and the energy and attitudes

I display when I'm around women.

Look at the feelings you would most like to change. Try to follow each feeling back to a thought or belief. Most of our self-destructive feelings are related to guilt, fear, anger, hostility, helplessness, hopelessness, and loneliness.

Compare how much of your time and energy is spent on negative and how much on positive feelings. Remember that anger is not a negative emotion if it is appropriately expressed. If you're angry at someone, you need to tell them. If that's not possible, you can do it in a visualization. A lot of problems come from the routine *suppression* of anger. Anger is only a problem if it is chronic, unfocused, and not released in a healthy way.

Start with the assumption that you *do*, on some level, know the beliefs behind the feelings. When you find the belief, write it down. Now you're in a position to change the belief. Remember that it's just a belief, just a thought. It can be changed. If you associate it with a childhood experience or pattern of experiences, write that down. If there's a way to state the opposite belief, perhaps as an affirmation, do so. Perhaps you can do a symbol transformation exercise in order to get a symbol to represent the new belief. Whenever you're trying to change a belief, it's important to try to take small actions or have small experiences from the point of view of the new belief. Pretend you are the person with the new belief until the new belief becomes established.

Is there a different feeling attached to the new belief? Practice that feeling. As an actor practices for a role, you can pretend you believe something new and even pretend to *feel* different. After a while you won't have to pretend any more—the new belief and feeling will have taken hold. Studies have shown that our bodies react differently to different facial expressions even when we're faking the expression. Smiling is good for us, even though we may not feel like smiling. Beliefs and feelings can be "faked" in the same manner.

One way to change a persistent negative feeling is to personify it as a monster-pet. Visualize your "friendly" monster and do a closure ceremony in which you thank it for protecting you all these years and tell it you're now ready to set it free and let it go back into the "wild" where it belongs. Of all our monsters, fear is probably the most common and, for many of us, the most well fed, healthy, and robust.

> If I could give one gift to people, it would be to liberate them from their fears . . . because fears create illness.—Norman Cousins[2]

Fear and Love

Love/fear, one of the greatest polarities we face, is probably common to all people and may encompass all other challenges. It's almost a cliché to say that God is Love, yet love is the greatest emotion we are able to experience in physical reality. Some of those who have had near-death experiences perceive God or the energy they meet as light. Some describe it as love.

If we think of Spirit flowing through mind to create the physical, we can think of that Spirit as love. Whatever Spirit-suppression devices we have are suppressing love. If we remove those devices, love can create miracles. That which is the greatest suppressor of love is fear. Love and fear cannot occupy the same space.

As the Bible says, " . . . perfect love casts out fear." (I John 4:18) We might agree that love is the antidote to fear, that love is the energy that creates miracles in our life, but how do we extricate ourselves from fear and move toward love?

Overcoming fear and moving toward love means changing our beliefs and attitudes so that we can give up fear's false protection, remove our armor, and knock down the walls of our fortresses. Love makes us vulnerable; it strips us bare. It does not place us in danger, however, because of one of the great paradoxes of love: the more vulnerable we are, the safer we are. Total vulnerability equals total safety. The fearless self is the loving self.

Do You Want to Be Healed?

This question can be answered in your healing journal. Earlier we asked related questions: "How does this illness serve me?" "What would happen if I gave up this illness?" In answering the question, "Do you want to be healed?" list the "no" reasons as well as the "yes" reasons. Remember that healing, in the sense I'm using it here, goes beyond simply healing the body.

Remember also that the "yes" and "no" reasons are polarities that can easily exist within the same individual. If someone were to ask you if you wanted to be healed, the "yes" would most likely come easily and quickly to your lips. If there is a "no," it is in the shadows, beneath normal awareness. It will take a lot of courage to find and acknowledge the part of you that does not want to be healed. If it exists, it may be small and offer no great impediment to healing. If it's large and has a lot of energy, you will need to deal strongly with it.

The "yes" answers should be in a form such as, "Yes, I want to be healed so I can…" The "no" answers, similarly, should be put in the form, "No, I don't want to be healed because…" or something similar.

This exercise provides another way to pose the question that will get a more honest answer. It will take courage and high motivation to see what's in your way, not just in healing your illness, but in living the loving, healing life.

Exercise: Do You Want to Be Healed?

Close your eyes. Take a few deep breaths and allow your

body to relax. This exercise is based on your ability to be sensitive to bodily sensations, so take as much time as you need to get your body in a relaxed state. If you have aches and pains or any discomfort, tell your body to let them go, to put them aside for the time that you're doing this exercise.

While our conscious minds are not always honest, our bodies don't know how to lie. Ask your unconscious, "Do you want to be healed?" Do not answer the question with your rational mind; let your unconscious answer the question through your body.

Repeat the question three times, aloud or just in your mind, and then be still. Feel what happens in your body in reaction to the question. Notice every place where there's a physical and/or emotional response to the question. Where does the question go in your body? What feelings are attached to that place—both bodily sensations and emotions? The question will generally lodge in one major body area and give rise to one primary feeling.

Before you do anything else, allow yourself to fully experience the feeling. Don't suppress or reject it. Emotional suppression equals dis-ease and illness. Emotional expression equals health.

If you're a more visually oriented person, allow an image or symbol to form in your mind's eye to represent your unconscious answer to the question. You may have a full-blown imagery experience, a mini-dream. Any images you get can be treated like dream symbols. Dialogue with them or try the symbol transformation exercise. Use any of the noninterpretive methods from chapter 8 that appeal to you.

If you're more verbally oriented, you might speak to either the bodily sensation itself or the emotion. What you will be in touch with is the part of yourself—the monster or alternate personality—who is unwilling to be healed, afraid of life after health.

Find out which part of yourself it is and what it's afraid of. What can you do to make it feel safe? What does it need? For your own healing to go forward, you need to heal that inner, obstructive self. What actions can you take? What beliefs can you change? What fears do you need to face?

The feelings that come up can be quite intense. If you find that your feelings are too intense or overwhelming, you might want to talk with a professional counselor or therapist. In such feelings lie the potential for our greatest healing. They are not to be avoided.

Remember, you can stop any of these exercises any time you want. If you get a strong bodily reaction to the question, it doesn't necessarily mean you don't want to be healed. It certainly doesn't mean that you want to die. It means that there's some inner opposition to your healing, some part of you that does not want to be whole. Your healing process can be helped immensely by contacting that particular "monster" and finding out what it wants and needs. Once you confront and deal with this obstacle, it can become one of your strongest healing allies.

Obviously, you can use this same technique with any number of questions to try to see how your unconscious feels about something: "Do you really want this job?" "Do you really want this relationship?" "Do you really want to have a lot of money?" This kind of inner work is important because it is one way to gain access to inner information. We know much more than we think we do. We just have to learn different ways to access the information.

I did this exercise with my client Grace, the adoptee who re-experienced and changed her own birth scenario. I took her through a brief relaxation and then asked the question: "Do you want to be healed?" Grace immediately burst into tears. I let her cry as long as she wanted. In fact I urged her to let the feelings out, not to hold back. Whatever the source of the tears, they needed to be released.

After Grace stopped crying, I asked her where the feeling of sadness came from in her body. She said it came from her heart. I asked her to imagine going to her heart. (Some individuals will experience parts of their body in a relatively anatomically correct form, while others will have a more symbolic or metaphorical image. The image that arises spontaneously is the best one.) Grace's heart was partly realistic and partly metaphorical. It looked like a regular heart, but it had a door.

I suggested that Grace enter her heart through the door, but she was too frightened. I urged her to open the door, telling her that her healing lay in her heart. (This is where courage comes in. I don't know if Grace would have gone into her heart without my urging. If you find yourself frightened in this exercise you can choose to proceed, even though you're afraid, or stop the exercise and go back another time. In some cases I will stop the exercise myself. As a counselor, I have to respect my clients' fears even as we work together to overcome them. While I *will* try to persuade people to take actions that are frightening to them, I will not try to force them. The inner battle can be engaged at another time.)

Grace did finally open the door and go into her heart. Inside she found an extremely angry and ugly woman. She wanted to turn around and run out as fast as she could. I urged her to stay. The woman screamed at Grace almost incoherently. I encouraged Grace to talk to the woman, to try to calm her down and reassure her. Behind such anger you will almost always find fear.

The anger began to subside, and the fear began to emerge. The ugly woman was like a frightened caged animal. She didn't trust anyone; she wouldn't let anyone get near her. She knew how ugly she was, and she rejected all others so that they would have no opportunity to reject her. I told Grace to ask the woman if she would allow Grace to return again and speak with her. The woman fearfully and hesitantly agreed to another visit, and Grace left.

Grace had enough information to work on for the moment. My job is to help individuals find out what work they need to do, not to do it for them. I knew that the healing of this angry, frightened, ugly woman was going to take some time, and Grace was going to have to do it on her own.

I told Grace she would need to go back and visit this woman, perhaps many times, and begin to establish a relationship, begin to develop some trust between them. Grace was the only one who could heal the ugly woman and whatever she might represent.

Grace accepted the fact that this ugly woman represented some part of herself, but with as much reluctance as I at first accepted my dream shadow, Bob One. It was hard for Grace to believe that such an ugly self resided in her heart. At the same time she recalled that her older brother's nickname for her was "Ugly." Grace is a very attractive woman and had been a pretty girl; remember, we are not dealing with truths but beliefs.

The ugly self also explained many of Grace's painful experiences growing up, as evidenced by her dream about Karen and caring. No wonder she believed that her friends didn't care about her. How could anyone care about someone who was so ugly? This belief in her basic ugliness also interfered with her physical healing.

Grace *did* return to the ugly woman in her heart many times and eventually transformed her and was herself transformed. Each time Grace entered her heart, she would hold the ugly woman, talk to her, and tell her she loved her. In Grace's words, this is what eventually happened: "I was able to recognize that the ugly self was not ugly at all. She had become ugly after years and years of me denying my fear of being that ugly person. She didn't represent my ugly self. She represented the fact that I believed I was ugly."

Grace eventually saw the woman in her heart as beautiful, and the two of them danced together and celebrated. This represented a significant healing in Grace's life, in her body, and her relationships. The task was not yet done, though.

The ugly woman represented protection, a significant monster-pet. Grace's life metaphor, triggered by the "rejection" by her birth mother, was that something was wrong with her. Transforming the ugly woman meant removing that protection. To Grace, the expectation of rejection by others represented a kind of safety, a sense of control: "I know I'm going to be rejected because something's wrong with me. I'm ugly. I will avoid rejection by keeping people at a distance." The last thing Grace wanted to do was let someone into her heart. Look what they would find!

Transforming the ugly woman into a beautiful woman is only the first step. Grace must find the courage to accept that new image as a truth about her, to expand into it, to live it on a daily basis. She must allow her former image to be shattered. The new, beautiful self must go into the world with her heart open. She must risk the very thing that Grace has spent her entire life avoiding, the possibility that when you allow people to get close to you they may reject you.

Grace is involved in that ongoing healing process. And healing *is* a process, a way of being in the world on a daily basis. Perhaps our illness evolved in a matter of a few months or a few years; the AIDS virus can incubate for at least ten years. But the *reason* for any illness, its underlying *purpose*, comes from a lifetime of acting on certain assumptions, of believing in a self and a world that are no more than thought fabrications.

An illness may be cured with a pill, a ray, or a knife. Or it might be cured with more unconventional means. A life, however, can only be healed from the inside out. A life is healed *only in the transformation of the self* and the resultant transformation of your personal world.

"Do you want to be healed?" Only you can answer that question. If you can honestly answer it affirmatively, you will remove any healing-suppression devices and open the way for the Spirit to perform its healing work.

11

Some Healing Techniques

There is a wide variety of healing techniques and modalities, from mainstream medical interventions to holistic healing, to religious or spiritual methods such as faith or psychic healing. All of these modalities address symptoms. Holistic healing tries to address more than the immediate symptoms by looking at diet and other lifestyle issues. A truly holistic approach to healing would also take into account our religious/spiritual life and emotional life, our work life, family life and other relationships, issues with finances, with sexuality, and all the other factors that affect our physical, emotional, material, and spiritual well-being.

Our thought diet, the food for thought we take in and the thoughts we put out, is more important than the food we eat or other lifestyle issues. Healing an illness, in the most holistic sense, means healing the thoughts and feelings that created it. Healing your body and healing your life are the same thing. The healing techniques that are most effective in this regard are those that lead to healthy changes in your thoughts, feelings, and attitudes.

I see all healing techniques and modalities as focusing agents. When you become ill, especially if the illness is serious, suddenly a great deal of your time, energy, and attention is directed toward your illness. The energy is mostly emotional energy, although physical energy is often involved. The illness has become a focusing agent, centering your attention on the problem. Healing interventions, whether surgery or a prayer circle, focus an individual's energy and attention on healing. It is not the healing technique that heals. The individual, focusing his or her thoughts and feelings, hope and healing intentions on a healing outcome, cooperates with the body's natural healing abilities.

I realize that theory may seem quite radical to many. I don't expect every reader to be able to come all the way with me. I *do* want you to recognize that your thoughts, feelings, and intentions are more important than any physical healing method. Because of that, however, your choice of healing method is very important. You need to follow a course that most fits what you *believe* will work. For most in Western society, that means mainstream medical intervention.

None of the techniques in this book, or any other healing techniques, should take the place of proper medical intervention. Alternate healing modalities, however, can be used to supplement or augment medical intervention. When medical intervention has done all it can do, other techniques may still be effective in the healing process.

Through my own studies and the work I have done with individual clients and in groups (as well as my own self-healing work), I have developed a number of healing techniques that may be helpful to you. You will find some of these in the second part of this chapter. First, I want to look at a number of different healing approaches or healing attitudes.

It is impossible for an illness not to be a focusing agent for us. Even the smallest injury or physical symptom attracts our attention, and we spend time, emotional energy, and thought energy on the problem. There is a point of diminishing returns, however, and that energy focus can begin to feed the illness, contributing to *its* "health" and longevity. Whatever healing process we may be involved in, it is important to invest time, emotional energy, and attention in the desired outcome, the healed self.

The Yin and Yang of Healing

There is some debate in the alternative or holistic healing community as to whether it is better to pursue more aggressive or more receptive healing techniques. I call them *yin* and *yang* healing approaches, respectively. In Chinese philosophy, *yin* is the feminine, dark, receptive force in nature, while *yang* is the masculine, light, aggressive force. In traditional Chinese medicine, illness is believed to be the result of imbalance between an individual's yin and yang. Healing results when those forces are brought back into harmony in the individual.

The yang methods pioneered by the Simontons in the 1970s have been criticized for their violence. Cancer patients were encouraged to visualize symbolic representations of their white blood cells fighting and killing symbols representing the cancer cells. The patients chose their own images. The fact is, the Simontons' methods were successful in prolonging the lives of their patients. Their methods worked, like the Senoi teaching their children to face, fight, and even kill their nightmare figures. But is the violence necessary? Stephen Levine, for example, believes in a more yin approach: " . . . when people can fight their illness, it becomes 'me' against 'my illness.' It becomes separation and anxiety. Our sense is that when you touch that which is in pain with mercy and awareness, there's healing. Where there's awareness, there's healing."[1]

Levine uses meditation as a primary healing tool, including certain guided meditations he has created. He feels that doctors who single out their successful patients as "superstars" or "exceptional patients" create a framework in which others are looked upon as failures, "second-stringers," or "losers."[2]

First of all, a distinction must be made between an individual's attitude toward his or her prognosis and toward the illness itself. Many of those who are successful in healing their illness fight against the prognosis, against the death sentence handed them. If you yield to the prognosis, if you accept the statistical percentages as authoritative, if you accept the illness as something out of your control, you have less power with which to heal yourself.

Not only have studies revealed cancer "personalities," those prone to the disease because of suppression of feelings and suppression of the self, but also profiles of those who are more successful in curing their disease or prolonging their lives. These patients *do* fight. They *do* question. They do not give their power over to a physician or a statistic but involve themselves in the healing process.

When Julie was diagnosed with breast cancer, she quit her job and left her marriage. Had she honored her feelings earlier and acted on them, the cancer and the operation might not have been necessary. While aggression or violent images may not be required in healing your illness, taking your power back and acting from that power *is*.

Patsy Robinson, one of the founders of the Center for Attitudinal Healing in Sausalito, California, tells about Joe Bauer, one of their group members: "I remember the first night that Joe came to our meeting. He said that he had recently gone to a physician who diagnosed him as having an inoperable brain tumor. Joe's doctor told him he had only

about two months to live. When Joe heard this, he told us, 'I
fired him. I did not want to go to a doctor with that little
optimism.'

Joe lived for another three years."[3]

The Institute of Noetic Sciences was founded by astro-
naut Edgar Mitchell in 1973; its purpose is "to scientifically
research the nature and potentials of the mind and spirit,
and apply that knowledge to the advancement of health
and well-being for humankind and our planet."[4] Toward
that end, the Institute funds research and gathers scientists
and scholars together to share methods and information.

Among other things, the Institute is studying so-called
spontaneous remissions in all diseases, a subject which has
been mostly overlooked in the past. If we can get some idea
of what people who go into spontaneous remission are like,
what qualities they may have in common, it may help us in
our search for helpful healing modalities. The Institute's
database on spontaneous remission is the largest in the
country.

The following story, like that of Joe Bauer above, illustrates at least one strong characteristic of survivors. Twenty-
five individuals who had survived a "terminal" illness were
interviewed by a doctoral student in Moscow, Idaho. Many
of the respondents were farmers' wives. One woman was
asked how she felt about the doctor's prognosis that she had
a terminal illness and would be dead in six months: "That
was *his* opinion," was the reply. The interviewer said,
"Would you like to say more about that?" She said, "Well,
you know we're told all these things by all these experts. We
live on a farm, and all these federal people come in and they
look at the soil and they tell us that nothing will grow and
we should put these fertilizers in and we should do all this
stuff. We don't do it and hell, things grow there anyway. So
why should I listen to an expert?"[5]

As Brendan O'Regan, former vice president for research
at the Institute, writes, "I'm not saying to ignore your physi-

cian, but I'm saying that people of an independent mind and spirit seem to be people who have a better prognosis in these matters."[6]

A friend of mine who was a hospital chaplain's intern told me about two women who were friends and were both diagnosed with uterine cancer at about the same time. One woman had an early case and was told she had a very good chance for a cure. The other woman, however, had an advanced case, and her prognosis was poor.

The woman whose cancer had been detected early was terrified by the possibility that she might die from her cancer, in spite of her doctor's assurances that her odds were very good. The other woman, however, refused to accept the negative prognosis. Their bodies, obedient to their minds and their beliefs, followed the expected course. The woman with the early case soon died, and the woman with the advanced disease survived.

As for doing battle with the disease itself, I think it's necessary to recognize the uniqueness and individuality of each patient. The same techniques will *not* work for everyone. Jodi, a woman who had breast cancer, came to me for counseling. She decided to do a healing ritual on her own. She performed a ritual cleansing and set out candles, incense, and various artifacts, mostly Native American. She played special music. She chanted, drummed, prayed, and meditated. Her ritual could be seen as an active or yang approach to healing, but it also involved the yin aspects of prayer and meditation. Most effective healing probably involves both elements.

At some point in her ritual a black, jelly-like substance began to ooze from the incision where the biopsy had been taken. A fair amount of this substance was ejected. The tumor was gone, and no operation was necessary.

Several years later, Jodi came to see me again. Her cancer had returned. A relapse can be more devastating than the original diagnosis. The feeling of elation over your remission is long gone, and the return of what you thought you had overcome for good can be very discouraging.

After we talked about the situation, she decided that she needed to approach it differently this time. The first time she had approached her healing in a mostly yang or aggressive way. This time she decided to heal herself in a yin or receptive way by accepting the cancer and allowing it to leave her body. She was still doing well when I saw her again many years later.

A person who is normally aggressive and angry might need to learn a more yin way of approaching healing, to learn patience, acceptance, and peace. A person who is normally passive or quiet might need to engage his or her illness in a more active and aggressive way.

Varieties of Healing Techniques

Body Healing Techniques. It's beyond the intent of this book and my expertise to go into body techniques or therapies. There are many things you can do for your body, either by going to a professional or doing things on your own. Osteopathy, chiropractic, massage, acupuncture or acupressure, yoga, stretching, breath work, or any of the many body-work treatments or body-energy techniques can be helpful in a total healing regimen.

Exercise, including walking, biking, or swimming, and healthy eating habits can all add to a healthy lifestyle. As far as physical healing is concerned, giving and receiving lots of hugs is probably one of the most beneficial things you can do for your body, regardless of what physical problems you may have. In fact it's a good disease preventive as well. We now know that infants cannot physically survive without human touch. Regardless of the meaning of your illness, doing good things for your body can help create a healing focus.

External Healing Techniques. These include writing exercises such as I've suggested throughout this book, the use of affirmations and other forms of positive suggestion, and self-hypnosis. External techniques also include painting, drawing, collage, and other arts, such as sculpting. Not only are drawing and painting useful dreamwork techniques, they are an excellent means of bringing what is inside, out. A drawing or painting is a like a frozen dream.

Dr. Bernie Siegel is a popular writer and speaker on alternative attitudes in medicine and founder of ECap (exceptional cancer patients), which offers individual and group therapy for patients with life-threatening illnesses. Siegel sometimes uses his patients' drawings to help with their prognosis, but also to get a sense of how patients perceive their doctors and/or their treatment. Siegel recognizes that patients with negative attitudes toward their doctors or treatment are going to have a rough time, unless they either change their attitudes or change doctors and/or treatment.[7]

The Center for Attitudinal Healing, mentioned before in the Joe Bauer story, utilizes drawings, with children especially, as a means of expressing their feelings about their life-threatening illness and treatment. Drawings can be used in a manner similar to my symbol transformation or rescripting dreamwork techniques. Children draw an image of their illness or their feelings about the illness. They then draw a second picture, or add to the first one, a representation of the healing of the illness or the feelings. It's an important part of the attitudinal healing process.

Drawing and journal-writing are therapeutic ways of dialoguing with the self, of putting aspects of the inner self where you can see them and interact with them. I recommend them as an ongoing part of living the healing life. Your illness is the result of thoughts and feelings you may not have been aware of. These techniques can help bring those thoughts and feelings into consciousness.

Internal Healing Techniques. These include techniques like visualization, feeling exercises, meditation, and prayer.

Affirmations can be included in this category because they can be said silently in a meditation. However, affirmations can also be spoken aloud or written down where they can be seen during the day. Affirmations and visualizations are helpful for changing the thoughts that built the disease in the first place.

The Cayce readings are sprinkled with affirmations, a common focusing technique given for physical and emotional healing, as well as for spiritual growth. One series of readings resulted in the *Search for God* books, numbers one and two. These books contain a series of lessons to be followed by study groups; each lesson has an affirmation.

A recent book by Jerry Jampolsky and Diane Cirincione, *Change Your Mind, Change Your Life*, has affirmations at the ends of some of the chapters. The book also lists twelve principles of attitudinal healing that can be used as affirmations, as can the eighteen weekly attitudinal healing lessons in the back of the book.[8]

Of course, I recommend that you create your own affirmations based on the information you have gained about your own issues.

Writing Exercises for Healing

Success Journal. Bragging is considered to be in bad taste in our culture. Humility is a virtue. Bad news and misfortune are more acceptable topics of conversation than successes.

When you begin to pay attention to your thoughts, feelings, and conversations, you might be surprised to find out how much of your time is spent in thinking and talking about what's wrong: wrong with you, wrong with your family and friends, and wrong with the world. It's understandable that our problems attract our attention and emotional energy, but that focus also gives us a distorted picture of the world and of ourselves.

One way to improve your life almost immediately is to begin paying more attention to the positive experiences in your life. Your life, right now, may be better than you think.

In order to speed or acknowledge this change, begin to write down your positive experiences, your daily successes. This should be a high-priority item in your healing journal. By consciously focusing on the positive experiences in your life, however small, you can begin to get a different impression of what your life is really like. If focusing on problems is a habit, you can create a new and healthier habit. You might even begin bragging to your friends, sharing your successes. If a family member or friend starts talking about woes, you might shake him or her up a bit by asking if anything good has happened recently.

You create *more* of what you focus on, what you give time and energy to. As you focus more and more on what's right, what's good, what's positive in your life, more will come to you.

The Universal Times. The *Universal Times* is an imaginary newspaper I invented some years ago. It's based on the idea that we are constantly putting out our thoughts and feelings and constantly receiving the thoughts and feelings of others. You could consider it the news organ of Carl Jung's collective unconscious. The *Universal Times* is a symbolic representation of the telepathic communication that constantly goes on among all of us at an unconscious level. As such, it is a "paper" that everyone in the world "reads" every day. It represents a way of concretizing the principles of "mind is the builder" and "thoughts are things." For example, if you're having a bad day, being abused by the world at large, you may have an "ad" in the *Universal Times* that says, "Kick me." If you have fears, they're right there in the *Times.* They may be shouted in a headline or whispered on the back page. All of your thoughts and feelings are in the *Times* for everyone to read.

The *Times* isn't just a passive vehicle, a tattler telling all your secrets to the world. It's also something you can use actively to make changes in your life. Is there something you want to create in your life? Put a want ad in the *Times.* You can use the *Times* to project a positive future. For example, you might create an imaginary headline that reads, "San Francisco Man Miraculously Healed!" You can create your own headlines, your own stories, your own ads. Writing down what you want makes it more real. Because everyone reads the *Universal Times,* others will cooperate with the changes you wish to make.

Forms.   We live in the information age. It could be called the age of forms. You can create forms as a way of focusing your desires and intentions and making life changes. Visualize the desired form and what it says, as a meditation, or create it in your journal. I think the more concrete journal technique is more effective.

Identification Form: Create and fill out an identification form to describe the new you, the self you are becoming. List all of the important qualities and characteristics of your emerging self. Don't be shy or overly humble. Don't just write down a physical description of the healed self; give personality characteristics, abilities, and attitudes. You might want to give a secret or inner name to this new identity.

Résumé: To go along with your new identity, you might want to upgrade your résumé. Don't just list your accomplishments and qualifications from the past but things you intend to accomplish in the future. Think of it as your idea résumé. It needn't be aimed at securing a particular job. It's more a statement of your qualifications for being in the world.

Requisition Form: Is there something you want to create in your life? You can put an ad in the *Times,* or you can create and fill out a requisition form. Requisition forms are great! Write down what you want and forget about it. Trust the universe to provide.

Wish List/Shopping List/Treasure Map: For those of

you who want a lot of things, the requisition form method may be too cumbersome. You can simply make a wish list or shopping list of what you want. You could also make a treasure map, which can simply be a collage of things you want to have or do within a certain time period—the next year, for example.

A minister friend did a treasure-map collage and put it in his closet. About a year later, he ran across it and found that everything on it had been materialized in his life except one thing. (OK, the one thing was skydiving.)

You can approach forms in a yin or yang manner. You can energize your desires by going over your lists or looking at your treasure map every day—yang—or you can put them away and trust that they will be manifested—yin. Do what seems best to you. Try both ways.

The Shredder or Incinerator Form:　Old attitudes and beliefs that just aren't working any more really need to be destroyed. This form is a request to have something sent to the shredder or incinerator. Just write down what it is you don't need any more—a habit, belief, attitude, or fear. It will be destroyed, and you can forget about it.

Contracts:　Sometimes our present difficulties are due to contracts we made as children, often with our parents, but sometimes with God. These were one-sided contracts, because the second party wasn't aware of it and didn't agree to it. A contract with a parent might be, "If you'll love me, I promise not to surpass you," or "I'll be unhappy because you were unhappy."

Grace had made a contract with God when she was a little girl. She couldn't find her Barbie doll anywhere, so in frustration she finally prayed to God and told Him if He would help her find the doll she would never sin again. Immediately after praying for help she found her doll. It was in plain sight. Too late, the little girl realized she had made an impossible deal. She decided that God hadn't really found the doll for her, since it had been there all the time.

Years later, however, Grace was struggling with her spiritual growth. We decided to visit her inner child in a visualization and ask what she thought about spiritual growth. Because spiritual growth to her meant getting closer to God, the little girl was afraid that if she got closer to God, He would whack her because she broke the contract (repeatedly).

I'm not suggesting that the incident caused her problem with spiritual growth. Grace may have chosen spiritual growth as a life issue or challenge before she was born. The incident with the doll became a life metaphor, the trigger for that issue. The same issue came up in other experiences at other ages. For example, as a teenager she had prayed to God to let her die because of ongoing physical and sexual abuse. Because God did not kill her, she became angry at God. Both anger and fear became blocks to her spiritual growth.

If we can uncover some of our old contracts, we can break them. We can write them down and then ritually burn them. We can also, however, create new contracts, deals with ourselves about the wonderful things we intend to do for our bodies and our lives. Write a contract which lists a number of specific things you intend to do to bring more pleasure into your life, some specific healing actions you will do on a daily or weekly basis. Keep track of your success in honoring the contract and write that in your journal as well.

Pink Slips: It may be necessary to fire some of your personalities, those who are not helping with your healing process. In firing them you will have to take on the job you gave them, take back whatever fears and doubts they are acting out for you. You can ease their burden by promising some kind of retraining program. There's no reason why a former shadow can't perform some very positive and useful function once you've taken their formerly protective, now obstructive, job away.

Cancellation Form: This form can be used to cancel old contracts that are harmful to you or can be used like the pink slip. I like to think of it as an energy cancellation form.

If you're aware that your energy is going into a certain fear or you find yourself worrying a lot about something, create a cancellation form in which you essentially say, "I don't need that worry or fear any more. Please cancel my original order." Use it to cancel a bad habit.

You can even cancel your illness. Write in your journal that you appreciate what the illness has taught you and that you are already acting on its lessons. You now cancel it and give the illness permission to leave. Request that the resources formerly being used to maintain the illness now be channeled into its healing.

Dream Request Form: You can use this form to program for a special dream. Be as specific in your request as possible. These forms work best when put under your pillow.

Job Description: You can use this to describe your new "job" in life, the way you want your life to be after you have healed your body. How will the healed self be different from the dis-eased self? You can also use this form as a request for personnel. If you need a particular type of guide or helper, you can describe your needs on this form and "send" it to Personnel. They can put a help-wanted ad in the *Universal Times* for you.

Use this technique to create a helpful personality, subpersonality, or aspect of yourself who has qualities you wish to develop. Remember that you have a huge pool of personality characteristics, abilities, and qualities to draw from. Be specific about what you want. Watch for this character to show up in your dreams or meditations. (For example, you can create an inner personal physician, as suggested under *Parallel Processing* later in this chapter.)

Special Degrees and Awards: Give yourself a diploma! Unfortunately, our culture tends to value us for what we do, produce, or accumulate. Living the healing life means loving and accepting ourselves and others just for *being*. We are all experts and authorities on our own lives, and we

FREE *CATALOG OF BOOKS* AND *MEMBERSHIP ACTIVITIES*

Fill-in and mail this postage-paid card today.

Please write clearly

Name: _____

Address: _____

City: _____

State/Province: _____

Postal/Zip Code: _____ Country: _____

358-9
1/99

Association for Research and Enlightenment, Inc.
215 67th Street
Virginia Beach, VA 23451-2061

For Faster Service call 1-800-723-1112
www.are-cayce.com

should have the "sheepskin" to prove it.

Regardless of educational achievement, income, or any other external yardstick, there is one degree that everyone is born with, and it's the only one that really matters. I call it the "I AM" degree. Create an I AM degree for yourself, the degree that's named after God. It's really the only diploma you'll ever need. It gives you the rights, privileges, and responsibilities inherent in being a spirit.

If anyone asks you what degree you have, you can tell them you have an I AM from the Universal University. Put a story in the *Times* about your graduation, and be sure to mention the various honors bestowed upon you. If there are specific abilities or qualities you wish to develop, create a degree stating that you have those qualities. Put it in a frame and hang it on your wall.

Give yourself awards for any successes you have with your healing. Buy a trophy or award yourself in a more substantial way by going out to dinner or giving yourself some other special treat.

Obviously there are all sorts of forms that can be devised to help focus your energy in a healing direction. Be creative, and let me know of your successes.

Visualization Exercises

Shapechanging. Multiple personalities, stigmatics, and the others discussed in chapter 3 demonstrate the amazing plasticity of the human body. As a fan of science fiction and fantasy, I am fascinated by such magical abilities as shapechanging or shapeshifting. One day I decided to try shapechanging in order to lose some weight. It seemed the quickest route to take, and I am sometimes guilty of impatience.

I lay down on my bed, took a few deep breaths, and relaxed my body. I then spent a few minutes—probably no more than ten—imagining that I had the power of shapechanging. I imagined using my power to change the shape of my body, not into that of another person or creature, but just into a slimmer version of myself.

The exercise was fun and relaxing. I then left my apartment to walk to town. As soon as I left, a friend of mine from a nearby town drove by and saw me. She stopped her car and parked it, and we went back to my apartment to talk.

The whole time she was there, she kept remarking on how good I looked and how much weight I had lost. She was genuinely surprised and impressed. As soon as she left, I had to run into the bathroom and weigh myself. I found, to my great disappointment, that I hadn't lost any weight at all! (I believe I *could* have changed my shape and lost weight instantly if my belief had been strong enough.) Nonetheless, I was very impressed by the effect *my* fantasy had on *her!* It was a powerful example of how our thoughts influence not only ourselves but others as well.

By using the shapechanging exercise, along with other techniques, including exercise and changing my beliefs, I *did* lose weight. The shapechanging exercise is very helpful in focusing your intent on a specific outcome. When you're successful, you can change the way you feel about yourself as well as get more positive feedback from others, as I did.

Exercise: Shapechanging

Get yourself into a relaxed and receptive state. Determine ahead of time what you want to do. If you have a serious illness, you can use this exercise to experience yourself as being disease-free. Shapechanging can remove or diminish pain for as long as you maintain your changed self. If you have a tumor, you can shapechange into a version of yourself who does *not* have the tumor.

First, imagine yourself to be a magical being who has the power of shapechanging. This magical character can be useful for many different things so take your time and create this version of yourself as vividly as possible. Visualize yourself wearing special clothing and carrying magical implements such as a wand, staff, or crystal ball.

Once you have become the shapechanger, begin the process of changing your body. Simply focus on the end result. Imagine yourself to be disease-free. Feel the change happening in your body. Once the exercise is over, remind yourself throughout the day that you have changed your body. Allow others to respond to the change.

Repeat the exercise as needed. This can be a powerful healer to the extent that you are increasingly able to accept the shapechanged self—the healed self—as real. The trick is to believe more in the healed self than in the diseased self. Pay attention to the feedback you get from others, especially in the first hour or so after you do the exercise.

Journey to a Cell.   It's helpful, in working with an illness, to get some sense of the resources available to you. In this exercise you will visit a single cell in your body to discover how much and what kinds of energy might be available to you in your body's cells.

I've done this exercise a number of times on my own and in the Mind Development group. It has always been a great energizer. The first time I did the exercise, I was surprised to see that my cells had attitudes quite different from my own. When I first imaginatively looked at a wall of cells inside my body, they were glowing with energy and were continuously "singing." I saw a cell dividing, and when it was finished all of the neighboring cells cheered. Then I saw a cell's light go out, the cell apparently dying. All of the other cells cheered again!

When I entered a single cell in the exercise I was amazed, not only by how much energy I felt in that one cell, but also by how much love was present. I felt more love in that one cell than I experienced in the rest of my life at that time.

Exercise: Visit to a Cell

Get comfortable and relax. When you're ready, you will imagine yourself as a point of consciousness, separate from your body, that is very tiny and capable of entering the body at any point. Once you're inside the body, find an organ or tissue that will present you with a wall of cells. Find healthy cells this first time.

At first the cells will seem to be the size of a large honeycomb. As you continue to get smaller and the cells appear to get larger, pay attention to what the cells are like, how they look and feel. Finally, you will be small enough to travel inside one of the cells. You have the capability of passing through the cell membrane. Do so when you're ready.

You can explore the cell as fully as you like. The most important thing, however, is to experience the feeling of the cell itself. Feel its energy. Try to get some sense of its feelings, attitudes, and even desires. You might even dialogue with the cell. You may receive some healing information.

At another time you can enter a diseased portion of your body. If you have a tumor or virus, you can enter them and see what *they* feel like. You already know how you feel about them. See if there's something you can do for them. See if you can find out what they're doing for you. You may be able to do some healing work by praying for the diseased cells, sending healing energy to them, laying your hands on them, or perhaps just giving them permission to leave your body.

You can also enter any organ or body part that's affected, as Grace entered her heart. You may have a more or less anatomically correct experience or a more symbolic one. See what's in that part of your body, and again see what is needed. What can you do for your diseased organ or body part? What is it doing for you? Use your imagination, and do any repair work that seems needed.

Parallel Processing. I've already mentioned that those

with MPD sometimes heal more quickly and may age more slowly than the general population. One multiple named Cassandra provided a possible answer to this mystery. Since some "multiples" are still aware even when they're not "running" the body, they can be busy doing other things.

This allows Cassandra "to 'think' on a multitude of different channels at once, to do things like work on several different term papers simultaneously, and even 'sleep' while other personalities prepare her dinner and clean her house."[9]

"[Cassandra] even has a subpersonality named Celese who possesses a thorough knowledge of anatomy and physiology, and whose sole function is to spend twenty-four hours a day meditating and imaging the body's well-being."[10] I decided it would be very advantageous to have someone working on my health (or anything else I needed to work on) twenty-four hours a day. I did the following exercise and got in touch with my personal physician. I was pleasantly surprised when I didn't get one that I expected.

I thought I would get a healer like the god Asklepios because of my interest in dreams, or possibly Paian, healer to the gods. Instead I got the name of a physician I had heard of before but with whom I wasn't familiar—Galen. Imagine my surprise when I found that Galen was a Greek physician who had practiced in the second century A.D. Furthermore, he had worked with dreams and visualizations. He believed in the meaning of illnesses. This points again to the Divine speaking to us when we allow it and take the time to listen.

I have used this exercise with individuals and in groups. The results, as expected, have varied with the time and energy individuals are willing to put into the creation and maintenance of the relationship.

Exercise: Meeting Your Inner Physician

In this exercise you will create (or discover) a healing personality, a personal physician or healer who will work on your healing twenty-four hours a day. She or he will give you reports on your progress and give you healing suggestions any time you wish to check in.

Get in a relaxed state with your intention clearly in mind. You may wish to go to a special place, a healing temple or shrine or a holy place in nature. Allow an individual to appear in your mind's eye. Don't reject whatever you get. You may even get an animal. Ask your healer if he or she is willing to perform healing functions for you. Proceed if the person or animal agrees.

In this first meeting you can get acquainted and see if your healer has some advice or information for you. The value of the healer grows as you talk and develop the relationship. Write down your interactions and conversations in your healing journal.

In the future you can interact with your inner physician in visualizations or in writing, whatever is easiest and most effective for you. If you receive specific advice, try to follow it if it seems helpful. Sometimes your physician will do something directly to your body during your visualization. Try to be receptive to such inner interventions.

Yin Healing. The next exercise is a visualization that can also be done as a daily affirmation. It's based on the idea that your illness is not evil, but is simply a bearer of messages, of information about what's going on in your head. Don't shoot the messenger!

In this yin healing exercise, you simply use your illness as a focusing agent for loving yourself and for releasing the illness.

Exercise: A Yin Healing Exercise

There are two parts to the exercise: loving and releasing. In the first part, you will choose whether to focus on the illness itself or the affected body part. Get into a relaxed state, and try to visualize the disease or body part. If you're focusing on the disease itself, let a symbol or image appear that represents the disease. This representation can, in itself, be very revealing and healing.

Once you have an image of the organ or body part, or a symbol in your mind, reach deep within yourself and try to find your ability to love the disease. Affirm it as a messenger, thank it for the message, and imagine pouring love into it. You might visualize this process by making the love into white light or some other color or form of energy.

In the second part, which can be done at a different time, practice releasing your disease. Visualize your illness as before, or simply feel it in your body. The disease is there because you're holding it, keeping it there. Imagine simply letting it go. Instead of feeling the illness *in* your body, feel it flowing *through* your body, and out. You can imagine it flowing out the bottom of your feet or the top of your head, or it may dissipate out through every cell in your skin. You may feel a physiological change as you do this.

If this feels helpful, continue as long as needed. During the day you can also send love to your disease and perhaps think of an affirmation for loving and releasing it. I'm not saying that this exercise will cure cancer or any other serious illness, but it can contribute to the healing process. I have successfully used this technique to prevent simple illnesses or headaches from taking hold. When I feel the symptoms of the flu beginning, instead of resisting them and tightening my body against them, I relax, acknowledge the feelings of impending disease or headache, and imagine the disease and its symptoms flowing through my body and out again. It's usually very effective.

Path Work

Path work can involve writing, visualization, dreamwork, affirmations, and other waking work. It can be quite complex, but I will lay out the basics as simply as possible. You can be creative with this information and find what works best for you.

If we turn around from where we're standing right now and look into our past, we will see that we have followed a certain path. We have taken many turns, run into some obstacles, climbed a few hills or mountains, and forded streams and rivers. We can see how certain decisions or actions led us down one fork rather than another. We went to one school rather than another, took this job rather than that, married this individual rather than another.

It is clear that our path would look different if we had made other choices. In some cases it might be *very* different. The choices we made along the way were based on our perceptions of ourselves and others, based on our values, what we thought was best. Sometimes we faced choices that were difficult, in which one direction led to greater risk and possibly greater reward while the other choice represented more security at the price of a lesser reward.

All of those choices led up to our present situation, to the person we are today. Many paths were taken without much thought, as we allowed ourselves to be moved by circumstances. The more we allowed other people and external circumstances to choose our path for us, the less capable we felt of making our own choices or the more difficult it became to make decisions in opposition to those other voices.

Look back on some of the significant choices in your life, such as educational, career, or relationship decisions, and ask yourself what might have happened if you had chosen differently. You can imaginatively follow a path-not-taken and find out what that version of yourself might be like today. You can dialogue with this alternate self and see what you can learn, what attitudes, abilities, and other gifts this self might have to share with you.

While it's easy to see that we have followed a certain path which led us to the present moment, we have a tendency to see the path into the future as a kind of blank. Yes, we have certain expectations about what might happen in the next week, month, or year. We might have some idea of where we'll be living five years from now, whether we'll be in the same house or city, etc.

Still, the future seems to be something determined by the choices we make every day as well as by people, things, and experiences that impinge on us, including natural and world events. Those of you with life-threatening illnesses know that life can take sharp and unexpected turns at times.

Because you, the chooser, operate on a whole complex of attitudes, beliefs, expectations, and feelings, your future path is more fixed than you might expect. Unless we change our thoughts and remove our Spirit-suppression devices, our life tomorrow will be pretty much the same as it is today. We'll just be a day older.

One way to visualize this process is to imagine yourself as a searchlight or movie projector. As a searchlight, you are illuminating your future path according to your present thoughts and feelings. You only see the path that your mind is building. Other perfectly legitimate and possibly more positive paths may lie just to either side of the path you are lighting, but you can't see them.

As a movie projector, you are watching a screen showing the ever-popular *This Is Your Life*. But you're not just watching it, you're creating it and projecting it onto the screen. The movie onscreen—the outer world—isn't going to change until you change the film—the inner world, your thoughts and feelings. It's going to be a life of reruns until you make a new movie.

There are a number of different metaphors for path making that I use. Use the one that feels right for you, or combine them as I do.

The Compass. This can be done as a visualization and also as a reminder during the day to get yourself back on course. In this metaphor Spirit is magnetic north. Your highest potential for healing and spiritual growth is magnetic north. You are the compass.

Your needle *wants* to go to magnetic north, to live with Spirit unsuppressed, because of the bias of creation. With our free will, however, we are capable of pointing that needle in any direction. Our thoughts and beliefs determine the direction of the needle. It should be clear in this metaphor that it takes energy to get off the path of Spirit.

Exercise: The Compass

Get into a relaxed state. Imagine that you are a compass. Visualize the face of the compass, and see if you can find which direction the needle is pointing. You might at least get some idea how far off from north you are. This is primarily a feeling experience, a yin exercise.

Feel your body as the compass. Feel what it's like to be pointing away from your greatest potential, from your ideal self. What emotions are you experiencing? Now imagine you are able to release the needle. Just let it go. Imagine it swinging wildly as it seeks a new resting place. Allow yourself to relax, to release your suppression devices so completely that the needle is able to point to north.

If you are able to get the needle pointing to north, which might say "God" or "Spirit" on the compass, simply allow yourself to feel the sensation. Remember, *if you can feel what it feels like to be healed, you can be healed!* Stay with the feeling as long as possible.

If you are unsuccessful after a few minutes, don't work too hard. Don't try to force it. Come back another time and try again.

If you were able to get the needle to point north, you can use the metaphor during the day. When you're feeling harassed and harried, off course in any way, call up the image of the needle and let it return to magnetic north.

Path as Prophecy. The compass stays in the present and gives you a feeling about whether you're going in the right direction. Another way of getting to a desired end—such as healing or spiritual growth—is to have a clear image of the desired outcome. The outcome becomes a beacon which draws you. Wherever you are standing, you can see the end of the path. If you can create a picture of the end of the path, you have a much better chance of getting there.

Our beliefs, including our self-image, act as prophecies. We behave according to our thoughts. We expect certain outcomes, consciously or unconsciously. The mind makes prophecies, and they almost always come true. If we don't like what's happening in our life right now, we need a new prophet and some new prophecies.

Exercise: Creating a Prophet and a Prophecy

The prophecy cannot be vague. You must clearly set out your goals, whether short term or long. What exactly do you want awaiting you at the end of your healing path? Remember, it isn't enough just to be symptom free. You want to be healed *for* something. What will the prophet say about your future? How will your life after illness be described?

You can visualize this, but it might be helpful to make a list of what you want to do once you're healthy. Once you have your list completed, see if you can put it in terms of a prophecy. Turn your list into a paragraph describing what's going to happen once you're healed. Use words like "It shall come to pass" or "In those days Bob will . . . " and give the prophecy as much dignity and weight as you can. You might set a date for its fulfillment.

Every prophecy has a prophet. Visualize a meeting with your prophet, just as you met your inner physician. Talk to your prophet about how things stand now. What do you need to do in order to get onto the path of this positive prophecy? Check in with your prophet periodically to see how you're doing and get frequent path-correction advice.

The Future as a Gestalt Personality. Another way the prophecy can help you is in terms of personifying the outcome. The changes you wish to make in your life will make a difference in every area of your life and will affect all of those close to you. There is a "being" who represents your life right now. This being is made up of all of your relationships, all of your activities, and all of your thoughts and feelings, including any thought-monsters that may be around.

It can be thought of as a gestalt consciousness, a combination of consciousnesses and/or personalities which make up one being. If we freeze the movie *This Is Your Life* at any point, we will see a picture of this gestalt consciousness, a personification of all the elements in your life.

The fulfillment of your prophecy represents a new gestalt consciousness, a new personification. There is not just a prophet helping you fulfill your desires; there's a being who represents the prophecy itself. Not only can you call upon your prophet for advice and direction, but you can call upon your positive prophecy itself and give emotional energy and attention to it because *it has as much desire to be as you have desire to create the life it represents.*

This gestalt personality may be more of a spirit than a person, but it might have some form. That's up to you. The advantage of having a prophet with you in the present giving you guidance, and the prophecy in the future beckoning you forward, is that you complete an energy circuit.

Your desires, represented by the prophecy and the prophet, reach toward the future, direct your energy toward a specific outcome. The prophecy itself, as a being representing fulfillment and manifestation, reaches back from the future. *Your desire to create meets the creation's desire to be.* In just such great cooperative ventures are positive futures created.

Please feel free to alter any of these exercises to fit your needs. Some of them may suggest further techniques that you can develop on your own. Allow yourself to get in touch with your great creative self. See your healing process, not as a battle to be fought every day, a struggle to survive, but as a creative challenge, an opportunity to dig down and find resources of strength, courage, and creativity you never knew existed.

Imagine yourself to be in a great cooperative, creative endeavor. All of your experiences and all the people involved in those experiences are cooperating with you in your healing. Look for the healing cooperation in everything that happens to you, even experiences which seem negative, and use everything presented to you as fully as possible.

PART 5

LIVING THE HEALING LIFE

12

Attunement

According to the dictionary, *attune* means "To bring into a harmonious or responsive relationship," or, in reference to music, "To put into correct tune."[1] For our purposes we're going to focus on three levels of attunement: coming into a harmonious relationship with your body, coming into a harmonious relationship with your mind, and coming into a harmonious relationship with your spirit.

Living the healing life doesn't just mean being healthy. It is an ongoing awareness, a healthy way of viewing oneself, others, and the world. It is a healing way of being in the world on a daily basis. An important part of living the healing life is practicing daily attunement.

In music you attune to the correct tone. As the definition suggests, attunement is a relationship. One is harmonious with and responsive to something else. What could represent a healing or harmonious "tone" for us?

A musical tone is a vibration. Ultimately, the most healing tone or vibration would be the First Vibration, the
"sound" of Spirit. Living the healing life means daily attuning to this vibration, to this sound within the self. There is
one tone to attune to. There are, however, a number of levels or gateways to attunement, and each should be explored
and worked with for maximum benefit.

Body Attunement

There are two different aspects of body attunement. One
is the idea of attuning the body to the Divine. The other is a
matter of body awareness or mind/body attunement, consciously being attuned to your own body. In the cell exercise, you attuned to a single cell. Edgar Cayce suggests that
our cells are conscious and each contains the Divine within:
"For all healing, mental or material, is attuning each atom
of the body, each reflex of the brain forces, to the awareness
of the Divine that lies within each atom, each cell of the
body." (3384-2)

In the world of subatomic physics, consciousness is being pushed to even more fundamental levels. Aside from
the fact that photons (light particles) behave sometimes as
particles and sometimes as waves, subatomic particles
seem able to share "information" faster than the speed of
light. Since information, in the form of energy, cannot move
faster than the speed of light, these apparent communications provide a mystery for physicists to solve. Henry Pierce
Stapp suggests that energy is not required to move because
the process of communication exists outside of space-time
and only the results exhibit themselves within space-time.
This led physicist E.H. Walker to speculate that subatomic
particles may be conscious! "Consciousness may be associated with all quantum mechanical processes . . . since everything that occurs is ultimately the result of one or more
quantum mechanical events, the universe is 'inhabited' by

an almost unlimited number of rather discrete conscious, usually nonthinking entities that are responsible for the detailed working of the universe."[2]

Because the body is conscious, aware of itself and its workings, body attunement is a source of ongoing information for the healing and maintenance of the body. The body is sending us messages all the time. Unfortunately, we often do not hear these messages, especially when they're at the whisper stage. The body frequently doesn't get our attention until it shouts at us through some serious malfunction. One benefit of attuning to your body is increased sensitivity to body whispers.

Body messages sometimes come in dreams, where we can get specific dietary suggestions as well as suggestions for specific physical exercises. Pay attention when you dream of specific foods or physical activities. (I dreamed of eating carrots this morning, probably partly in anticipation of this chapter.)

Pay attention to your waking feedback. Are you getting messages from the universe during the day about diet, exercise, or lifestyle changes? Are you getting feedback from others about your body or your health? The universe/Spirit knows what your body needs and will tell you in every way possible. It is up to you to listen.

Exercise: Body Attunement

Ideally, this would be done every morning as part of your regular morning routine, even before you eat breakfast (in case the body suggests something different for breakfast). You can do this lying down or sitting up. You should have as few outer distractions as possible since body attunement requires your full attention and concentration in the beginning.

Relax your body and still your mind as much as possible.

There are two ways to approach the exercise. The first time you do it, you should take the time to explore your entire body. Start with your feet and let your consciousness explore them inside and out. See how they feel. Be open to messages as well as feelings.

Do this for your entire body. Notice if there are places that are particularly tense or in pain. Try to release the tension or pain and/or see if you can receive a message from the body part. You might try loving the problem areas and then releasing the pain or tension from your body.

If you're able to get specific dietary or other physical suggestions from your body, be sure to follow them if you can. The more you cooperate with your body, the better the relationship and future communications will be.

Once you become accomplished at this attunement exercise, you can begin going immediately to the trouble spots. They will act like magnets and draw your attention to them. Some of you may be able to do this right away.

The human body is a self-healing mechanism. It "knows" how to heal itself. It's possible that the body could heal itself of any illness if we were able to get our contrary thoughts and feelings out of the way. Attuning to the Divine in the following exercise is one way to get out of the way. Our body is currently attuned to the mental conditions that made the body sick. By attuning to the Divine, we allow the body to respond to a different attunement and aid in the natural healing process. Attunement to the Divine can also help us experience our bodies, ourselves, others, and the world in a healthier way.

Exercise: Attuning the Body to the Divine

Relax your body as before. Go to a single cell as you did in the cell exercise, if you like. Experience the energy and divinity of that single cell as fully as you can. Once you've done that for a minute or two, allow that energy to expand throughout your body. Imagine that every cell in your body is on fire with divine love, light, and energy. Allow yourself to experience this attunement for several minutes, at least.

You may experience a particular vibration when this is happening, or you might experience an actual tone. Remember the vibration or tone, as it may help you get into attunement more quickly in the future. Once you become experienced at this body attunement, you will be able to do it in a matter of seconds, while driving or even at work. This attunement can also result in images or messages.

Another way to do this exercise is to imagine a spark of the Divine somewhere within your body. Experience that spark as you did the cell, as fully and vividly as possible. Then allow the spark to grow until it fills and overflows your body. Again, there may be an associated feeling, vibration, or tone.

I often do "aspect" visualizations in groups. These aspects are parts of you which personify particular abilities or qualities you would like to manifest in your life. They may be past-life characters, subpersonalities, or just fantasy characters that personify certain qualities. Because fear is one of the greatest blocks to spiritual growth and to living the healing life, I did an aspect visualization in the Mind Development group to get in touch with our Fearless Selves.

Most people had a very powerful experience. To my surprise, my Fearless Self showed up in my dreams shortly after I did the exercise. Since then he has appeared many times in my dreams. He is recognizable because he looks the same each time—like Bob Two, the idealized version of myself who appeared in the dream with Bob One, my shadow who opposed my philosophy of life.

My Fearless Self presents me with a very positive, self-confident, calm, detached, and even amused approach to life. He also has an idealized body. In the following exercise you will get in touch with your Fearless Self. You may want to call it your Courageous Self or even your Ideal Self.

Although we're focusing on body attunement, you will find that your Ideal Self is attuned in body, mind, and spirit. I place the exercise here in order to give you an ideal body to focus on.

Exercise: Ideal Self Exercise

You might want to prepare with a writing exercise. You can write down the qualities of the Ideal Self which you wish to get in touch with, or look at your values list from chapter 6. This isn't really necessary, however, as this self is already aware of those qualities.

Get relaxed and centered. Open yourself to this aspect of yourself. Although this is an Ideal Self, it is very real, and its qualities and characteristics are available to you if you have the courage to expand into them.

Allow an image of the Ideal Self to appear in your mind's eye. In this exercise, as in many others, the *feeling* of the aspect is more important than the appearance. You can work on the appearance, if you like, but be sure to get a clear and strong feeling for this version of you. The feeling will draw you most quickly toward manifestation of the Ideal Self.

You may want to have a conversation with your Ideal Self, whether you can see her or him clearly or not. The Ideal Self can become another guide and helper in your healing process.

Write your experience down in your healing journal. Watch for your Ideal Self in your dreams. During the day, try to experience yourself as the Ideal Self. Try to act from that perspective. See if you are able to get different feedback from people as a result.

The body is alive and conscious and seeks the healing life as much as we do. It is willing to assist in our healing as much as we will allow. Attuning to our body in order to receive body messages and attuning our body to the Divine in order to move toward the Ideal Self is not difficult and is worth whatever effort it takes. It can also be fun!

Mind Attunement

In a way, this whole book is about mind attunement. Understanding the meaning of our illness and the meaning of our life requires attunement of the mind to itself, its own thoughts and attitudes, attunement to the body, attunement to waking and dreaming reality—what the mind has built—and, finally, attunement to the spirit.

Attunement of mind means awareness. Living the healing life requires awareness of what's going on at every level of being—spirit, mind, and body—as well as what's going on in the world around us. Unconsciousness is the bane of attunement. Living the healing life requires that we wake up to our own thoughts and behavior.

The meaningful world is a metaphorical world. The mind becomes attuned as we're able to recognize other people and all of our experiences as metaphors for parts of ourselves. We become free to live the healing life as we stop blaming others and the past for our current life. Everyone and every experience becomes our teacher. We see all of life as a great cooperative venture. There is no neighbor to be in conflict with because we *are* the neighbor. There are no enemies to do battle with because they're all within us, paper dragons made out of our own fears.

What Jeremy Taylor does with dreams, using the words "part of me" to describe different characters and objects, we can do with our waking-life experiences and persons. The Hindus practice this by saying "I am that" to every person and experience they meet. We are always meeting self. When we really understand this, we will approach attunement of the mind very quickly.

Another aspect of awareness that determines mind attunement is self-awareness. Our self-image and expression of the self will either be attuned to the Ideal Self or to some level of disharmony. "Know thyself," one of Socrates' dictums, is still important today. The secret of attunement is to strip away the false beliefs about ourselves and find the core of our being.

An ongoing part of living the healing life is to consider all our cherished ideas about ourselves, others, and the world to be beliefs so that we can have the opportunity to make changes, to move toward our own core being, our true selves.

Peter Lemesurier wrote a book on beliefs, *Beyond All Belief*, in which he pushes the idea of belief to its logical extreme. Nothing is absolute, he claims. "Consciousness alone is real. The reality that remains after belief is burned away is evolving consciousness itself, the summary mind that perceives."[3] I would argue that this "summary mind" is Spirit or the Mind of God. Once belief is burned away, what is left is the mind attuned to its Creator.

Spirit Attunement

Underlying and forming the pattern for all attunement is spirit attunement. The Divine is the template upon which our being is based. The fulfillment of our being requires a movement toward that template, toward the underlying divine energy and pattern. Even in physics this underlying pattern is beginning to be recognized: " . . . the tangible reality of our everyday lives is really a kind of illusion, like a holographic image. Underlying it is a deeper order of existence, a vast and more primary level of reality that gives birth to all objects and appearances of our physical world in much the same way that a piece of holographic film gives birth to a hologram."[4]

Indian teacher, Sri Aurobindo, drawing from many religious traditions, put it this way: "If it be true that Spirit is involved in matter and apparent Nature is secret God, then the manifestation of the divine in himself and the realization of God within and without are the highest and most legitimate aims possible to man upon earth."[5]

Edgar Cayce confirms my own experience that the Fearless Self is also the Ideal Self or the Attuned Self: "For as has been so oft quoted, and so little interpreted in people's lives, the consciousness of God's presence, as manifested in Christ, casteth out fear . . . " (3691-1) Cayce says that fear causes us to lose consciousness of our spiritual heritage.

In this story from Gerry Jampolsky and Diane Cirincione's book, this process of losing consciousness is poignantly played out: A newborn infant was brought home for the first time. The couple's three-year-old daughter insisted on going into the baby's room by herself. The parents were surprised by the strength of her insistence. They were somewhat concerned for the well-being of their newborn, but the room had an intercom so they let the little girl go in. "The little girl tiptoed into the baby's room alone as the parents listened in. They heard their daughter close the door and then listened as her footsteps approached the crib. There was a moment of quiet, and then they heard their daughter's voice softly whisper to the baby: 'Baby, remind me what God is like. I am beginning to forget.'"[6]

Spirit attunement means remembering what God is like. More important, it is remembering what *we* are truly like as expressions of God. One of the things we can do is to try to experience ourselves as the Ideal Self, to experience and express ourselves from that point of view as often as possible.

Another important part of spirit attunement has to do with how we see others. The attuned spirit sees the Spirit in others as well. In Matthew 25, Jesus gives a number of parables or metaphors for the kingdom of heaven. One is the parable of the separation of the sheep and the goats. The sheep are placed at the right hand of the Son of Man, the goats on the left. To the sheep he says, "'Come, O blessed of my Father, inherit the kingdom prepared for you from the foundation of the world; for I was hungry and you gave me food, I was thirsty and you gave me drink, I was a stranger and you welcomed me, I was naked and you clothed me, I was sick and you visited me, I was in prison and you came to me.' Then the righteous will answer him, 'Lord, when did we see thee hungry and feed thee, or thirsty and give thee drink? And when did we see thee a stranger and welcome thee, or naked and clothe thee? And when did we see thee sick or in prison and visit thee?' And the King will answer them, 'Truly, I say to you, as you did it to one of the least of these my brethren, you did it to me.'" (Matthew 25:34-40)

To those on the left he says the opposite. What this revolutionary teaching means is that every time we look into the face of another, we are not *just* seeing ourselves—meeting self—we are also seeing God. Mind attunement means seeing the self in others. Spirit attunement means going beyond the human face to see the face of God behind it.

The Sufis have a dance in which two concentric circles of individuals face one another. Each person dances with each individual in the other ring as the circles move in opposite directions. While touching palms and looking into the eyes of each partner, they sing a song that means, in essence, "The God in me greets the God in you."

When we can see and greet the God within us *and* see and greet the God within others, we will truly be attuned in body, mind, and spirit, and we will be living the healing life.

13

Action

In Matthew 7:16, Jesus tells us that individuals are known their fruits. Attunement leads to action. Certain actions are the fruits of being attuned to the Spirit. Other actions can *lead* toward healing and attunement. Still others lead to disharmony and dis-ease.

Unhealthy Actions

Our actions always come from our thoughts and feelings. There are many thoughts and feelings that can lead to "crimes" and "barriers," to unhappiness and illness. Chief among them is fear. Many of our unhealthy actions, if followed back to their mind-source, will lead to fear.

Serious illnesses almost always represent a response to fear, some constriction, restriction, or binding of the self. We build fortresses to protect ourselves and our fortresses, over the years, become prisons. They are built one fear at a time, one day at a time, one choice at a time. By the time we finally realize that we're in a prison, we don't know how we got there or how to get out.

One way to begin setting ourselves free may be to say "no." Healing begins when we say "no" to dishonesty and "no" to fear. Saying "yes" can be the beginning of healing also, when we say "yes" to ourselves and "yes" to life. Bernie Siegel speaks of the importance of independence, assertiveness, healthy choices, and healthy actions: "People who always smile, never tell anyone their troubles, and neglect their own needs are the ones who are most likely to become ill. For them, the main problem often is learning to say 'no' without guilt. Many only become able to live for themselves, to tell others what they really feel, after the shock of the diagnosis. One patient, who never expressed displeasure at *anything*, began to improve when she was able to tell her husband that she didn't like the family dog."[1]

This may sound rather trivial, but it's not about the dog, it's about an unhealthy denial of the self. When you don't make your wishes known and let others make choices for you, you lose a little bit of your self, and your self-esteem sinks a little lower. In this next case the stakes were higher than the family dog, but the meaning is the same.

Thelma, one of my friends, was controlled most of her life by a mother who manipulated through martyrdom. Guilt and shame are right behind fear on the list of crippling emotions. The martyr uses his or her "weakness" to control others. Beware of people who see themselves as victims. They will often attempt to victimize you.

The mother used the ultimate manipulation a number of times: suicide threats and attempts. Finally, the daughter reached the end of her ability to respond. Because she wasn't responsible for her mother's feelings or actions, she needed to stop responding to them as if she was. One day her mother threatened suicide by putting a gun to her head and saying she was going to shoot. The daughter finally found the courage to get out of the game. She said to her mother, "Go ahead and shoot, but if you do I will hate you for the rest of my life."

The mother didn't shoot herself and never tried that manipulation again. A situation like this represents a feedback loop or "game." To get out of such a loop, we need to feed something different into the loop, to change the rules of the game. To participate in a situation as if one is responsible for another's actions is called *codependency* or *enabling* in the addiction literature. When we find ourselves involved in such unhealthy actions, we need to make another choice. Of course, the earlier it is in the game, the easier it is to make choices and change the game or get out.

Unhealthy Choices. Every situation in your current life is the result of choices you made in the past, choices that are reaffirmed every day. How do we end up with a serious illness? Do we, at some point, decide to get cancer, for example?

Remember the whispers? The self whispers to us as soon as we begin to make negative choices in our life. If we continue to make those choices, the self will "speak" more loudly. We don't decide to get cancer. We decide not to express our anger at a loved one. We decide to go along with something we really don't want to do, like the woman who disliked the family dog. As we repeatedly give our power over to others in small ways, we are in the process of building an illness. Whispers tell us when we're off track in the beginning. The whispers respond to what I call micro decisions and micro actions. To prevent illnesses and other life problems, we need to develop micro awareness.

This process became clear to me during the terrible events that occurred outside Waco, Texas, involving David Koresh and the Branch Davidians. That tragedy was the result of a different kind of illness, but like any other illness, it was a spiritual dis-ease.

I couldn't understand how intelligent adults could so totally give their power away to another individual. How could men allow Koresh to have sex with their wives and possibly even their children? How could the women allow themselves and their children to be used in that way? I thought they must have checked their brains at the door. But I was wrong.

None of those people made a decision to leave their homes, join a cult, give their wives away or allow themselves to become concubines to a religious leader, subject their children to abuse, arm themselves, and hold off the authorities. They didn't decide to die in a fireball. That conclusion was the result of micro decisions and micro actions. Perhaps they decided to go and listen to David Koresh. Then they chose to go back a second time. At some point they decided to join the church. Then they decided to move to Texas, and so on.

They didn't make one decision that resulted in the final outcome. They gave their power away in small pieces and then found themselves in a situation where small decisions and small actions would not be enough to extricate them. They had invested time, energy, and emotions in the church and in Koresh. It would be difficult to admit that they made a mistake, difficult to stop the inertia created by their micro decisions and actions. Similarly, people will stay in a bad relationship or unhappy job situation because of the "investment" they've made over the years.

Healing requires that we make new decisions. We need to make new micro decisions and take new micro actions, but we also need to make macro decisions to extricate us from the macro outcome—disease—that our earlier decisions and actions have created.

Once we have experienced a life-shattering illness, small choices will no longer be enough. Fortunately, the illness itself creates a whole new playing field and the possibility of a new game. Our old loop is broken by the disease. In the healing process our choices are important because it's tempting to re-create the old self and the old life, to go back to the comfort of our familiar monsters.

Life before illness wasn't an inevitability. It was the result of choices and actions in the past. Many were unconscious and habitual. A life-shattering experience gives us the opportunity to make choices more consciously, to focus on outcomes that are more positive and desirable, on not just a healed body, but a healed life.

Unhealthy Attitudes and Emotions. Our actions follow our feelings. Fear causes us to act in certain ways, as do hatred and anger. A negative self-image, with low self-esteem, results in unhealthy actions. Guilt and shame are unhealthy emotions. One of the most important emotional pathways to healing is that of forgiveness: forgiveness of self and others.

Worry is probably the most common and most useless unhealthy emotion around. Worry never changes anything for the better. It takes a lot of time and energy and ruins our days. We're capable of being unhappy every day of our life because of something that *might* happen. Cayce said this: "Do not burden self with that as is unnecessary to be met until the time arises, for *worry* killeth." (900-345) Worry kills! Or as Jesus put it: " . . . do not be anxious about your life, what you shall eat or what you shall drink, nor about your body, what you shall put on. Is not life more than food, and the body more than clothing?" (Matthew 6:25)

Worry is related to fear. Anger is another emotion whose origin is often fear. People who are violent and angry are often fearful beneath their violence. Anger is a healthy emotion when it's expressed in an appropriate and timely manner. It becomes unhealthy when it's held inside, expressed inappropriately, or when it becomes chronic.

The meaning of our illness will often be found in the associations traditionally made with the organ affected. It is not surprising to find a prevalence of heart problems among men. The heart is the seat of the emotions in our culture, and men in this culture have traditionally had problems expressing their emotions. One of the most popular surgeries in our country is the coronary bypass. When men stop bypassing their hearts in their relationships, fewer such operations will be necessary.

Unhealthy Diet. The combination of diet and emotions is probably more important to our health than diet alone. Anxiety, anger, and stress of any kind produce chemical changes that are not compatible with good digestion. For some American families, the evening meal is one of the most stressful times of the day so it is no wonder that we have so many gastrointestinal problems.

Under the topic of diet I include negative lifestyle choices such as excessive smoking, drinking, drug use (illegal as well as prescription and over-the-counter) and other unhealthy excesses. It's beyond the scope of this book to go into diet in detail.

Many unhealthy diets are the result of a lack of consciousness or awareness, not just in the choice of foods, but in the process of eating itself. Many of us eat so fast and have our attention divided in so many directions that we're not even aware of what we've eaten. We may actually taste very little of our meals. We may feel psychologically hungry, even after a relatively large meal, simply because we didn't consciously participate in eating it.

You may need to change your diet. An important healing action, however, is to simply eat more consciously, both in terms of choosing your foods and in terms of experiencing what you eat. Ideally, meals should be taken in silence or with quiet conversation, without the TV or other distractions. We might find ourselves eating less as we eat more slowly, and eating better foods as we eat more consciously.

Healthy Actions

If poor choices and unhealthy actions in the past have created an illness in your present, healthy choices and actions can change the present *and* the future. I believe your illness, in fact, has that intention. It came to give you the opportunity to make different choices, take different actions, to step onto a healing path.

Some of the healthy actions you can take are mini-actions. Your illness was built from many small decisions and actions. Making small healing decisions and taking mini-actions will help put you on a healing path.

For those who wish to delve into healing actions in more depth, I recommend *Healthy Pleasures* by Robert Ornstein and David Sobel. The authors cover a variety of healing actions and attitudes and present research in support of their healing benefits.

Healing and the Senses. Many healthy pleasures involve the body and its senses. I've mentioned touch in terms of hugging and various body therapies. Studies have shown that Americans do not touch one another as much as people in some other countries. In the 1960s, psychologist Sidney Jourard observed couples in cafes in a number of countries and counted the number of times they touched one another. In San Juan, Puerto Rico, couples touched at a rate of 180 times per hour. In a cafe in Paris, France, the number was 110 per hour. In Gainesville, Florida, it was *twice* an hour, and in London, England, Jourard *never* observed a couple touch. According to the World Health Organization, although Americans spend more money per capita on health than any other industrialized nation, we are in the poorest health of any of those nations. A lack of touching may be one part of the reason for that standing.

Because of the current focus on child abuse, sexual harassment, and other *touching* crimes, touching in this country may become even more restricted. It's possible that we lead other nations in murders, violent crimes, and sexual crimes precisely because we don't touch *enough*. From my experiences with perpetrators of incest and child abuse, I have found that many of them are restricted in their ability to touch. They were not touched as children themselves or were only touched in a violent or inappropriately sexual way.

Being touched is not just good for our health, it's a necessity of life: "During the early nineteenth century, if a child was separated from its parents, it was sent to a foundling institution. This was, in effect, a death sentence. A study of ten such institutions in 1915 revealed that in all but one, every single baby under the age of two died."[2] This was the result of touch deprivation. When Bellvue Hospital in New York changed this practice, the death rate dropped to under 10 percent.

Sex is another form that healthy touch can take. Healthy sex is an experience in which both love and intimacy are expressed. Even without intercourse, holding and cuddling can contribute to the healing life. More than any other interaction, sex can be the primary source of physical and emotional intimacy with another human being. It provides the foundation for sharing confidences and for social support, both vital for health.

Increasing your daily touch quota can represent an important healing action. Treat yourself to a massage or even a facial. Ask for and give lots of hugs.

Much has been written about the importance of visual stimulation in the healing process. You can buy a video that shows nothing but fish swimming in a tank. It's a fairly effective stress reducer. Of course, you can also buy real fish. Having something to take care of and talk to will undoubtedly increase the benefits greatly.

What are you feeding your eyes? What do you look at most of the day? Put up pictures or posters of beautiful nature scenes. Whenever possible, feast your eyes on nature herself. One of the most healing things we can do is spend time in nature, which can be one of our most direct visions and experiences of the Divine. In nature we can engage all of the senses: vision, hearing, smell, touch (by touching trees or water and being touched by wind), and even taste, if we know what's edible.

If you can't get out in nature, bring nature to you in the form of pictures, cut flowers, or plants. You can experience any form of nature you wish in a meditation or reverie. In the visualizations I do in groups, I always invite people to create an inner quiet and safe place in nature in order to help them relax before beginning the visualization. You can create such a place for yourself, whether it's a place where you've actually been or one created completely in your imagination. Simply imagining yourself in this place can be a quick and effective stress reducer.

The healing power of music has been known and practiced throughout recorded history. "Primitive" peoples played instruments, sang, chanted, drummed, and danced as part of their healing rituals. A number of studies have documented the specific physiological effects and benefits of music. "Music influences respiratory rate, blood pressure, stomach contractions, and the level of stress hormones in the blood. Though people react differently, slow, quiet, non-vocal music generally lowers bodily reactions to stress, while the faster variety heightens alertness and arousal."[3] Make music a daily part of your healing actions. Spending only ten to twenty minutes a day listening to music you love can be beneficial.

Most of us don't pay much attention to smells unless we're annoyed by them, yet it's one of our most important senses. We are more likely to recall past experiences through the olfactory sense than any other. Although aromatherapy has been a part of many ancient cultures, it has only recently made a comeback in this country. Evidence is mounting for the power of aroma to bring about specific physiological responses. "Patients with insomnia, anxiety, panic attacks, back pain, migraine, and food cravings are now being treated with modern aromatherapy. For example, some patients with chronic pain are instructed in deep muscle relaxation while inhaling peach fragrance. Later, the patients simply take a whiff of peach, and the relaxed state is quickly induced."[4]

You can pursue aromatherapy through books or a professional aromatherapist, but the simple conditioning exercise of pairing a pleasant smell with a relaxed state is easy to do on your own. Use the relaxation visualization above, or anything that will get you into a relaxed state, and then smell something you already like and is easy to obtain. Pairing the two only three or four times should make the conditioning stick. If it begins to fade, you can repeat the conditioning. Most health stores carry various oil essences, with descriptions of their purpose. The easiest path is to just surround yourself with smells that you like. Cut flowers or living plants in the house can combine aromatherapy with visual therapy.

Other forms of aromatherapy include smelling pleasant herbs and spices, smelling favorite fruits, or burning incense or scented candles. Experiment with different smells to see which ones are the most healing for you. Ask your dreams for aromatic suggestions. It's relatively rare but possible to experience smell and taste in your dreams.

Food is another pleasure that involves smell. Actually, most of the pleasure we derive from food is a result of smell, not taste. If you hold your nose while eating, the taste of food is diminished drastically. In terms of food as a healthy pleasure or healing action, it can be helpful to change our attitude about what foods are good and bad for us and also what constitutes being overweight.

Part of our dieting mania is the result of cultural ideals. In the past a plump woman, for example, was the ideal. Today many individuals aim for a physical ideal that may not only be unattainable but unhealthy. According to Ornstein and Sobel, "Sixty million adult Americans are trying to lose weight. *More than half of these people are not overweight.*"[5]

Diet is something that should be considered part of living a healing life—but not necessarily *dieting.* If you choose to follow a particular diet for your health, be sure it includes at least a few things that you can eat for pure pleasure. Occasionally eating something for pleasure can sometimes have an overall healing effect even if the food is considered "unhealthy." Of course, any food that is really harmful to your health should not be eaten.

Make a list in your healing journal, not just of pleasurable foods, but of all of the things that bring you pleasure. Be honest, and even include things that you think would be pleasurable even though you may never do them. This is your private journal, and you can let your imagination run wild.

At least once or twice a week, if not every day, deliberately do something physically pleasurable. It could be a solitary pleasure such as taking a walk or listening to music, or a joint pleasure such as going shopping or having lunch with a friend. These pleasures are not frivolous. They are good for you in and of themselves. Beyond that, however, they send a message to the self which says, "I care about myself. I believe I deserve to have fun and feel good." Such healing actions will become positive habits, a regular part of your healing life.

Healing Actions. Go to school; live longer. There is a surprising relationship among education, health, and longevity. One Irish study, for example, looked at the risk factors in heart disease:

"The results confirm a strong association between education and cardiovascular disease which is not entirely explained by differences in age, cigarette smoking, diastolic blood pressure, weight or plasma cholesterol. *Indeed, on the basis of the logistic analysis, the independent effect of educa-*

tion on cardiovascular disease is as strong as the effects of smoking, blood pressure, weight, and cholesterol combined."[6]

It's possible that more education gives an individual more information and options. The more knowledge and information we have, the more sense of power we have, the more choices we are aware of. Since we're basically on earth to learn anyway, anything we do to increase our knowledge can be good for us. A formal education isn't necessary, but taking classes for pleasure and learning about things of interest, regardless of your age, can be an important healthy action.

A related health factor is satisfaction in our work. As we've already seen, some people may contract a serious illness just to get out of an unhappy work situation.

"People report low job satisfaction as one of the greatest sources of unhappiness. It is associated with high rates of anxiety, depression, psychosomatic symptoms, and coronary heart disease. Furthermore, a study of several hundred volunteers revealed that work satisfaction and feelings of happiness were better predictors of longevity than *health habits.*"[7]

What about exercise? As with the diet craze, exercise has become associated with hard work and sometimes unattainable results. As a result of this craze, we have a number of new industries including not only personal trainers, but sports medicine for all of the self-inflicted injuries of the "no pain, no gain" generation.

Studies have shown that a modest amount of exercise can be as beneficial as heavy workouts, especially if you have been used to a sedentary lifestyle. Furthermore, mild exercise can be gained in doing things that you enjoy doing already. For example: "According to another study of twelve thousand middle-aged men, those who used about sixteen hundred calories a week had nearly 40 percent fewer fatal heart attacks than those who burned less than five hundred calories a week. That's only a half-hour a day of walking, gardening, dancing, doing chores, fishing, golf, or bowling. However, logging in over two hours a day of more intense activity and consuming a hefty forty-five hundred calories a week in hard exercise *did not further decrease cardiac fatalities.*"[8]

After exercise comes rest. Rest and sleep are necessities of life. Science still has not discovered why we sleep, although many important recuperative functions occur during sleep. My own bias is that we sleep in order to dream and make a nightly connection with the Divine. Still, it appears that there *are* some health benefits in deep sleep related to the stimulation of the immune system. The need for rest and sleep when we're sick may be related to this immune system arousal in deep sleep.

The importance of healing your relationships for life healing has already been stressed. Beyond our personal relationships, we are part of a larger community. A number of studies have confirmed that belonging to a tight-knit community has a very positive effect on health, even when that community is the nation you live in.

The Japanese, for example, have the highest life expectancy in the world and a heart disease rate of only one-fifth the rate in the United States. When Japanese move to this country, however, their life expectancy and rate of heart disease more closely approach that of Americans, *except for those who maintain their traditions and close ties to the Japanese community.*

Studies of communities within the United States confirm the importance of social support. Diet seems to play less of a role than such support systems. Vegetarian Seventh-Day Adventists have less colon and rectal cancer than other Americans. Mormons, who eat slightly more beef per capita than the U.S. average, have even fewer of these cancers.

Many studies indicate that people who attend church are healthier than those who do not. Recognition of the importance of social support in the healing process has spawned a number of groups around the country. I have listed some of them at the back of this book. With a little effort, I'm sure you can find support groups specific to your needs in your area. Check with local churches, holistic healing organizations, or hospitals and clinics.

Remember Cayce's admonition to be good *for* something? One of the most healing actions you can take is to help someone else. One problem with a serious illness is that of putting too much time and energy into it and therefore keeping it "healthy." Helping someone else is an excellent way to start changing the direction of your energy, and it's good for you!

One study on men who did regular volunteer work found that they had death rates two-and-a-half times lower than those who did not. It's important that the work be truly voluntary. When you feel forced to care for someone, like an invalid parent, the results can be the opposite of healing. It can be quite stressful. Volunteering can get you out of your home and keep you from focusing on your illness.

Many cities have agencies which monitor volunteer needs. It needn't take a lot of your time. An hour or two a week helping someone in need can be highly beneficial for you as well as those you help.

Rachel Naomi Remen is the medical director of the Commonweal Cancer Help Program, a yoga-based retreat in Bolinas, California, run by Michael Lerner. Commonweal was featured on the Bill Moyers's TV special, *Healing and the Mind*. In her work, she has noticed that people who come to heal their cancer have often closed off a part of themselves. In the process of healing their cancer, they begin to heal themselves as well. "It is as if the process of illness, limitation, suffering, the shocking isolation of a brutal disease, awakens in us the seeker, which is so much more than the scientist. We begin to sort values, what matters and what doesn't. We become open to looking at the meaning of life, not just the meaning of pain, of one's own pain, but even the meaning of life itself."[9]

Healthy Choices. We can gain understanding of the healthy choices we need to make as we discover the unhealthy choices which led to our illness. The antidote is almost always found in the problem. The woman who finally admitted that she didn't like the family dog was making a healing choice that was the opposite of her previous choice not to speak up and express her needs and wants.

Grace made the choice to reject herself because she thought she was ugly, and therefore experienced rejection by others. Her emotional and physical healing required a different choice. She had to learn to accept and love her ugly self, to transform it into a thing of beauty. She feels she now experiences love from others at a much deeper level.

This story from Rachel Naomi Remen beautifully illustrates the need for and possibility of making new choices. Previous choices were made from fear and serve to protect us. This example shows how that protection can hurt us when it is maintained beyond its usefulness.

A Polish man, Harry Rose, was a survivor of Auschwitz. Even through the horrors of such experiences come some of our most powerful stories of courage, love, and even forgiveness. Harry was a brilliant chemist, a very mental man. Remen, of Polish descent herself, says, "He wanted to see if he could use his mind to heal his cancer. At first he was taken aback by the Commonweal approach, because we do a lot of touching. He would say, 'Vot is this luffy, vot is this huggy, huggy, huggy, vot is this huggy the strangers, vot is this?' And we continued to hug him anyway."

On the fourth day, in a yoga meditation, Harry "experienced himself inside a large field of shifting energy." He called it a "big rose" and located it in his chest. It generated a large energy field around him and frightened him. He described it as having "a hemorrhage of energy." "When he told us about it later, he said how vulnerable it made him feel, because since his experience as a twelve-year-old boy in Auschwitz he had lived very cautiously with regard to his heart and loved only close people, only family."

On the last day Remen asked Harry how he was doing with the big rose. "And he said, 'Better.' I said, 'What happened that helped?' He said, 'I took a valk and talked to God. It's better.' 'Harry,' I said, 'What did God say?' He said, 'Ah, I say to God, "God, vot is this, is it OK to luff the strangers?" And God said, "Harry, vot is this 'strangers'? You make strangers, I don't make strangers."' "[10]

What a wonderful story! And it's true. God doesn't make strangers. When we're afraid of someone, we're really afraid of ourselves. When we're angry at someone, we're angry at ourselves. When we hate someone, we're hating ourselves.

Look at your previous choices and see if you can change some of them. The antidote to your unhealthy choices will be found *within* those choices. Making new choices will take courage, because you must face whatever caused you to make the unhealthy choice in the first place. If a choice was made out of fear, your healing requires that you face the fear and make a different choice. You have to risk the frightening outcome that closed you down in the first place, as Harry did.

Healthy choices lead to healthy actions. Healthy actions always direct us toward a greater manifestation of spirit, to an experience of fewer Spirit-suppression devices. Try to be aware each day of the choices you are making with your thoughts, words, and actions. The way that you express Spirit, throughout the day, is the way you will experience Spirit.

Healthy Attitudes and Emotions.   Many people think their attitudes and emotions are fixed. Attitudes and emotions come from our thoughts and beliefs, and they can be changed. The development of new and healthier attitudes and emotions should be a high priority for the healing life. I've already mentioned confession as one means for healing feelings of guilt. Following are some other attitudinal healing actions.

Norman Cousins used laughter as an important part of his healing process. Ten minutes of deep-down belly laughter, while watching old TV comedies, equated to two hours of pain-free sleep.

While there may be nothing funny about your illness, laughter can help in the healing process. Good moods boost immunity, and bad moods or depression suppress it. Healthy actions are actions which lead to healthy attitudes and emotions. Happiness is something we have a constitutional right to pursue, but it seems elusive for many. We tend to think of happiness in terms of major actions or experiences: getting married, having a child, getting a new job, or buying a new car or home. If we have a serious illness, getting well would certainly make us happy. But were you happy *before* you got sick?

By identifying happiness with major life events, we put it in the category of a temporary high. Happiness, as part of the healing life, is made up of small daily experiences that make us feel good. In your healing journal, list the things that make you happy, make you feel good. These may be some of the healthy pleasures mentioned above. Think of small things you do that make you feel good about yourself. Try to incorporate more of these into your daily routine.

Two attitudes that can lead to more happiness are hope and optimism. Such feelings have a strong positive effect on the immune system and contribute to success in treatment and long-term survival. Hope and optimism create positive expectations. Whereas a realistic view of oneself used to be considered an important factor in mental health, current studies show this is simply not true.

People who have a high opinion of themselves and their abilities, even when those opinions aren't shared by their friends, tend to be in better health. Those who are more realistic about their shortcomings are often mildly depressed and may be headed for deep depression. Optimism and high expectations are not unrealistic if they result in good health. Good health is very real.

I'm not suggesting that you lie to yourself *about* yourself or your life situation. Because thoughts are things, optimism, hope, and positive expectations will lead to more positive outcomes. Many people keep expectations low in order to avoid disappointments such as they have had in the past. Unfortunately, low expectations lead to *more* disappointment! It's better to have high hopes and high expectations and accept occasional disappointment.

Also, there's the value of "pretending," or, as one woman put it at one of my talks, "Fake it until you make it." By pretending we're different, that we feel different, or our situation is different, we set in motion energies which can bring about the difference we're pretending. *You have to be able to imagine it before you can create it.* Imagination, used in a positive way, can be your best friend.

Healthy Diet.   Diet is an important part of healing and also of living the healing life. Keep in mind, however, the power and importance of thoughts and attitudes. If you try to follow a diet that you hate, the benefits of the healthy food will be considerably diminished. Try to find a diet that allows you to continue to enjoy food. Changing eating habits can be important by itself. Practice eating with more awareness. Keep a food log in your healing journal, at least for a while, to see what you're currently eating and how you eat. Make eating a more conscious action.

You can find dietary suggestions in Bernie Siegel's book, *Love, Medicine, and Miracles,* which come from the American Institute for Cancer Research and are endorsed by the National Academy of Sciences. He also includes some recommendations from health researcher Nathan Pritikin.[11]

In the Cayce health readings, dietary recommendations and other healing applications were specific to the individual receiving the reading. Certain recommendations showed up repeatedly, however, regardless of the physical problem being addressed.

The treatments advised many times over seem to revolve mainly around the following (in addition to the staple advice concerning attitudes, emotions, and prayer):

1. Proper diet—often cleansing diets.
2. Water intake—seven to eight glasses a day.
3. Regular exercise—proper circulation.
4. Proper eliminations and release of toxins (colonic irrigations were recommended for all).
5. Castor oil packs (used externally, on the abdomen, primarily), Epsom salt packs, Glyco-Thymoline packs, hot salt packs, etc.
6. Massage—spinal oil rubs.
7. Herbs, tonics, inhalants—in great variety.
8. Vibrational therapy—color, sound, music, electrical appliances.
9. Spinal manipulation and proper alignment was recommended in most of the physical readings.

Repeated emphasis was placed on proper body balances and balanced activities. Moderation in all things and recommendations to achieve balance were customarily given for the following:

1. Diet and food combinations.
2. Proper assimilation and utilization of foods.
3. The cerebrospinal and autonomic nervous system (spinal manipulation recommended).
4. The endocrine system (herb tonics).
5. Liver/kidney activity (acid/alkaline)—cleansing diets and castor oil packs recommended.
6. Elimination and excretion of waste substances and toxins.
7. Circulation of blood and lymph (exercise, massage, hydrotherapy recommended).[12]

There are many healing actions you can take, far more than I have mentioned here. Healing is based on small daily awarenesses, decisions, and actions. The healing life is about being more conscious of what you're doing with your thoughts, emotions, time, and energy on a daily basis.

In the next chapter, we'll look at the question of what we're healing ourselves for. Who is the self being healed? Who are we, and who are we becoming? What are the fruits, the actions, of one in attunement with Spirit?

14

Being-Becoming

A lot of the problems we create in our lives have to do with our attitudes and focus. Illnesses are no exception. As I've already mentioned, we tend to look at what's wrong with ourselves, what's wrong with others, and what's wrong with the world. When we're sick, it's hard to think of anything but our illness. We watch the bad news on TV. We focus on what we haven't accomplished rather than our successes and accomplishments.

For those consciously on the spiritual path, it can actually be worse. Because you have a sense of what is possible for you—spiritual goals and ideals to attain, the gap between the present self and those ideals can be very discouraging. In the United States especially, we are very goal oriented. We move from one goal to another, never allowing ourselves the time to enjoy the fruits of our accomplishments. Our successes give us a sense of satisfaction for a few days at most, and then we're back to being discontented. We spend a lot of time beating ourselves up for not fulfilling our potential.

In our spiritual life, we seem to think there's some ultimate goal out there, and we can't be happy until we attain it. We may call it enlightenment, oneness with God, or some other ideal. We believe that once we reach it, we can relax and stop struggling. We will be happy, even blissful, from that time on.

This is clearly not a healthy situation. It means we spend most of our lives thinking we're not OK. Is this just the way things are or are we missing something? I don't believe we're here to struggle with our spirituality and then be miserable most of the time because we haven't made it, whatever "it" is. I think a different perspective is called for, one that will allow us to have more fun in life and actually enjoy our spiritual quest.

A lot of our problems in this area are the result of a belief in perfection. We expect to arrive at some point where we'll understand everything, and from that time on we'll . . . what? Play harps and sing God's praises for eternity? Even the most devoted religious fanatic would tire of that after a while.

The Unfinished God

The Creator doesn't present a picture of perfection, and neither does the creation—nature. The problem with perfection is that it leaves no room for change, for growth, for creativity, for new experiences. To be perfect would be a terrible fate!

If you knew everything, had seen everything, done everything, and knew everything that was going to happen, existence would be intolerable. It would be like seeing the same movie over and over again for eternity.

God isn't perfect, isn't finished. A perfect God no longer

learns, no longer grows, no longer creates or experiences. There are no surprises, no new joys, no challenges. God is a living God precisely because He/She/It continues to change, to learn, to grow, to create, and to experience. And we are one of God's channels for learning and experience. In our own great creativity, we give God new experiences to add to Its Being.

Moses asked God for a name so the Hebrews would know that Moses was bona fide and had been sent by God to free them from Egypt. God said, "I Am that I Am." The Hebrew phrase can also be translated, "I will be what I will be," or "I am becoming what I am becoming."

God is characterized by Being. God's existence is Its most important characteristic. God is characterized by Becoming. While Being is God's noun, Becoming is God's verb, the arena of God's action.

We are like God. God is our model. Our being is our most important characteristic. We are important and make a difference in the universe *just because we exist!* If we were to live life in a coma or profoundly retarded, our existence would still be meaningful. There are no meaningless individuals and no meaningless lives. There are no meaningless experiences, including illness.

Because the roles by which some individuals value themselves are sometimes lost through serious illness, they are often confronted with the question of whether they are valuable, whether they are lovable, just because they exist. It would be good for all of us to ask ourselves that question, whether or not we're ill. Can we love ourselves for simply being, regardless of accomplishments, position, attractiveness, income, or possessions?

Many of those who go through the life review in a near-death experience report that what they experience is their impact on other human beings. They see their life from the point of view of the people they have affected, for better or worse. When they come back from that experience, they

find themselves much more interested in human relationships than in accomplishments or possessions. Many with
serious illnesses reorder their values and priorities in the
same way.

As unfinished beings, we can recognize that we, like God,
will *never* stop growing, learning, creating, and experiencing. Perhaps we can lighten up a little bit and recognize that
every goal and accomplishment is temporary. There will always be a new one once the old one is reached. The art of
Being and Becoming lies in living in and enjoying the
present. It's been said so often that it's a cliché but, as with
many clichés, it carries an important lesson.

If we don't enjoy the journey to our various goals, we're
essentially not enjoying our lives. Enjoying our lives means
enjoying our days, enjoying the trip. As beings who are for-
ever becoming, the trip is all there is.

Be Content, Not Satisfied

Another frequent saying of Cayce's was "Be content, not
satisfied." This phrase represents the balance we need to
find in order to enjoy our days while continuing to learn
and grow and create a better future. We can be content with
our accomplishments and give ourselves credit for what we
have done, where we have brought ourselves. We need to
periodically pay attention to our growth and accomplishments, our positive creations, and pay homage to the selves
who brought us where we are. Doing this gives us the kind
of energy we need in order to make more positive steps into
the future. When we operate from a sense of failure, our successes become even more difficult.

A friend of mine was badmouthing her old self, the self
who lived in the shadow of her husband and played the role
of housewife, mother, and a pretty woman to be shown off
by her husband. I told her that she shouldn't look down on
that former self. It was that self who had had the courage to

make the changes and take the actions that led to her new life.

In your healing journal, write down some of your accomplishments from the past, both large and small. Allow yourself to feel pride in what you have accomplished. Recognize yourself as the individual who created those experiences. Recognize your capacity for creating more in the future.

Any movement toward growth, change, and healing will be faster and less of a struggle to the extent that we are able to love and respect ourselves now. You might practice with an affirmation along these lines: "I love and respect myself and others," or "I'm OK the way I am now, and I'm changing for the better every day."

We may never be satisfied with our lives, because there will always be more to learn and experience, more to accomplish, even after we die. We can be content, however, by recognizing that we are in the process of becoming and we're doing the best we can each day.

Self-Image

I've written of the power of self-image before. Your self-image has a lot to do with what you are creating in the world. It will strongly affect the progress of any illness and its healing. Your self-image is nothing more than the ideas you have about yourself. Even though our self-image is a collection of ideas, we tend to act as if it were something real and true, something fixed. Your ideas about yourself, as with any other ideas, can be changed, but self-image is one of the more tenacious idea complexes. It will take some courage and energy to make those changes as well as a strong willingness to become someone different from who you thought you were.

Are you basically a good person or a bad person? What do you really think of yourself? Is your opinion correct? If you think poorly of yourself, your self-image is almost certainly off the mark. We are all basically good, although we can stray from that goodness through the use of our will. I think it's helpful and correct to assume you're a good person. Anything you don't like about yourself represents a distortion of your basic goodness. Such distortions can be corrected.

"This is the first lesson ye should learn: There is so much good in the worst of us, and so much bad in the best of us, it doesn't behoove any of us to speak evil of the rest of us. This is a universal law, and until one begins to make application of same, one may not go very far in spiritual or soul development." (3063-1) What Cayce says about speaking evil of others also applies to speaking evil of ourselves.

Self-condemnation is a waste of time and energy, like worry. That's why it's counterproductive to blame yourself for your illness, to beat yourself up simply because you chose this avenue for growth and learning. At the same time, it can be liberating and an important part of the healing process to take full responsibility for your life and illness, because responsibility is the doorway to freedom.

One of the worst things we can do is to try to establish our self-image by comparing ourselves with others. If we compare ourselves with those we consider superior, for any reason, we will feel inferior. If we compare ourselves to those we consider inferior, we are guilty of judging others, and that's not healthy either.

A serious illness can change an individual's self-image quickly and sometimes drastically. In chapter 5, I mentioned the concept of identifying with your illness as a negative use of illness. This sometimes happens because the illness robs individuals of some of the actions and roles that were important to their pre-illness identity, to their former self-image. It may be natural to identify with your illness in the beginning, but the breakdown of identity due to a serious illness represents an opportunity to re-create yourself, to develop a new and healthier self-image than the one you had before.

One of the most important characteristics of being is the uniqueness of individuals. There is no one on the face of the earth, nor has there ever been, nor will there ever be, who is quite like you. You can do things in a way that no one else before or since can ever match. No one in all of existence experiences life in quite the way you do. Every human being has a unique contribution to make to the whole, regardless of their station in life.

Recognizing and acting from our individuality can be one of our most healing attributes: "Psychologists estimate that less than 20 percent of the population has an 'inner locus of control,' the kind of self-possession in which persons are guided by their own standards rather than beliefs about what others may think. This integrity is a large part of the survivor personality. . . . As Elida Evans observed in her groundbreaking 1926 study of the cancer personality, 'Development of individuality is a safeguard to life and health. It lifts a person out of the collective authority.'"[1]

The Qualities of Being

In terms of self-image, what are some of the qualities of being for living the healing life? I think everyone can come up with a list of virtues that would represent a high quality of being in the world, virtues representing a healthy attitude toward self, others, and the world. Your values list probably has some of these virtues on it. Instead of trying to follow a list of virtues, it might be easier to have a virtuous framework, a way of looking at oneself and others, that would lead to virtuous being.

In a meaningful world, a metaphorical world, perhaps the qualities of being can be summed up in the Golden Rule. This law is found in every world religion and in just about every culture. It contains the idea that we are not only always meeting self, but we are always meeting the Divine: "So whatever you wish that men would do to you, do so to them; for this is the law and the prophets." (Matthew 7:12) "'As a man soweth, so shall he reap.' As an attitude is held towards another, that is gradually builded within self . . . " (451-1)

We can always check out the current quality of our being by looking at our lives, by looking at those around us. The quality of being associated with living the healing life is to see every individual, no matter how negative he or she appears to you, as a reflection of yourself and, further, to see every individual as a reflection of the Divine.

Love

There is no difficulty that enough love will not conquer; no disease that enough love will not heal; no door that enough love will not open; no gulf that enough love will not bridge; no wall that enough love will not throw down; no sin that enough love will not redeem. . . .

It makes no difference how deeply seated may be the trouble; how hopeless the outlook; how muddled the tangle; how great the mistake. A sufficient realization of love will dissolve it all. If only you could love enough you would be the happiest and most powerful being in the world. . . . —Emmet Fox[2]

What a powerful affirmation! Most people agree that love is the answer. If that's the case, why is love so difficult? Our Spirit-suppression devices can be called love-suppression devices. Our problems protect us from Spirit and from love. Love is difficult precisely *because* love is associated with the Divine. We run from love as we run from the Divine.

If illness can be life shattering, love can be even more life shattering. Love shatters our limited self-images, breaks us open, strips us bare. The Hebrews who left Egypt with Moses were unable to look upon Moses' face after he'd been in the presence of God. It was too bright. Love brings us face to face with God, or at least with our own God self. Perhaps it's too bright for us as well.

I believe we're more afraid of our divinity than we are of our fears and troubles. In fact, one of the primary functions of problems, including illnesses, may be to protect us from our divinity, to protect us from the intimacy represented by divine love. To avoid the brightness of that light is to avoid our own spiritual heritage, the divine light of our own being.

Living the healing life, the becoming life, requires that we get in touch with our courage and face the reality of our being, that we accept our birthright. We are made of God stuff, which is love stuff, and as we learn, grow, create, and change, we become more and more like the Creator. Our reason for being *is* to become creators in our own right and co-creators with the Spirit.

Attunement/Oneness

According to mystics from around the world, each moment of enlightenment (grace/insight/samadhi/satori) reveals that everything—all the separate parts of the universe—are manifestations of the same whole. There is only *one* reality, and it is whole and unified. It is one.[3]

The healing life involves experiencing our uniqueness and separateness, the holy integrity of our being. It also involves recognizing and being in attunement with the reality of our connection to Spirit and all of creation. This is one of the paradoxes of creation, a kind of tension that helps to drive our physical experience. We are unique and individual, separate from our Source in freedom of choice and action. Yet we are one, part of that great whole from which we emerged. The healing life is characterized by a skillful dance with that paradox, a smooth and natural movement between individuality and oneness.

Our being is guaranteed. It is who we are, and it cannot be taken away. Our becoming is also part of us, but we can ignore it. We can try to stay stuck and not move toward a fuller expression of our greater being. But we are not here to suffer and struggle, to feel pain and loneliness. We are here to experience, to learn, to grow, to create, and, most of all, to love and be loved.

We choose our experiences. We also choose how we will respond to those experiences. Living the healing life means being more conscious choosers, conscious creators, and conscious co-creators. It means having the courage to face our fears of success and failure and to face the ultimate fear of accepting our divinity.

Whatever else your illness means, it means changing your life for the better. It means finding out what you're really here for and getting on that path. It means gradually opening to your divine heritage, being and becoming more and more from the perspective of that heritage. Whatever other specific meaning and purpose your illness has, it always has the purpose of healing your life, even if you eventually die from your illness.

We're here to discover and live our divine nature, and we will continue to come back until we "get it." Why not go for the Divine in us now? Why not open to the God self? Nothing bad can possibly happen. Perhaps we're actually here to have fun, to play with our creativity the way a child plays with building blocks.

Remember the three-year-old girl who was beginning to forget God? Living the healing life means beginning to remember God.

NOTES

Introduction

1. Unless otherwise noted, all Biblical quotes are from the Revised Standard Version.

2. "What Keeps Me Alive" by Bernard Gavzer, *Parade,* January 31, 1993, p. 6.

Part I—The Birth of an Illness

1
Mind Is the Builder

1. *As a Man Thinketh* by James Allen, The Peter Pauper Press, p. 7.

2. *The Edgar Cayce Guide to Self-Healing* by Patrick J. Berkery, Ph.D., Contemporary Mission, Inc., 1979, pp. 5-9.

3. *Edgar Cayce—The Sleeping Prophet* by Jess Stearn, Doubleday and Company, Inc., 1967, p. 28.

4. The Cayce readings are identified by two numbers. The first number represents the person seeking the reading, the number insuring anonymity. The second number is the number of the reading itself; first reading, second reading, etc.

2
The Mind-Body Dance

1. *Marilyn Ferguson's Book of Pragmagic,* adapted and updated by Wim Coleman and Pat Perrin, Pocket Books, 1990, p. 35.

2. *The Healing Brain* by Robert Ornstein and David Sobel, Simon and Schuster, 1987, pp. 141-142.

3. *Marilyn Ferguson's Book of Pragmagic,* adapted and updated by Wim Coleman and Pat Perrin, Pocket Books, 1990, p. 163.

4. *The Healing Brain* by Robert Ornstein and David Sobel, Simon and Schuster, 1987, p. 148.

5. *Marilyn Ferguson's Book of Pragmagic,* adapted and updated by Wim Coleman and Pat Perrin, Pocket Books, 1990, p. 43.

6. *Love, Medicine, and Miracles* by Bernie S. Siegel, Harper and Row, 1986, p. 69.

7. *Health and Light* by John Ott, Pocket Books, 1973.

3
The Outer Possibilities of the Mind-Body

1. *The Holographic Universe* by Michael Talbot, HarperCollins, 1991, p. 105.

2. *The Future of the Body* by Michael Murphy, Jeremy P. Tarcher, Inc., 1992, p. 350.

3. *Ibid.,* pp. 472-475.

4. *Ibid.,* p. 534.

5. *Ibid.,* p. 532.

6. *Love, Medicine, and Miracles* by Bernie S. Siegel, Harper & Row, 1986, p. 194.

7. *The Holographic Universe* by Michael Talbot, HarperCollins, 1991, p. 104.

8. *The Future of the Body* by Michael Murphy, Jeremy P. Tarcher, Inc., 1992, p. 234.

9. *Noetic Sciences Collection: 1980-1990,* edited by Barbara McNeill and Carol Guion, Institute of Noetic Sciences, 1991, "Inner Faces of Multiplicity: Contemporary Look at a Classic Mystery" by Tom Hurley, p. 13.

10. *Ibid.,* "Etiology of Multiple Personality: From Abuse to Alter Personalities" by Tom Hurley, p. 17.

11. *The Holographic Universe* by Michael Talbot, HarperCollins, 1991, p. 99.

12. *Marilyn Ferguson's Book of Pragmagic,* adapted and updated by Wim Coleman and Pat Perrin, Pocket Books, 1990, p. 92.

13. *The Future of the Body* by Michael Murphy, Jeremy P. Tarcher, Inc., 1992, p. 249.

14. *The Holographic Universe* by Michael Talbot, HarperCollins, New York, 1991, p. 135.

15. *Ibid.,* p. 129.

16. *Ibid.,* p. 129.

4
Birth Choices

1. *Reincarnation: Claiming Your Past, Creating Your Future* by Lynn Elwell Sparrow, Harper & Row, 1988, p. 21.

2. *The Nature of Personal Reality* by Jane Roberts, Prentice-Hall, Inc., 1974, pp. 53, 54.

3. *Jung and the Story of Our Time* by Laurens van der Post,

Vintage Books, 1975, p. 118.

Part II—The Ways We Use Illness

5
Negative Uses
1. *Edgar Cayce—The Sleeping Prophet,* by Jess Stearn, Double-day and Company, 1967, p. 107.

6
Positive Uses: The Gifts of Illness
1. *The Future of the Body* by Michael Murphy, Jeremy P. Tarcher, Inc., 1992, p. 210.

Part III—Understanding Your Illness

7
Doing Dreamwork with Your Illness
1. *The Healing Power of Dreams* by Patricia Garfield, Fireside, 1991, pp. 258-296.
2. *Ibid.,* pp. 297-327.
3. *You Can Heal Your Life* by Louise L. Hay, Hay House, 1984, pp. 149-188.
4. *Where People Fly and Water Runs Uphill* by Jeremy Taylor, Warner Books, 1992, p. 267.

9
Illness as Spiritual Teacher
1. *Noetic Sciences Collection: 1980-1990,* edited by Barbara McNeill and Carol Guion, Institute of Noetic Sciences, 1991, "The Case Against Competition" from a talk by Alfie Kohn, p. 85.
2. *Ibid.,* p. 85.
3. *Future of the Body* by Michael Murphy, Jeremy P. Tarcher, Inc., p. 209.
4. *Ibid.,* p. 209.
5. *Change Your Mind, Change Your World* by Dr. Richard Gillett, Fireside, 1992, p. 135.
6. *Marilyn Ferguson's Book of Pragmagic,* adapted and updated by Wim Coleman and Pat Perrin, Pocket Books, 1990, p. 7.

7. *Future of the Body* by Michael Murphy, Jeremy P. Tarcher, Inc., p. 450.

8. *Jung and the Story of Our Time* by Laurens van der Post, Vintage Books, 1977, pp. 216, 217.

Part IV—Healing an Illness

10
Do You Want to Be Healed?

1. *Love, Medicine, and Miracles* by Bernie S. Siegel, Harper & Row, 1986, p. 99.

2. *Marilyn Ferguson's Book of Pragmagic*, adapted and updated by Wim Coleman and Pat Perrin, Pocket Books, 1990, p. 142.

11
Some Healing Techniques

1. *Noetic Sciences Collection: 1980-1990*, edited by Barbara McNeill and Carol Guion, Institute of Noetic Sciences, 1991, "Conscious Living, Conscious Dying," with Stephen Levine and Jeffrey Mishlove, p. 72.

2. *Ibid.*, p. 72.

3. *Change Your Mind, Change Your Life* by Gerald G. Jampolsky and Diane V. Cirincione, Bantam Books, 1993, p. 44.

4. *Noetic Sciences Collection: 1980-1990*, edited by Barbara McNeill and Carol Guion, Institute of Noetic Sciences, 1991.

5. *Ibid.*, p. 53.

6. *Ibid.*, p. 53.

7. *Love, Medicine, and Miracles* by Bernie S. Siegel, Harper & Row, 1986.

8. *Change Your Mind, Change Your Life* by Gerald G. Jampolsky and Diane V. Cirincione, Bantam Books, 1993.

9. *The Holographic Universe* by Michael Talbot, HarperCollins, 1991, p. 100.

10. *Ibid.*, p. 100.

Part V—Living the Healing Life

12
Attunement

1. *The American Heritage Dictionary of the English Language,* Third Edition, Anne H. Soukhanov, Executive Editor, Houghton Mifflin Company, 1992.

2. *The Dancing Wu Li Masters* by Gary Zukav, William Morrow and Company, Inc., 1979, p. 88.

3. *Marilyn Ferguson's Book of Pragmagic,* adapted and updated by Wim Coleman and Pat Perrin, Pocket Books, 1990, p. 20.

4. *The Holographic Universe* by Michael Talbot, HarperCollins, 1991, p. 46.

5. *The Future of the Body* by Michael Murphy, Jeremy P. Tarcher, Inc., 1992, p. 190.

6. *Change Your Mind, Change Your Life* by Gerald G. Jampolsky and Diane V. Cirincione, Bantam Books, 1993, p. 99.

13
Action

1. *Love, Medicine, and Miracles* by Bernie S. Siegel, Harper & Row, 1986, p. 172.

2. *Healthy Pleasures* by Robert Ornstein and David Sobel, Addison-Wesley Publishing Company, Inc., 1989, Chapter 10, p. 42.

3. *Ibid.,* p. 59.

4. *Ibid.,* p. 69.

5. *Ibid.,* p. 85.

6. *Ibid.,* p. 191.

7. *Ibid.,* p. 195.

8. *Ibid.,* pp. 106, 107.

9. *Noetic Sciences Collection: 1980-1990,* edited by Barbara McNeill and Carol Guion, Institute of Noetic Sciences, 1991, "Spirit: Resource for Healing," by Rachel Naomi Remen, p. 65.

10. *Ibid.,* p. 65.

11. *Love, Medicine, and Miracles* by Bernie S. Siegel, Harper & Row, 1986, pp. 140, 141.

12. *Edgar Cayce's Story of Attitudes and Emotions* by Jeffrey Furst, Coward, McCann and Geoghegan, Inc., 1972, pp. 184, 185.

14
Being-Becoming

1. *Love, Medicine, and Miracles* by Bernie S. Siegel, Harper & Row, 1986, p. 167.

2. *Ibid.*, p. 205.

3. *The Dancing Wu Li Masters* by Gary Zukav, William Morrow and Company, Inc., 1979, p. 271.

Bibliography

BIBLIOGRAPHY

BIBLIOGRAPHY

Allen, James, *As a Man Thinketh*, Revell, 1957, or The Peter Pauper Press.

Berkery, Patrick J., *The Edgar Cayce Guide to Self-Healing*, Contemporary Mission, Inc., 1979.

Coleman, Wim, and Perrin, Pat, adapters and updaters, *Marilyn Ferguson's Book of Pragmagic*, Pocket Books, 1990.

Furst, Jeffrey, *Edgar Cayce's Story of Attitudes and Emotions*, Coward, McCann and Geoghegan, Inc., 1972.

Garfield, Patricia, *The Healing Power of Dreams*, Fireside, 1991.

Gillett, Dr. Richard, *Change Your Mind, Change Your World*, Fireside, 1992.

Hay, Louise L., *You Can Heal Your Life*, Hay House, 1984.

Jampolsky, Gerald G., and Cirincione, Diane V., *Change Your Mind, Change Your Life*, Bantam Books, 1993.

McNeill, Barbara, and Guion, Carol, Editors, *Noetic Sciences Collection: 1980-1990*, Institute of Noetic Sciences, 1991.

Murphy, Michael, *The Future of the Body*, New York, Jeremy P. Tarcher, 1992.

Ornstein, Robert, and Sobel, David, *Healthy Pleasures*, Addison-Wesley Publishing Company, Inc., 1989.

Ornstein, Robert, and Sobel, David, *The Healing Brain*, Simon and Schuster, 1987.

Ott, John, *Health and Light*, Pocket Books, 1973.

Roberts, Jane, *The Nature of Personal Reality*, Prentice-Hall, Inc., 1974.

Siegel, Bernie S., *Love, Medicine, and Miracles*, Harper & Row, 1986.

Soukhanov, Anne H., Executive Editor, *The American Heritage Dictionary of the English Language*, Third Edition, Houghton Mifflin Company, 1992.

Sparrow, Lynn Elwell, *Reincarnation: Claiming Your Past, Creating Your Future*, New York, Harper & Row, 1988.

Stearn, Jess, *Edgar Cayce—The Sleeping Prophet*, Doubleday and Company, Inc., 1967.

Talbot, Michael, *The Holographic Universe*, HarperCollins, 1991.

Taylor, Jeremy, *Dream Work: Techniques for Discovering the Creative Power in Dreams*, Paulist Press, 1983.

Taylor, Jeremy, *Where People Fly and Water Runs Uphill,* Warner Books, 1992.

van der Post, Laurens, *Jung and the Story of Our Time,* Vintage Books, 1975.

Zukav, Gary, *The Dancing Wu Li Masters,* William Morrow and Company, Inc., 1979.

American Self-Help Clearinghouse—St. Clares-Riverside Medical Center, Danville, NJ 07834, 201-625-7101

Provides current information and contacts for getting in touch with various self-help groups across the country. You might want to try them first.

Association for Research and Enlightenment (A.R.E.)—P.O. Box 595, Virginia Beach, VA 23451-0595, 804-428-3588; 800-333-4499.

Dedicated to researching the thousands of readings given by psychic Edgar Cayce and related materials from other sources. Many of these readings were health readings, and the A.R.E. has a library of readings based on various diseases. There are also study groups around the country which focus on a specific course of study as well as sharing dreams and meditating. Call for groups in your area.

The Biofeedback and Psychophysiology Clinic—The Menninger Clinic, P.O. Box 829, Topeka, KS, 66601-0829, 913-273-7500

Offers services for a wide variety of stress-related and other health problems. Learn appropriate relaxation and activation responses, stress management, and performance enhancement. Biofeedback machines measure and feed back information about internal responses and mind-body interactions affecting muscle tension, circulation, brain rhythms, heart rate, or blood pressure. There are probably clinics, hospitals, and/or private practitioners of biofeedback in your area.

Center for Attitudinal Healing—33 Buchanan, Sausalito, CA 94965, 415-453-5022

A nonprofit center based on the principles found in *A Course in Miracles*. Support groups for children and adults with life-threatening illnesses as well as groups for family members. There are over eighty related groups around the country. Call for one near you.

Commonweal—P.O. Box 316, Bolinas, CA 94924, 415-868-0970

A nonprofit center for service and research in health and human ecology. Among its activities are The Commonweal Cancer Help Program, a yoga-based retreat program for people with cancer who seek physical, mental, emotional, and spiritual healing.

ECap (Exceptional Cancer Patients)—1302 Chapel Street, New Haven, CT 06511, 203-865-8392

Founded by Dr. Bernie Siegel, offering individual and group therapy utilizing patients' dreams, drawings, and images. ECap is based on "carefrontation," a loving, safe, therapeutic confrontation which facilitates personal change and healing. Groups are available for people who have cancer, AIDS, or other life-threatening or serious chronic illnesses. Call for Dr. Siegel's national workshop schedule or for regional ECap-like referrals.

Esalen Institute—Big Sur, CA 93920, 408-667-3000

Workshops devoted to mind-body interactions, including breathing and body awareness, yoga, dance, centering, movement, and meditation. Its Healthspring project offers a global referral system linking visitors to Esalen with bodyworkers, counselors, and teachers from their home areas.

Institute of Noetic Sciences—P.O. Box 909, Department M, Sausalito, CA 94966-0909, 800-383-1294

A research foundation, educational institution, and membership organization committed to the further development of human consciousness through scientific inquiry, spiritual understanding, and psychological well-being. Although it does not have healing support groups, it does support local member group activities. Many of these groups discuss issues related to healing and the mind-body connection.

Interface—55 Wheeler Street, Cambridge, MA 02138, 617-876-4600

A holistic education center which explores trends in health, personal growth, science, and religion. It offers lectures, courses, workshops, and conferences featuring teachers who do work on the borderlines between the major disciplines—between physical and mental health; science and religion; and psychology and spirituality.

National Hospice Organization—1901 North Moore Street, Suite 901, Arlington, VA 22209, 703-243-5900

Represents hospice providers and addresses such questions as the quality of care, licensing and reimbursement, public information referral, legislation, ethics, research and evaluation, and education. Currently in the United States there are 1,800 hospice programs serving over 200,000 terminally ill persons.

New York Open Center—83 Spring Street, New York, NY 10012, 212-219-2527

Dedicated to spiritual, ecological, and social awareness and change, this is one of the major clearinghouses for holistic ideas and practitioners in the United States. Offers classes, lectures, performances, and other programs on topics such as holistic health and nutrition, bodywork, psychology, world religion and philosophy, the environment, the arts, and spiritual aspects of our everyday lives.

Oasis Center—7463 North Sheridan Road, Chicago, IL 60626, 312-274-6777

A growth center and a community interested in exploring the most effective ways of unlocking dormant human potential and providing opportunities for heightening self-awareness. Provides workshops and courses on subjects such as personal growth, spiritual practice, myth, ritual, health and healing, creativity, and human potential.

Omega Institute for Holistic Studies—260 Lake Drive, Rhinebeck, NY 12572, 914-266-4301

Offers week-long and weekend courses, workshops, and retreats from June through September. Subjects include health, social action, spiritual awareness, and professional development.

Preventive Medicine Research Institute—900 Bridgeway, Suite 2, Sausalito, CA 94965, 415-332-2525

Offers training programs and conducts clinical research in mind-body medicine for health professionals and the public. Founded and directed by Dean Ornish, author of *Dr. Dean Ornish's Program for Reversing Heart Disease.*

RISE Institute—P.O. Box 2733, Petaluma, CA 94973, 707-765-2758

Works with people with immune-related illnesses such as cancer, HIV, chronic fatigue syndrome, rheumatoid arthritis, diabetes, hypertension, and cardiovascular illness. Based on the work of meditation teacher Sri Eknath Easwaren, the RISE program is delivered primarily through courses, workshops, and seminars.

Spiritual Emergence Network (SEN)—5905 Soquel Drive, Suite 650, Soquel, CA 95073, 408-464-8261

An information and referral service for individuals experiencing intense nonordinary states of consciousness, psychospiritual crises, and the transformative experiences of spiritual emergence.

The Stress Reduction Clinic—Department of Medicine, University of Massachusetts Medical Center, Worcester, MA 01655, 508-856-1616

An outpatient clinic in the form of an eight-week course. Patients must be referred by a physician for such things as high blood pressure, ulcers, cancer, chronic pain conditions, and heart disease. Mindfulness meditation and hatha yoga are taught for developing awareness between emotional and physical tension and to help patients deal with stressful life situations. Programs for professional training and five-day patient programs are available periodically.

Reading List

Allen, James, *As a Man Thinketh*, Revell, 1957, or The Peter Pauper Press. (This is a classic little power-of-positive-thinking book first published in the early 1920s. It can be found in a number of different editions in your bookstore.)

Chopra, Deepak, *Ageless Body, Timeless Mind: The Quantum Alternative to Growing Old*, New York, Harmony Books, 1993. (I had read very little of the popular healing literature before writing the first draft of my book. I have found that Chopra's interpretation of Ayurvedic healing is very compatible with my own views. The focus of this book is the idea that even aging is primarily a thought problem.)

Chopra, Deepak, *Quantum Healing: Exploring the Frontiers of Mind/Body Medicine*, New York, Bantam Books, 1989. (Another bestseller, you will find a number of interesting stories demonstrating the power of the mind over the body.)

Coleman, Wim, and Perrin, Pat, adapters and updaters, *Marilyn Ferguson's Book of Pragmagic*, by Pocket Books, 1990. (This large paperback is loaded with good information on mind-body stuff. It's modeled on Ferguson's *Brain/Mind Bulletin*, a collection and condensation of current information in the brain/mind field.)

Faraday, Ann, *Dream Power*, New York, Coward, McCann and Geoghegan, Inc., 1972. (Both of these books by Ann Faraday, despite their age, are the best introductions to dreams available. The sampling of different dreamwork theories lets you decide which ideas appeal to you and which you might want to pursue further.)

Faraday, Ann, *The Dream Game*, New York, Harper & Row, 1974. (The earlier book presented a number of psychological theories such as those from Sigmund Freud, Carl Jung, and Fritz Perls. This one looks at some more metaphysical sources for dreamwork including Edgar Cayce and Jane Roberts's Seth material.)

Furst, Jeffrey, *Edgar Cayce's Story of Attitudes and Emotions*, New York, Coward, McCann and Geoghegan, Inc., 1972. (I don't know if this is still in circulation. It's a good compilation of Edgar Cayce's comments about the effects of attitudes and emotions on health and well-being.)

Garfield, Patricia, *Creative Dreaming*, New York, Ballantine Books, 1974. (Also a classic, this book focuses on using dreams to make specific changes in your life. Includes a good section on the Senoi method of dreamwork.)

Garfield, Patricia, *The Healing Power of Dreams*, New York, Fireside, 1991. (A good book for seeing how dreams can give you accurate information about your illness and can help in the healing process. There's good information about the ancient Greeks and their use of dreams with illness.)

Gillett, Dr. Richard, *Change Your Mind, Change Your World*, New York, Fireside, 1992. (A practical and understandable guide for making life changes by changing thoughts and feelings.)

Gregory, Jill, *Dream Tips*, The Novato Center for Dreams, Novato, 1988. (This is a rich and compact booklet of dream tips covering dream recall, journaling, dream sharing, incubation, flying dreams, lucid dreams, and much more. This and the following booklet can be ordered from: Jill Gregory, The Novato Center for Dreams, 29 Truman Drive, Novato, CA 94947 or 415-897-7955. The Novato Center for Dreams is a clearinghouse for information on dreams from around the country. If Jill can't tell you about a dream resource in your area, she may be able to tell you who can.)

Gregory, Jill, *Lucid Dreaming Tips*, The Novato Center for Dreams, Novato, 1988. (In this booklet Jill has culled techniques from many sources including many of her own. You will find "Suggestions for Encouraging Dream Lucidity," "Techniques to Maintain Lucidity," and "Applications of the Lucid Dream State," as well as actual dream samples of various types of lucid dreams.)

Hafen, Brent Q., Frandsen, Kathryn J., Karren, Keith J., and Hooker, Keith R., *The Health Effects of Attitudes, Emotions, and Relationships*, EMS Associates, Provo, Utah, 1992. (The title of this book says what it's about very well. It contains a great deal of research on attitudes, emotions, and relationships. The authors cover the relationships between health and emotions, personality styles, social support, spirituality, and perceptions.)

Hay, Louise L., *You Can Heal Your Life*, Santa Monica, California,

Hay House, 1984. (Already somewhat of a classic, this book has lots of good affirmations that can be used as is or modified for your purposes. I would use her list of the meanings of different illnesses with caution. Only you know what your illness means.)

Jampolsky, Gerald G., and Cirincione, Diane V., *Change Your Mind, Change Your Life*, New York, Bantam Books, 1993. (Jampolsky is the founder of The Center for Attitudinal Healing. His philosophical foundation is the *Course in Miracles*. There are some uplifting stories and useful affirmations in this book.)

Lidell, Lucinda, with Thomas, Sara; Cooke, Carola Beresford; and Porter, Anthony, *The Book of Massage: The Complete Step-by-Step Guide to Eastern and Western Techniques*, New York, A Fireside Book, Simon and Schuster, 1984. (This is a good introductory book to massage. It covers three major types of bodywork: massage, shiatsu, and reflexology. Included are tips for touching, from infancy to later life, body reading, and anatomy [including information on auras and chakras]. At the back are addresses for information regarding courses, workshops, and individual treatments.)

McGarey, William A., and associated physicians, *Physician's Reference Notebook*, Virginia Beach, A.R.E. Press, 1968. (Both of these books by McGarey deal with the Edgar Cayce health readings. Bill and Gladys McGarey founded a clinic in Phoenix, Ariz., where the Cayce readings were put into practice.)

McGarey, William A., *Healing Miracles: Using Your Body Energies*, San Francisco, Harper & Row, 1988.

McNeill, Barbara, and Guion, Carol, Editors, *Noetic Sciences Collection: 1980-1990*, Institute of Noetic Sciences, 1991. (This excellent collection of articles draws from ten years of research and dialogue on consciousness and the mind-body relationship. Information on the Institute of Noetic Sciences (IONS) can be found in the list of groups and organizations. Also available from IONS is a paper on the results of a study on spontaneous remissions, perhaps the most thorough study on this subject now available.)

Murphy, Michael, *The Future of the Body*, New York, Jeremy P. Tarcher, 1992. (This is a big book and will take some dedication to get through it. It's well researched and has a wealth of information on extraordinary human functioning. If you're interested in pursuing any of the topics in more detail, Murphy has a thorough bibliography on each subject area. An excellent reference book.)

Ornstein, Robert, and Sobel, David, *Healthy Pleasures*, Reading, Massachusetts, Addison-Wesley Publishing Company, Inc., 1989. (Ornstein and Sobel come from a very scientific point of view. They cite studies to back up the value of the various healthy pleasures in the book. A welcome change to have someone tell us that the things that feel good to us are good *for* us.)

Ornstein, Robert, and Sobel, David, *The Healing Brain*, New York, Simon and Schuster, 1987. (Some good mind-body information in this book. What I found of interest here is information about how many of the major diseases that have been virtually wiped out were not necessarily stopped with medical breakthroughs. They were already on the way out when new drugs and vaccinations were discovered.)

Ott, John, *Health and Light*, Pocket Books, 1973. (John Ott is a pioneer in full-spectrum lighting. This book has studies and anecdotes on the use of natural light both in healing and illness prevention.)

Reilly, Harold J., and Brod, Ruth, *The Edgar Cayce Handbook for Health Through Drugless Therapy*, New York, Macmillan, 1975. (Edgar Cayce sent people to Dr. Harold Reilly before Dr. Reilly knew who Cayce was or how he got his information. They finally met and had a long friendship. This is a very complete book dealing with the Cayce approach to many different kinds of illness.)

Roberts, Jane, *The Nature of Personal Reality*, Englewood Cliffs, New Jersey, Prentice-Hall, Inc., 1974. (This is the "Bible" for the Seth material. It clearly lays out how we create our own reality on a daily basis and has exercises to help with that process.)

Sechrist, Elsie, *Dreams—Your Magic Mirror*, New York, Cowles Education Corp., 1968. (I read this book a long time ago. It has a lot of information on the Edgar Cayce approach to understanding dreams, including what he had to say about colors, numbers, and other common dream symbols.)

Siegal, Bernie S., *Love, Medicine, and Miracles,* New York, Harper & Row, 1986. (Both of Siegal's books are inspirational. He has lots of wonderful stories. He also talks about the efficacy of using dreams and drawings for working with illnesses. There are many examples of the meaning of illnesses and also examples of the power of suggestion in healing and in making us sick.)

Siegal, Bernie S., *Peace, Love, and Healing,* New York, Harper & Row, 1989.

Sparrow, Lynn Elwell, *Reincarnation: Claiming Your Past, Creating Your Future,* New York, Harper & Row, 1988. (For an understanding of reincarnation from the Cayce perspective. There are many books on reincarnation if you find yourself drawn to that subject.)

Stearn, Jess, *Edgar Cayce—The Sleeping Prophet,* New York, Doubleday and Company, Inc., 1967. (This is an excellent story of Edgar Cayce's life. Another biography is available by Thomas Sugrue called *There Is a River.* Both will give you an idea of what Edgar Cayce was all about and how he got into the work that became his life.)

Talbot, Michael, *The Holographic Universe,* New York, Harper-Collins, 1991. (Like the Murphy book, this book has lots of examples of extraordinary human functioning. It's smaller and much more readable. I found it quite inspirational.)

Taylor, Jeremy, *Dream Work: Techniques for Discovering the Creative Power in Dreams,* New York, Paulist Press, 1983. (Lots of good dreamwork tools plus one of the most thorough annotated bibliographies on dreams available.)

Taylor, Jeremy, *Where People Fly and Water Runs Uphill,* New York, Warner Books, 1992. (This later book by Taylor has much more information on working with dreams in groups, one of Taylor's strengths. He also updates his earlier bibliography.)

Thurston, Mark, *How to Interpret Your Dreams,* Virginia Beach, A.R.E. Press, 1978. (This is another book presenting the Edgar Cayce approach to dream work. Mark Thurston has been on the staff of the A.R.E. for many years and has worked with the readings, including those on dreams, for a long time. This is a good how-to on dreams from the Cayce information.)